bedfellows

bedfellows

Nivita Chaliki

NEW DEGREE PRESS

COPYRIGHT © 2022 NIVITA CHALIKI

BEDFELLOWS

ISBN 978-1-63676-837-3 *Paperback*
     978-1-63730-205-7 *Kindle Ebook*
     978-1-63730-281-1 *Ebook*

To the person who gave me their old typewriter on a Thursday afternoon—you gave my hands new inspiration to write, to create. You gifted me something precious, and this book is a product of it.

To the person who taught me how to see beauty through a camera lens, and in turn find beauty in all that I see—your influence is everlasting in all that I do, all that I am.

To the people who held out their hand even when I pushed it away and always when I needed it most—you are everything.

Contents

*"because the bird flew before there was a
word for flight, years from now there will be
a name for what you and I are doing"*

—MARCELO HERNANDEZ CASTILLO, CENZÓNTLE

author's note

It starts in my friend's car. We're parked in my driveway. It's long past midnight. Her headlights are on (we realize too late, hours later, that having the engine turned off and the headlights simultaneously on is less than wise, and after it dies, we spend a good thirty minutes during the graveyard hours trying to jumpstart her car).

It starts with a thought that sticks to the walls of my mind like fly paper. We've just come back from watching a movie, still emotional from scream-singing all the way to my house, and in the dim glow of the headlights, I notice her nails are painted red.

That's the first sentence. It exists now somewhere in the middle of this book, so when you find it, you can know that that was the real beginning.

I think this book has the potential to be quite incriminating. It's more or less my inner everything laid bare in the guise of fiction. Everything that happens, everything that is felt and expressed, said and unsaid, is thinly appropriated from the truth. After reading this, you'll know me likely better than I know myself (given, that's not too high a bar).

This book is a mind unraveled. Kash's mind, in particular, but mine, too. I lost myself countless times in the swirling mess of writing this story. It was like pinning down needle-thin memories in some moments and like pulling teeth in others. It left a sour taste sometimes, but sometimes it was the sweetest thing I could ever have. I hope reading this book is a little bit like that for you.

And in that hope, I also want to make sure that you take care of yourself while reading. All of us come to terms with the difficult parts of our being at different times in our lives, I think, and Kash is the same—we watch her come to terms with herself and the people around her, with her own worth, her sense of self, her sexuality, and her wants and desires, all through a multitude of ups and downs—so for the people who struggle with these things themselves, I hope this can be somewhat of a reassuring reflection rather than a painful deconstruction (or if it's painful, at least in a productive way). There's no conclusion, or end of the tunnel, I think, but there is something to be said about sharing stories and knowing you're not an alien in yours.

And for the kids (we're all *kids*, aren't we?) who don't know what they are yet and feel like they never will—you don't have to. I know everyone says that. As someone who has resigned all attempts to know myself, it may seem like a false attempt at reassurance or self-satisfaction. It's not.

But then again, maybe this entire book is an attempt at reassurance and self-satisfaction, and if that is the case, I hope you find truth in it regardless. Things are okay. We are okay.

Thank you so much for reading.

With love and warmth,
Nivita

high school: senior year.

where did you go—across the ocean?

Kash's feet pounded down the stairs, anxiety eating her up from the inside and leaving a shell of burning doubt. She'd called him two times just in the last hour, twelve overall in the past week, and the sense of foreboding she'd been harboring since last Friday was at its peak.

He wouldn't have.

Kash shook her head, rushing through the kitchen and into the family room with purpose.

Her parents were sitting on the floor in front of the couch, leaning against it comfortably while they watched some old Telugu movie. Her sisters, twin in appearance and their affinity for annoying her, were lounging on the couch, watching the TV with indifference. Kishori was playing with the end of her braid, and Kumari's legs were sprawled over an armrest.

"Does anyone know where Levi is?" Kash asked out loud, fisting and flexing her hands repeatedly.

"Levi?" Kishori asked, picking her head up leisurely from its place on a decorative cushion.

Kash rolled her eyes.

"Yes, Levi, that's what I said," she all but snapped. The sounds from the TV and the squeaking of leather as her sisters sat up laboriously grated against her ears. Kash felt an abrupt need to throw something.

"Hey," her father said, pausing the film, finally, and looking up at her with a frown. "What's wrong?"

"Does anyone know where Levi is?" Kash repeated through gritted teeth, holding onto her composure by a thread.

"Out of all of us," her father responded, "shouldn't you know the answer to that question?"

"Makrand," her mother said softly to him, putting a hand on his shoulder in a knowing way that made Kash's skin crawl with heavy anticipation.

"What is it?" she immediately asked her mother. "What's going on?"

Her mother looked at her with the kind of guilt a doctor regards their patient with before they say the word terminal, and it made Kash positively shrink.

No, no, no, no.

"I'm going to hang out with Raza for a bit," Kash declared, digging her feet into the ground and summoning every shred of willpower to appear firm and normal. Like she wasn't caving in on the inside.

Her father frowned.

"Okay?" he said. "Is he coming over? Or—"

"No, no, no," Kash assured her father, already grabbing her keys from where she'd last left them on the side table. "We're just going for a drive."

"Wait, Kash," her mother called out, and Kash halted midstep.

"What?"

"*Itu raa*," her mother beckoned her over with one hand.

Kash didn't move for a second. She contemplated leaving without saying anything. After a moment of grinding her teeth together in indecision, she walked over and kneeled next to her mother, who smiled softly.

"*Dha, juttu katuko.*" Her mother slipped a rubber band off of Kash's wrist and took her hair into her hands. "Tie your hair up before you go."

Kash groaned and turned around as her mother gently brushed her hair into a smooth ponytail with her fingers.

"How long are you going to be out?" her mother asked, twisting Kash's hair tightly as she tied the elastic in the slowest possible way.

Kash wanted to yank her head forward until her hair fell out of her mother's grip.

"I don't know," she mumbled, wincing when her mother tugged too hard on a few tangles.

"*Jada vesukuntechikku padadhu,*" her mother said in a slightly stern tone as she tried to work her fingers through the tangled knots of Kash's hair. "It's so *tangled*. Do you want me to—"

Kash groaned and swatted her mother's hands away before roughly slipping another elastic from around her wrist and tying her hair up carelessly. As soon as the elastic was firmly in place, she all but leaped up to stand and dismissed the elastic her mother held out for her to take back.

She bid her family goodbye, ignoring the startled, intuitive look on her mother's face, and ran out to her truck, phone, keys, and wallet in hand. She phoned her only other childhood friend and sighed heavily when he answered.

"Hey, Raz," Kash said immediately, clumsily brushing a few loose strands of hair out of her face. "Have you seen Levi?"

There was some shuffling on the other line before Raza's sleep-roughened voice croaked, "What?"

Kash huffed as she got in the truck and clicked her seatbelt in place.

"Did I wake you up?" she asked incredulously, starting up the engine and peeling out of her driveway.

"Yeah, wait," Raza grumbled. "One second."

Kash muted herself so she could pull over and groan loudly into her steering wheel, hitting it in frustration, before continuing to drive out of her neighborhood.

"Hey," Raza spoke after a few moments, "sorry, I'm back. Levi?" He sounded incredibly sleepy, and, at another time, Kash would've found it endearing, but she was filled to the brim with anxiety and anger and the frayed beginnings of betrayal.

"Yes."

"Why is he not answering?"

"*No*, he is *not*. If he was, why would I be waking you up at two o'clock in the afternoon?" Kash hissed.

"I was taking a *nap*," Raza insisted. "Maybe he's just busy getting ready for college, man, I don't know. He seemed busy two days ago, so I haven't—"

"You talked to him two days ago?" Kash asked, heart thudding.

"Yeah, why?"

A small strip mall came into view, the one they would sometimes drive to after school when they weren't quite ready to go home yet. Her eyes caught on a pair of people walking along the pavement, arms swinging, and for a second, she pictured the three of them instead, running around in the parking lot with the kind of illusive liberation only seniors in high school had. Raza with his keys jingling from his swinging lanyard, Levi with his hair long and curly and blazing in the golden sunset, and Kash with her cheeks flushed and laughing with all the fondness in the world.

"I haven't heard from him for over a week."

"Oh."

The strip mall passed out of view, and Kash suddenly wanted to scream. She didn't *know* what was going on, but a small voice in the back of her mind was chanting the answer, and it made her want to swerve off the road or punch a hole in the windshield.

Maybe she shouldn't be driving.

"I just texted him," Raza said like he hoped that would help.

"Okay."

"I'll let you know when he answers," he said like it would clear things up.

"Sure."

"It's Levi. He's probably just ignoring you," he joked like it would lighten the mood.

"Thanks, Raz," Kash said stoically. "I'll call you in a bit. I'm actually on the road?"

After a moment, Raza answered, "Okay, but don't overthink it, all right? He's terrible at texting back. You know this. You both are. Have been your whole lives."

"Yeah, I know," she said in a hollow voice before ending the call.

She pulled into the nearest parking lot, in front of a gaudy chrome diner with neon signs that she always thought looked straight out of a movie set.

He left, he left, he left; the voice screamed louder as she turned off the engine and sat there in silence.

She winced at the sound of scattered voices from outside, people laughing and talking as they slowly made their way into the diner. Cars zoomed by on the road, and the whoosh of sound practically rocked the truck, and she could feel the movement in her bones.

He flew across the ocean and didn't have the compassion to call you first, so you could talk him out of it.

Kash made a noise of angered helplessness and jammed her palm against the windshield. She wasn't expecting any, but the lack of cracks in the glass made her chest feel heavier and her heart squeeze painfully. She shook her head and dug the heels of her palms against her eyes until her vision dazzled with multicolored spots like a dark kaleidoscope.

Another ragged sound ripped itself from her throat, and she curled in on herself.

Her fingers itched to find his name again and call him. It wouldn't take effort. He was right at the top, the person she texted most, the person she called the most. *Levi.* His name would be *right there.*

She stopped swallowing back her tears and sobbed in between staccato breaths and hoped that anyone who walked by her truck and saw her crying would be a stranger.

wait for me when i leave.

There were a few places within reachable distance where reality and time felt a bit altered to Kash.

Her bedroom at four in the morning, on Sundays, when the light shining in through her windows still came only from the moon and stars.

The odd sculpture garden in the forest behind her house led to a small pond where the sky reflected like a painting on the water.

Levi's attic where it smelled like ancient history, with the window that made it easy to climb out onto the rooftop without his grandparents knowing.

The large courtyard behind the town public library looked like a part of Hogwarts when it snowed.

The abandoned car wash at the end of Kash's street, where she, Raza, and Levi would pretend the hollow gray tunnels were their own apartment in the city.

And the old playground down the street from their high school; although, like most things, it felt all the more surreal at night.

The playground had three sets of creaky swings and a wide, twisted plastic slide with visible metal bolts that would shock a person at their touch. Kash loved sitting tucked away in a shadowy corner underneath the yellow concave structure.

But the three of them would spend most of their time up on the tall blue monkey bars closer to the tree line. Sitting on them meant you were just high enough to see the roof of their school through the gaps in the foliage.

They could see it now, windows glowing warmly, lit up from the inside in contrast to the dark night sky. It was slightly breezy outside, adding a chill that colored their cheeks. Raza was well prepared—like always—in a warm fleece jacket with his hands tucked into his pocket. Levi and Kash, dressed only in thin shirts, huddled together to preserve body heat.

"There's something about being at school at night," Levi said, teeth chattering slightly, "it's so much better."

"Because there's no class?" Raza asked plainly.

Kash chuckled and pulled Levi closer until her shoulder dug into his warm chest.

"No, it's just different," Levi insisted, unconsciously draping an arm around her. "It just feels different, like when we turn off all the lights in the hall, and all we see is the red exit sign."

"It's 'cause night makes everything better," Kash said as she glanced over at Raza, who contemplated the night sky.

"Yeah, things are quieter," he mused. He looked down at her after a moment, and she smiled.

"Come over here," she murmured with a friendly pout and grabbed at him. "Give us warmth."

Levi hummed in agreement and opened his arms.

Raza rolled his eyes and maneuvered carefully across the cold metal rungs until he was close enough to wrap his arms around Kash with fond annoyance.

"Hey, me too," Levi whined, arms still open and waiting. After a moment of Raza willfully ignoring him, he huffed and dropped them.

Kash laughed as Levi clumsily clambered over the bars, so he was lying halfway in Kash's lap and halfway in Raza's, with his legs dangling precariously off the side. She yelped and grabbed at him as he began to slide off the bars.

Raza, half laughing, shook his head, and they both held onto their friend and hauled him back onto the bars, until his body weight rested comfortably between them.

"I could catch myself if I fell, you know," Levi said. "I'd just stand up." He kicked his long legs in emphasis, and Kash slapped him until he stopped.

They rested together, Raza and Kash holding Levi close, and all three of them relished the cool night air before their parents—grandparents in Levi's case—came back from their event and the reality of homework and projects came crashing down on them.

"Last back-to-school night we'll spend like this, huh?" Kash remarked.

"I'm glad," Raza said matter-of-factly.

Kash rolled her eyes at him.

"Leave a little room for nostalgia, Raz," she said.

Levi scoffed. "I don't want to feel nostalgia for high school. I'm ready to move on."

Kash stared at him.

Really? she wanted to ask him. *Even the plans to run away we made on the park bench next to the tetherball? A castle with plants?*

"All of it?" she asked instead.

Levi and Raza nodded in sync.

"You both are empty," she huffed.

"I'm not empty. It's just—what's so great about it?" Levi asked.

Kash stared at him, trying to put her answer into words.

What's so great about predictions and plans and doing everything together?

"Us. We're what's so great about it," she blurted, eyes darting over to Levi. "You're what's so great about it for me, at least."

Heat flooded up her neck and across her ears and cheeks and she froze, fingers tight around the bars below her. Regret doused her like an instinct, and she bit into her lip to stop from saying anything else.

"Yeah, you guys are all right," Raza said casually, absently brushing a piece of grass off of Levi's jeans.

Levi shrugged and smiled slowly, teeth glinting in the moonlight.

"Likewise," he said, grabbing Raza's hands just to flick them away with a soft laugh.

Kash let out a slow, inaudible sigh of relief and watched them descend into a mild catfight.

It felt natural, watching them, and she grimaced, resisting the urge to cower into herself. She felt wholly embarrassed, and it itched at her, made her feet flex up and down, and her fingers tap quickly against the hollow metal of the monkey bars.

As Levi and Raza descended further into laughter, their catfight escalating into a precarious tickle war, Kash felt the urge to walk. She wriggled out from underneath Levi, who made a confused sound as she pushed him unceremoniously onto Raza. She jumped down to the ground with a less than graceful landing, wincing as her heel smarted slightly.

"Kash," Levi called out, "where're you going?"

Kash wrapped her arms around herself and kept walking, making her way out of the playground away from her friends. She tilted her head to the sky and relished the cool darkness, a small chill going down her back. It was the time of year where the days were warm and the nights were less so. She heard Raza call out her name and then two muffled thumps that signaled her friends had both jumped down too.

Her phone buzzed in her pocket as she walked briskly down the side of the street back to school. She saw the notification and stopped in her tracks.

Oh.

Her heart began to race with excitement, embarrassment immediately forgotten. She always got like that whenever Lani's name popped up as a notification, and it was silly because it was never anything significant. Never any *'you up, let's go for a drive'* texts, or *'wanna spend the night looking at the stars?'*, or *'i like you, and absolutely in the way that you're thinking.'*

She opened it.

'hey are you still at school?'

It was a text from Lani, and it wasn't suggestive or exciting in any way, as expected, but that didn't stop her from fumbling over the keyboard as she typed out a response.

'yeah, how's dance class going?'

Two sets of loud, flat footsteps echoed behind her, slow and arrhythmic. She glanced over her shoulder to find Raza and Levi jogging over to her, as silly as possible, with lazy feet and flailing arms. She chuckled and glanced back at her phone.

Three little dots appeared. She held her breath.

'good. we're almost done.'

Kash nodded as if Lani could sense her body language through the screen.

Just as the boys caught up beside her, her phone rang, Lani's name displayed in bold across the screen above her picture.

She answered.

"Hey," Lani said, slightly breathless like she'd just finished a long routine or exercise.

"Hey," Kash responded, barely holding back her smile.

Raza gestured at her phone animatedly and mouthed, "Who is it?"

Kash shot him a vexed look and shoved him away.

"Hey, are you at practice?" Lani asked, and Kash could picture the questioning frown on her face.

Kash shook her head as if Lani could see.

"No, no," she assured, "I'm just wasting time with Raz and Levi."

"Oh. Can I ask you for a favor?" Lani asked with a mild urgency.

Anything.

The word almost fell from Kash's mouth.

"Yeah, what's up?" she said instead.

"I left a part of my calc set in homeroom," Lani explained. "Could you maybe drop it off after? I should be home in like less than an hour."

"Yeah, of course," Kash said, moving toward their school again. She was acutely aware of Levi and Raza trailing just behind her.

"Anything else?" she asked softly.

"No, no. Just that."

"Okay."

Kash felt a sharp jab at her shoulder, and she flicked her arm behind her.

"Okay," Lani chuckled, the sound soft and fuzzy through the speaker. "I'll see you later tonight, then?"

"Yeah."

"Thanks, Kash."

"Yeah." Kash waved a hand dismissively. "Yeah, of course. I'll see you later." The line went dead, and Kash whipped around to find Levi midmotion with his hand in the air.

"What are you doing?" she asked him coolly.

He dropped his hand and responded with an innocent smile.

"Who was that?" Levi teased. "Who're you seeing later?"

Raza snickered beside him.

"No one," she answered before grinding her teeth at their questioning faces and quickly explaining, "I've got to go drop something off at Lani's."

The subsequent looks of realization blooming on their faces made her fingers and toes dance nervously. She turned around and walked as quickly as she could without running. The road ended at an intersection and, after quickly looking both ways, she ran along the crosswalk. The boys stayed noisily in tow, and Kash had to remind herself that they were her best friends and that she loved them no matter how much they irritated her sometimes.

"What're you dropping off?" Levi asked, like a five-year-old who wanted to know everything. Like a five-year-old who thought they already knew everything.

"A calc project," Kash said curtly, flying past their school's sign at the main entrance and down the relatively small front lawn.

She walked into the lobby moments later, the boys following closely behind.

"You don't need to come, you know," she snapped, shooing them away. "I'm the one that's going."

Levi laughed, holding his hands up in mock defense.

"Are you going to head out now?" Raza asked.

"Yeah," Kash said, nodding, "I'll just let my parents know. You?"

Raza nodded. "Yeah, I guess. And mine are probably with yours."

"Well, I'll head out, too, then," Levi sighed out, walking backward to the lobby entrance. "I'll just text Mam and Pop. Don't feel like going up and finding them."

Kash shrugged. "Okay."

Levi tilted his head, as if he was thinking, and rocked back onto his heels.

"Okay," he repeated. He saluted as he turned. "Bye, Raz."

Kash turned to Raza with a confused look as Levi left the building without another word.

"No 'bye Kash'?" she asked, slightly offended.

Raza shrugged and smiled.

"What?" he said. "We've known each other for our whole lives but don't expect me to have totally figured him out by now."

Kash hummed in agreement and looped her arm with Raza's as they walked together up to their homeroom. Lani,

Raza, and Kash were lucky to be in mostly the same classes. She only had one class with Levi, though, and a part of her wondered if that had caused an inherent unevenness in their relationship.

"Your voice gets really soft around her, you know that?"

Kash blinked. "What?"

"Your voice—I mean, you're so fucking obvious. It's kind of painful."

"Shut up," Kash blurted immediately before pausing and trying for nonchalance, "Obvious about what?"

Raza shrugged, voice mockingly casual. "Feelings and such. About this person and that."

Kash rolled her eyes and regarded him with a theatrical smirk. "You're terrible at subtleties. Too quiet of a person naturally, to be anywhere near subtle when you speak."

Raza laughed. "Yeah, well. I'm not the only who notices."

"Notices what?" Kash asked.

"You're acting dumb," Raza said with a grin. "Okay. I won't push."

The walk to homeroom was short and Lani's calculus folder was easy to find. Luckily, both of Kash and Raza's parents were in the same classroom, which made it that much easier to say goodbye and run back down and out to their cars in the senior parking lot.

"Bye, Raz," Kash called out as she got in her truck. She ignored his knowing glance and closed the door as loud as she could, taking care to glare at him mockingly through the windshield.

He rolled down the window and waved as he started his car. Music immediately blasted through the radio, startling him. He fumbled around for a few seconds before managing to turn it down.

Kash smiled fondly and watched him carefully pull out before driving off down the road and disappearing behind the tree line.

She sighed and braced herself, meticulously picking out a playlist and timing the songs according to her drive as approximately as she could. She typed out a text to Lani and hovered over the send button.

'hey, i'm heading out now. gonna stop at home and then head over to yours. be there in about forty minutes.'

She stared at it until the colors on her screen blurred and the letters popped out at her. She shook her head and backspaced.

'hey, i'm heading out. be there in about forty minutes.'

She dug her teeth into her lip and read the message over and over again.

'hey, i'll be there in about forty minutes'

She squeezed her eyes shut and pressed send before she could overthink any more. A flash of panic seared through her, spidering out through her chest. She chased it away by starting the car and pulling out of her parking space.

Her house was just less than twenty minutes away, but the nervous anticipation made it feel like hours.

As soon as she parked in the driveway, she hastily made her way into the house and up to her room, keys jangling in her pocket as she took the stairs three at a time. She looked around frantically for her favorite sweatshirt, pawing through piles of clothes around her room. For a split second, she regretted being so messy.

She found it after a few painstaking minutes and ran back down the stairs, wearing her sweatshirt and some of her favorite perfume subtly rubbed onto her wrists and neck. She fixed her hair into a ponytail in the floor-length mirrors they had in the living room and gave her overall appearance one more quick scrutinizing look before scrunching her nose in defeat and running out to her truck.

Her nervous anticipation, this time, made her take longer and she arrived ten minutes later than intended in Lani's driveway. The pavement was old and crumbly, so the tires of Kash's truck crackled as she pulled in, like a bad tape recording.

She paused before turning the key, engine going silent and headlights going dark. She grabbed Lani's folder from the passenger seat and drew in a deep breath. The truck door clicked loudly as she closed it before making her way up to the wraparound porch decorated with white string lights. She curled her toes and tried not to smile too much as she rang the doorbell.

Loud footsteps sounded from inside, getting gradually closer until the front door opened with a click. Kash couldn't help the grin on her face.

Lani had a beautiful freshness about her. She looked cozy, with her hair curling wetly around her face and neck.

"Hi," Kash said shyly.

Lani smiled back. "Hi, Kash."

Kash held out the folder in her hands like it was some sort of prize.

"Here's your problem set?"

"Oh my gosh, you absolute savior!" Lani gushed, grabbing the folder gently from Kash's hands.

Kash's cheeks warmed, and she pressed her sweat-shirt-sleeve covered hands against them.

"You wanna come in?" Lani asked.

Kash nodded, pulling her bottom lip between her teeth. She stepped in after Lani. As she followed her further into the house, she noticed Lani's bare feet peeking out from soft sweatpants. No socks, just cold toes with light pink painted nails.

"Do you want something to eat? I was just making some dinner after my shower. I'm absolutely starved."

Kash watched a blond curl slowly drip water onto the fabric of Lani's t-shirt.

"Kash?"

"What?"

Lani smiled and pointed to a pot on the stove. "Pasta?"

Kash nodded before she could think better and say no, but the glowing beam that lit up Lani's face, and the way it snatched the heartbeat right out of Kash's chest, was more than worth it.

"It's just going to be butter and cheese, unfortunately," Lani said, slouching against the kitchen counter. "I think we've got pesto sauce in the fridge, though. And pickles if you want."

Kash wrinkled her nose. "Why would I want pickles in my pasta?"

Lani laughed. "No, like, you always get pickles on the side of your meals. I just mean if you want any."

Kash shook her head and tried to keep the waver out of her voice. "No, no. I'm good. Thanks, though."

Lani nodded.

They stood there, making small conversation, with Lani occasionally stirring the pasta in the pot.

Kash tried not to focus too much on every detail of Lani's appearance. It took a painful amount of willpower not to stare at the slight fold in the neckline of her t-shirt or the shadow that fell underneath her collarbone, or the color of the elastic holding her hair back in a messy ponytail.

"Was it over when you left?"

Kash blinked. "What?"

"Back-to-school night?" Lani clarified.

"Oh," Kash said. "No. Not yet. We left early. I think it goes on until eight thirty or so."

Lani nodded, carefully pouring the pot of water out.

Kash watched as she scooped the pasta equally into two bowls.

"You should have more," Kash said quickly. "You're the one straight out of dance class. You said you were starving."

Lani waved her hand. "No, no. It's a thank you. For being a wonderful friend and saving my homework grade tomorrow."

Kash laughed, looking down at the ground.

A wonderful friend.

"It's fine, what are friends for, you know?" she said, trying to keep the wistfulness out of her voice.

"Sauce or butter?"

Kash looked up and cleared her throat before saying, "Butter." They sat down at the counter with their respective bowls of pasta, laughing and talking.

Kash idly twirled her fork as she listened to Lani speak about her dance class.

"We're performing at a cultural center in two weeks, so it's been a lot of practicing performances," Lani said. "I'm a bit nervous for it, actually. It's my last time performing there since we'll all be off to college next year."

Kash hummed and said, "I'm sure you'll be great."

Lani laughed. "Thanks. Hopefully."

"You will be," Kash insisted softly. "You're very talented."

"Thank you," Lani said just as softly.

Kash hoped she wasn't dreaming up the red blush staining Lani's cheeks.

"Of course," Kash said, tearing her eyes away and looking down at her pasta.

It didn't take long for them to finish their food. Kash got up and reached for Lani's bowl, but Lani protested, holding her bowl away.

Kash shook her head and leaned over her. She tried not to get caught up in their fleeting physical proximity and grabbed the bowl.

Lani relented with a fond eye roll and Kash could feel her gaze on her as she walked over to the sink and set the dishes down under running water. She rinsed them quickly and set them aside before turning around.

Lani was watching her with a smile, head nestled in her hands.

"You should come, if you're free, if you want," she said.

Kash nodded earnestly, gripping the edge of the sink behind her.

Of course, I want to.

She watched as Lani beamed and a stray curl of blond hair lazily fell over her forehead.

Of course, I want you.

"Well," Kash said, wiping her hands down her thighs, "I should, uh, I should get going."

Lani blinked. "Oh. Okay."

They both made their way to the front door, slowly.

"Thanks for bringing over my calc set," Lani said.

Kash laughed. "You've already thanked me for that."

"Yeah, but like. It was more than nice of you. You're wonderful for doing that for me."

"It's nothing, Lani," Kash said firmly.

I'd do anything for you.

"Okay," Lani conceded with a pretty smile.

Kash returned the smile softly. She tapped her fingers against her thighs and tried not to fixate on the girl in front of her and how unfairly beautiful she looked in old sweats and messy hair.

"I'll see you tomorrow, then?" Kash said, eyes darting back and forth between her surroundings and Lani's face.

"Yeah, see you tomorrow, Kash," Lani said as she opened the door.

Kash stepped out into the cold and shivered as she turned to face Lani. She murmured a goodbye and quickly walked over to her truck before her lingering became awkward.

Lani didn't close the door, and Kash smiled fondly as she got in and started her truck.

Kash rolled down her window. "Close the door! It's chilly out!" she called out to her, laughing.

"I want to see you leave!" Lani called back, hunching in on herself a little as the grass rippled with a slight breeze.

Kash shook her head and rolled the window back up in concession. She quickly plugged in her phone, picked a playlist, and reversed onto the road. She waved at Lani through the windshield, who waved back with a grin and finally closed the door. Kash couldn't help her fond laugh and pressed the back of her hand against her mouth.

She drove in a dream, accidentally missing a turn so it took longer to get home. She preferred it, though. Driving at night was one of her favorite things to do and the way Lani looked tonight, freshly showered, was still reeling in her mind. She wanted to savor it.

She laughed again and squeezed her fingers around the wheel. She was an idiot. An absolute idiot.

let's keep this quiescence for as long as we can.

Kash loved her mom's cooking more than anything. She would probably demand a supply of her favorite *sambar*, with extra vegetables, to keep in her freezer next year in college—and bottles of the spiciest *pachadi* to keep stocked in the fridge, so she could eat it with rice whenever she wanted.

But the inarguable fact was that Raza's mom made chicken *biryani* unlike any other and Kash absolutely revered it.

"Well, *you're* hungry," Raza whispered to her as she leaned over to spoon a large amount of biryani onto her plate, taking care to have an equal amount of rice and chicken and avoiding any bay leafs and *elaichi* pieces. "You can't just pick what you want and leave the rest, just take out the elaichi and stuff afterward."

Their two families were having a casual get together dinner at Raza's house, and all of the food had been laid out onto a long serving table in the kitchen.

Kash's mouth practically melted at the sight.

"It's not every day I get to eat your mom's cooking," she scoffed, "I'm just taking advantage of the present opportunity."

Raza laughed. "She makes it every month. We always give you some in a box."

"Not enough," Kash said, shaking her head. "This chicken biryani is god-tier. And—if anyone hears me saying this, I'll be skinned alive—but your mom's cooking is objectively better than my mom's and we all know it."

They both piled more food onto their plates before going back up to Raza's room to eat, away from the loud laughter and boisterous conversation of their parents downstairs.

"I'll ask my mom to pack some for you for college next year," Raza said, sitting down on the floor at the foot of his bed. Kash followed next to him.

Raza had a smaller TV in his room, which was Kash's favorite thing about staying at this house. He'd connected a DVD player to it so they could watch movies all night in the comfort of his bed, and it was probably one of the reasons she always insisted they stay over at his house whenever they had a sleepover.

"What're you watching?" Kash asked as she turned it on and some old Bollywood movie was paused on the screen.

Raza shrugged. "I don't remember. You can change it if you want."

Kash shook her head and pressed play. She turned the volume down until the voices were just audible. She looked down at her plate, mixing the rice a bit before satiating her anticipation with a mouthful of biryani.

"Let's talk," she said after chewing and swallowing and relishing in the flavor.

Raza snorted as he worked through his own generous mouthful. He shook his head at her fondly.

"What do you want to talk about?" he asked after a moment of chewing and swallowing.

Kash shrugged and said, "I don't know. How're you doing? I feel like I haven't asked you that in a while."

"Eh," Raza lifted a shoulder, "things are fine. I'm fine. I'm finalizing college apps. Deadline for NYU is coming up in less than a month."

"You think you'll get in?"

"I hope I do," Raza said earnestly. "It's the only school I want to go to. The alternative is… staying here and going to UMass Amherst."

Kash laughed drily. "Right. *Amma* and *Nanna* are being annoyingly insistent that I apply to Emerson early. Don't even want to go there, though, I think they just want me close by."

"There're plenty of good writing schools close by, though."

"I know," Kash said, with a small laugh. "Nothing wrong with Emerson, technically, I just—I want to go farther than the state border, you know?"

"Hey," Raza said with a smile, "at least if we fail, we can both stay here and be miserable together. I'll visit you on the weekends. It'll be nice. Amherst isn't *that* far from Boston."

"An hour forty, idiot," she told him plainly before breaking out into a smile. "I'll take you up on that, though. But only if you bring food."

"Likewise. I want your mom's chicken kebabs."

Kash perked up. "Look, I can't promise they won't be eaten by the time I get to you. I covet those things."

Raza laughed and nodded. "Deal."

A love song dance montage played on the screen and filled the room with muffled music. They watched in silence for a bit, eating their food and laughing occasionally at the cheesiness of the romance on screen.

"The older you go, the cheesier they get," Raza said, laughing as the main heroine theatrically played coy and the main hero waxed poetic about her features.

"You mean the better they get," Kash corrected. "What are you talking about?"

Raza laughed and nodded, adjusting himself so he leaned farther into the blankets hanging off the mattress. His blue *kurta* top almost blended into the pattern of his comforter, and he almost disappeared in the plushness.

The bed frame dug into Kash's lower back, but with the amount of times they'd sat at the foot of his bed to talk or hang out or play cards, she was used to it.

"I think Levi's applying to UMass too," Kash said. "So, you won't be completely alone in our worst case scenario."

"Really? He didn't tell me."

She nodded. "He's been really cryptic about it. Pretty sure he's applying to Columbia as his first choice. For film."

Raza whistled.

"Yeah," Kash said with a grin, "I know."

"He never told me. He'll get in, though," Raza murmured. "I'd believe anything he does."

"Me, too," Kash said. She looked at Raza knowingly. "And I believe you'll get into NYU."

Raza looked down at his food with a small smile. "Thanks. Fingers crossed."

"You will," Kash insisted, leaning into him so their shoulders pressed against each other.

"Yeah," Raza nodded. "Yeah, *InshaAllah*, it'll happen."

Kash nudged him and went back to eating her food.

"I think it's about being the only child, but I don't think I'll be able to go anywhere my parents don't want me to," Raza confessed. "I love them and they're supportive and everything, but. I think there's a limit to how loving and supportive parents can be, you know? No matter how good they are. There's a limit to good-*ness*."

Kash watched him for a moment.

"I agree," she murmured.

There's a limit to understanding.

"Yeah," Raza sighed out heavily, visibly deflating.

"It took me long enough to convince my parents on writing," Kash said, "I can't change that now. They'd treat me like—they'd start telling me what to do."

"I think it's just them reacting," Raza said carefully. "They don't want you to make the same mistakes."

The same mistakes as your brother.

"Yeah," Kash said. "I know, I know. It's just—"

I'm not my brother.

A painful silence ensued and Kash wished she'd never brought it up. That college apps didn't exist. That grades and growing up were lightyears away. She wished everything was different and she could disappear into that preferable alternate reality where her family was perfect and things felt possible.

She licked her fingers clean of *raitha* before digging into the lamb curry and mixing it carefully with rice.

Next to her, Raza turned up the volume of the movie and the loud Hindi dialogue was grating to her ears. She looked up at the TV through her lashes, watching the movie and reading the subtitles with a foggy attention.

"He's coming home for *Deepavali*," she said, digging her teeth into her lip. "My brother."

At Raza's slightly confused face she reminded him, "Deepavali's the one where we, like, light *diyas* and fireworks. Celebrate good over evil, and all that."

"Oh. How is Rafi?"

"I don't know," Kash said, voice a little harsher than it should've been, "I haven't seen him in months. And it's been almost a year since he was home."

Raza raised an eyebrow, like he was about to pick apart exactly why there was an edge in her voice, and somehow work his way through with logic until Kash wouldn't be able to hide under annoyed petulance.

She huffed and looked away, inspecting a framed picture on the side table in the corner, of her, Levi, and Raza from when they were in elementary school. She scanned their buoyant smiles, Levi's messy red hair, and Raza's missing front two teeth, and felt the edges in her recede slightly.

"Every time I see that picture," she said, jutting her chin toward it in emphasis, "I want to go back to those days."

"Yeah," Raza said, "no APs, no GPAs, no extracurriculars, no SATs—"

Kash barked out a laugh at that and waved her hand in refusal. "No, please, no SATs!"

"Yeah, man, I'm taking them again next week," Raza said.

"I thought you took them in August?"

"I just want to make sure my scores are good. Next week's my last chance to take it—to improve—and I'm sending them straight over, so I *have* to do well—exceptional, if I even want a chance—" Raza rambled, voice slowly falling into a panic.

"Hey," Kash grabbed his shoulder with her free hand and looked him straight in the eye. "You are brilliant and smart. There's absolutely no reason for you not to get a good score."

Raza awarded her a bright, pure smile, his face lighting up and smile lines becoming more prominent around the corners of his mouth. His features were dark and warm, and

Kash pictured him going off into the real world and becoming the quiet, mysterious, main attraction.

"I think you'll do well in college," she mused, looking him over.

Raza raised an eyebrow. "What makes you say that?"

"You're quiet, obviously," Kash said. "But you've got a warmth about you. It makes people want to get to know you."

Raza looked down, embarrassment coloring his ears.

"You're biased," he said.

"I'm serious," Kash insisted, patting him on the back with theatrical propriety before tucking her chin on his shoulder. "I think you'll be the best out of all of us in college. I can picture you in the city easily. You'd fit right in."

Raza shook her off and laughed. "No, I'm too antisocial for that."

Kash shot him an unimpressed look and he laughed again, louder this time.

"Well, it is the dream, though, so maybe I'll suddenly come out of my shell. Become famous, or something," he said, shrugging his shoulders.

"Famous?" Kash grinned, barely swallowing her next bite of food before descending into laughter.

"Yeah, why not!" Raza threw his hands up. "Go to New York and become a rock star, that's what everyone does, right?"

"Oh my god, please don't become a rock star," Kash begged through uncontrollable giggles. "You'd be a terrible one."

"Can't make promises now!" Raza declared.

They both fell into each other, laughing and basking in the anticipating wonder of college, pretending the daunting unknown of it all didn't exist. For a split second, she thought of her brother and wondered how he'd reconciled the dream with the reality, and then came to the conclusion

that maybe he hadn't, and that's why things had turned out
the way they had.

like you, like him.

"Do you know what the proper way to listen to an album is?"

Kash shook her head and shrugged at her older brother.

Rafi gestured smoothly in a line and said reverently, "From start to finish."

Her brother was laying on his side, going through a long horizontal bookcase filled with CDs.

Kash watched with attentive eyes as Rafi ran a finger down a particularly beat-up Tom Petty album.

"I like that one," Kash said, "*Nanna* always plays it on the way to school."

Rafi raised an eyebrow, pulling out an entirely different CD instead, with scratched plastic and a broken hinge.

"Well, this one *is Nanna's*."

Kash's eyes widened at the black graphic album cover. She could vaguely recognize her father among the four faces on the back.

No. Way.

"Like *Nanna's band*?" she asked in disbelief.

Rafi nodded with a conspiratorial grin.

"Can you play it?" Kash asked, face open in excitement.

"No," Rafi said gravely, shaking his head.

"Why not?"

He leaned in and whispered, "It's—honest to god—terrible."

Kash stared at him for a moment before bursting out laughing. She slapped a hand against her chest and rolled onto her back, looking up at the basement ceiling.

"But *Nanna* said he played all over the country and people liked it," Kash said breathlessly.

"Yeah," Rafi said. "Definitely an exaggeration. And there's a reason why he's never played it. It sucks."

"*You* suck. And what d'*you* know, you're only fourteen." Kash stuck her tongue out at him.

Rafi rolled his eyes and ruffled her hair.

"And what do you know, you're only *nine*," he mimicked her.

She slapped him away and insisted, "Ten in three days!"

Rafi raised an eyebrow, mockingly. "Oh right. All grown up, aren't you, with your double digits?"

Kash rolled her eyes and shrieked when Rafi pretended to tickle her for a moment.

They laughed and, after settling down, lay on the cool carpeted floor of the basement, looking up at the tiny holes in the false tiles like they were stars in the sky.

"You know what?" he murmured after a while. He got up, eyes glazed over in thought.

"What?"

Kash watched as he walked over to where his guitar was leaning against the old piano. He grabbed it and lay back down, positioning himself on his back opposite to her.

"I, uh, wrote this one," he said softly. "So, it doesn't suck."

"Okay," she whispered.

He strummed carelessly for a few moments, fingers catching strings randomly.

"It's a million times better than *Nanna's*."

Kash giggled and tapped her hand against the floor. "Okay, okay. Play it."

He played a few chords, aimlessly switching back and forth between the same four.

"I won't accept you saying anything less."

"*Anna*. Just *play* it," she demanded.

After a moment, he complied.

He started with soft, delicate plucks on the guitar, and Kash closed her eyes to listen with every fiber of attention she could muster.

> *"I'll have you, if you'll have me.*
> *Don't let go even if you bleed,*
> *because when you do,*
> *I'll fall right off the cliff."*

His voice had the residual lilt of a classically trained Carnatic singer and Kash wished, for a moment, that she'd learned how to sing too. Because this was beautiful, in all the meanings of the word she could think of.

> *"Constantly we crash beneath,*
> *the waves that always paint the sea,*
> *and we go under but*
> *you can have my breath."*

A part of her wanted to ask what it was about, what the emotion in his voice was, and her mouth opened with the urging curiosity, but she squeezed it shut after a moment, realizing that she never wanted to interrupt whatever surreal feeling was around them at that moment. The surreality of actually hearing her brother sing words he'd written from somewhere inside him.

"I haven't figured the lyrics out for this part yet," Rafi paused to say, "and honestly haven't totally figured out the tune of it either, but it's—"

He sounded the melody out in *das* and *ohs* and Kash listened in adoring rapture to the sweeping sound of his voice moving across musical scales, up and down, until it came to rest for a brief moment.

"—and then it goes," he said, before singing out the next part—

> *"I'll give you all of me,*
> *when all your dreams come*
> *crashing down below."*

His voice trailed off and he slowly stopped plucking the guitar strings before giving a soft, short strum to signal the end. The room around them softened, as if to give an awed ovation to his performance.

Kash took a moment to bask in it and listened as Rafi absently plucked at a few strings before setting the guitar aside.

"Do you think you'll write more?" she asked.

"This isn't the only one, just, like, the most recent. And yeah."

"Can I hear those too?"

"Maybe."

"What are they about?"

"Nothing."

Kash tilted her head and gave him an unimpressed look.

Rafi shrugged and added, "Stuff."

Kash rolled her eyes.

"That was really pretty, *anna*," she sighed and let her head loll to the side for a moment before looking back up at the ceiling.

When he didn't respond, she turned her chin up farther, stretching her neck and staring at her brother upside down.

"Are you okay?"

Rafi looked at her the same way, chin pointing toward the ceiling, eyes strange and alien-like from this angle.

"Yeah, why?"

"Do you think you'll make a CD like *Nanna* and play for people all over the country? All over the world?"

Rafi scoffed, "No, no. This is just—this is just for here. Definitely not the world."

After a moment he added under his breath, "Yeah, no. This is—these're different."

"I want to write songs," she told him. "Like you."

After a moment he smiled softly and said, "Okay, copycat, you better play them for me, too, then.

happy deepavali.

The blouse of Kash's *langa voni* was beyond uncomfortable, bejeweled and embroidered intricately. The sleeves themselves reached halfway down her arms and the langa weighed heavily against her waist, the thick fabric falling just above her toes. It was a bit short on her, like all her langas usually were.

"*Amma*," she complained with a wince as she tried to adjust the skirt so it wouldn't fall down.

Her mother slapped her squirming hands away and went to work pinning everything up, occasionally poking into Kash's skin to which Kash would give a dramatized cry of pain.

"*Aagu oka nimisham*," her mother admonished her fidgeting with an exasperated frown. "Just *wait*."

"I don't get why we have to dress up, we're not going anywhere, no one's seeing us—"

"Do you have to complain about everything?" her mother snapped, pulling the strings of the back of Kash's blouse harshly.

"That's too tight," Kash grumbled, eyes darting around the master bedroom and eyeing the sarees her mother had laid out on the bed.

Her mother loosened the tie minutely.

"Okay, how is that?" she gestured for Kash to look in the cheval mirror.

Kash slumped her shoulders defiantly, moving over to look at her reflection with disinterest. She scanned the way the fabric of her voni draped in neat pleats across her body and over her left shoulder, allowing a slight peek at her stomach. She tucked her skirt up and pulled the sleeves of her blouse down before sighing in defeat.

Her mother smiled and grabbed her chin to press a firm kiss on her cheek.

Kash pulled away from the affection with mild annoyance.

"*Elli nagalu vesuko*, I laid them out on your dresser," her mother ordered. There was a strange pride in her eyes that Kash brushed away with a fond groan of frustration as she made her way down the hall to her room.

A pair of gold *jhumka* earrings and a matching gold necklace glittered on her dresser. She put them on with a defiant frown, moving her head back and forth to feel the swaying movement of the earrings against her neck.

"Kash!" her mother called her, voice growing nearer until her head popped in through the doorway. She surveyed her appearance before smiling and tilting her head.

"*Dha, elli deepalu velliginchukundaamu*," she said. "Let's light the *deepams*."

Kash sighed and followed her mother downstairs, taking care to lift her skirt so she wouldn't trip on the steps.

"*Bottu petukunnavaa?*" her mother asked, turning around.

Kash indicated the decorative sticker *bottu* on her forehead, between her eyebrows.

Her mother nodded approvingly.

"When's Rafi coming?" Kash asked, effectively halting the comfortable air between them.

Her mother stiffened.

"Um, I don't know," she said, eyes darting down as she dusted off her saree.

They made their way into the kitchen, confronted by her beaming father.

"Happy *Deepavali*," Makrand said warmly.

Kash returned the sentiment, and the hug he pulled her into. She wrapped her arms around him and squeezed as hard as she could before letting go.

"Kishu *nu* Kittu *ekkada*?" her mother asked. "Where're the twins?"

Makrand shrugged before regarding her in a way that made Kash roll her eyes and look away in disgust.

"*Cheera boundhi*, Jai," he said with a disgustingly adoring voice. "You look beautiful."

"*Thelusu,* you're the one that bought it," her mother said wryly, waving the fabric of her saree that draped over shoulder.

"I know, that's why I said you look beautiful."

Jaisri smacked Makrand playfully before asking where the twins were again.

Kash zoned out as she watched her parents interact with their usual warmth. She wondered if they'd stay like this for the rest of the night. If they'd stay normal, loving, once the hidden source of tension for them all presented itself explicitly. Once Rafi came.

The twins came bounding into the kitchen not a minute later, wearing matching langas with puff-sleeve blouses that

Kash found incredibly childish. Their long hair was braided carefully down their backs in two decorated plaits and even their jewelry matched, save for color.

"I never understood the novelty of matching when you're twins," Kash mused out loud, leveling them with a plain gaze.

"I never understood the novelty of you existing," Kishori shot back in a mocking voice.

Kash grinned, more in a baring of teeth rather than amusement.

It took them longer this time to light the candles all around the house, Kishori and Kumari helping by accidentally dropping and breaking a few clay candle holders.

They used tall ones throughout the house. The traditional, shallower, decorated diyas, that Kash much preferred, were lit in the *devudu* room where the statuettes of gods and goddesses could see them, and where the danger of unawareness wasn't a problem.

The doorbell rang once when Kash was placing the candles along the entrance to the foyer, and she immediately knew it was him.

She opened the door quickly, meeting Rafi's soft, nervous smile with one of her own.

"Hi, *anna*," she said.

"Hey, Kash," he said as he entered through the doorway gingerly. "Feels weird to ring the bell to enter my house."

Kash brushed that away by pulling him into a firm hug, which he returned with tight, enveloping arms.

"Rafi?"

They froze at the sound of their mom's voice, disbanding just in time to see their parents and sisters eagerly come in through the hallway.

An impasse manifested and Kash could feel the tension in the room thicken around her as everyone stood stock still.

"*Amma, Nanna,*" Rafi said, voice uncharacteristically young and unsure, like he was suddenly her ten-year-old big brother again. "Happy *Deepavali.*"

Her mother's face broke out into a hesitant but warm smile. Her arms reached out in a motherly gesture and Rafi sighed out before stepping into them.

Anxiety tipped over Kash's heart, falling just over the precipice, as she scanned her father's face for any sign of acknowledgment.

Makrand's face remained stoic, unyielding. He caught Kash's eye, and she felt like a little kid again, eyes glittering with young tears, nervously awaiting her father's reaction. He looked more than a decade younger, too, like he was back to figuring everything out by trial.

She supposed they all felt a little immature, unprepared, in the face of moving on.

"*Enti... ela unnav?*" he asked Rafi carefully.

How are you? After almost a year?

"Good," Rafi said. He winced before adding, "Looking forward to fireworks?"

Makrand nodded at that and turned around, an indication.

"We have the blue and red ones this year," Kishori said excitedly as they made their way back through the hallway and kitchen, and to the deck outside, together. Like a whole family.

"Oh really?" Rafi asked, indulging Kishori and ruffling her head lightly. "Remember you using them all up last year."

Kishori scoffed, ineffectively hiding her adoring giggles. "We bought more, duh."

"Smuggled them in from New Hampshire," Kumari interjected with a suggestive grin.

Rafi laughed at that, nodding. "Yeah, yeah, I remember where we get them."

It was bitterly cold outside for everyone except Rafi, who was still wearing his thick coat.

Kash observed as the twins went about unpacking all the sparklers onto the weather-roughened wooden boards. She hung back with her brother, by the sliding glass door that allowed light to spill from the kitchen inside, into the night. Their clothing glittered softly, like they were each wearing fabric made from precious stones.

"Can we do a *chichibuddi* this time?" Kumari asked loudly, whipping one of her braids behind her back.

"No, we have to keep a low profile," Makrand told her with a conspiratorial flick of his brow. "*Chichibuddis* are loud. We're not even allowed to do fireworks, not even sparklers."

The reminder that they were all actively doing something illegal lit a fire in Kumari's eyes and Kash thought she should be worried by that, but a fondness overpowered her as she smiled at her younger sister. What a little demon, twin *demons*, both of them.

"*Raakshasi*," Kash voiced her thoughts out loud as she watched Kumari meticulously unpackage and organize the sparklers by their determined color.

"Yeah, they both are. So—you guys won?" Rafi said softly, nudging Kash. He smiled at her. "Soccer, I mean. Last week's game. My roommate told me, his sister goes to your guys' high school, turns out."

"Yeah," Kash nodded, "it was a good game. Um, I have one on Sunday, if you, if you want to come."

Rafi nodded back after a moment. "Sure."

Their parents had lit the *deepam* candles now, setting them down carefully on the thick wooden railing that surrounded their deck.

Kishori and Kumari eagerly grabbed a few sparkler sticks in each hand and lit them against the flickering flames.

"It's so fucking cold," Kash muttered under her breath, a violent shiver going up her spine. She was slightly more grateful for the longer sleeves of her blouse and tried to find some warmth in wrapping the thin fabric of her *voni* more fully around her torso.

"You should wear a jacket if you want to be warm, idiot," Rafi said, shaking his head, before wrapping his arms around her without warning to rub quickly from her shoulders to her elbows.

"I'm okay, I'm okay, jeez," Kash slapped his hands away after a moment. "Stop. I'll warm up with the fireworks."

Rafi snorted and shrugged as if to say "suit yourself" before digging his hand back into his pockets, shoulders hunched against a particularly strong gust of wind.

"Kashvi! *Ittu raa!* Fireworks *kaaluchukondhugani,*" their father called out to her distractedly, emphatically waving a sparkler in one hand and gesturing for her to come over with the other.

The omission was palpable.

"Go on," Rafi said softly, a tinge of resignation in his eyes.

Kash shook her head and stubbornly tugged him along with her.

He followed with his head hung slightly, eyes darting between all of them as Kash went to grab a few sparklers from Kishori.

"Here, take the normal ones," her sister said, hiding away the boxes of colored sparklers like they were something precious.

Kash huffed and reached for the colored ones but stopped as Kishori pulled them back farther out of reach.

"Give me some red ones," Kash demanded.

Kishori made a face. "No."

It took all of Kash's strength not to tug on both of her sister's braids until she relinquished the sparklers.

"Please, *chinna*," Rafi tried, voice soft and coaxing. He smiled softly and affectionately and outstretched his hand like one would to a beloved pet.

Kash rolled her eyes.

Kishori paused for a moment, mulling it over before outstretching a handful of sparklers to him with an adoring grin.

"Thanks, Kishu," Rafi said warmly, knocking his knuckles affectionately against Kishori's cheek.

Kash raised an eyebrow as Kishori suddenly glared harshly at her, like she was summoning the ability to burn Kash to ashes.

"Kishu," Kash demanded again, matching her sister's glare, and held her hand out.

Kishori shook her head adamantly and flipped her braids over her shoulders as she turned back to lighting her sparklers.

"Here." Rafi gave Kash a few sparklers, his chuckles turning into white puffs of warm air in the cold night.

Kash took some begrudgingly and went over to one of the flickering *deepams*, lighting one for her and one for Rafi.

He took it with a smile, face illuminated by the red light, casting shadows above his cheeks and nose like a mask.

To their right, Kumari shrieked as the sparkler burned to its end, too close to her finger for comfort.

"Careful," their mother warned fondly from somewhere behind them.

In complete opposition, Kishori grabbed four sparklers in one hand and lit them all at once. The billowing cloud of rancid smoke and heat that erupted immediately rendered them all coughing and shielding away while Kishori laughed and held the mass of light as far away from her body as she could.

A bubble of warmth bloomed slowly in Kash's chest, in contrast to the sudden, crackling sparklers, as she watched Rafi and their parents immediately scold Kishori in varying degrees of reprimand, to which her sister waved the sparklers around in mock warning.

The warmth trickled in slowly through the gaps of her ribcage, like crystallized honey, manifesting into fondness. She brought a hand up to press against her sternum, ignoring the bite of the decorative rhinestones embedded in her blouse.

She laughed as Kishori then chased Kumari around until the sparklers died out and Kumari tripped on her *langa*, falling knee-first onto the cold floor of the deck. At least the thick fabric would be a good barrier against splinters.

"Careful, idiot," Kash said through bouts of laughter.

The half hour they could bear in the cold, they spent totally consumed by the playful novelty of sparklers, just like they did every year. The deck was illuminated in varying colors, and the opaque clouds of smoke around them made it all feel like a dream. Like a warm bubble, something hidden from the outside world, from the darkness that faded into opaque black just beyond the deck. Like their backyard didn't exist, the neighbors didn't exist, the unspoken tension and its inevitable consequence didn't exist. Just them, happy and playful, the way Kash liked to think they all naturally were as a family.

And like pleasant clockwork, the six of them rushed back inside and huddled around Makrand's tablet to video call their family in India, wishing a *Happy Deepavali* to each groggy set of grandparents, and aunts and uncles, and cousins. The twins showed off their dresses and jewelry like little girls, and Kash supposed that maybe they were still young. Thirteen wasn't too far off from twelve, which wasn't too far off from being in fifth grade, which wasn't too far off from being a child.

"*Ela unnaru, Ammamma?*" Kash asked, as she waved at her grandmother on the tablet screen, still breathless from playing around with the sparklers.

"Rafi?"

The pleasant comfort of a dream melted away. *Ammamma*'s voice seemed to cut through all the noise, rendering everyone silent.

Kash could hear herself shiver and tried to stop, tensing her body against the cold that still seemed to cling to her clothes and skin.

"*Ammamma?*" Rafi answered shakily. He came out from behind the twins timidly, like he was afraid of being seen.

Their grandmother didn't respond for a moment, and Kash could see the emotions flitting across her weathered face even through the pixelated screen.

"*Deepavaliki vachavaa?*" their grandmother asked softly, voice frayed and perceptive. She wasn't unaware of the distance between Rafi and the family, and the fact that he'd come, the fact that they were celebrating as a family, was significant enough to be felt by everyone, even through the screen of the tablet.

Rafi nodded jerkily. His eyes glistened in the moonlight coming through the large family room window, and Kash thought he looked incredibly lost, unsure of what he was doing here.

"Yeah, I came for—*Deepavaliki vachanu*, yeah." He stumbled over his words and wiped his nose like he didn't know what else to do.

"We always celebrate together every year, *kadhaa*," Kash offered, smiling purposefully at the camera.

"*Avunu, anthele*," their grandfather agreed with a wise laugh, swiping his hand through the air teasingly. "*Elaa unnavu, raa?*"

Kash beamed at him. Heartache seized her as she watched him laugh, missing the way it sounded in person, missing the warmth of his hugs, the sarcastic nature of his way of speaking.

"*Nenu baane unnaanu,*" Rafi answered, voice warm, "I'm doing okay."

"*Enti, emichesthunnavu ippudu?*" their grandfather asked, and Rafi blanched at that.

What are you doing now? With your life? With yourself?

He didn't know how to answer that question. Kash could see that, could see it in his eyes and the way he opened his mouth to speak, but no words formed.

"*Emiledhu, Deepavaliki vachadu, anthe,*" their father said dismissively. "*Anthe.*"

Rafi recoiled at that and Kash felt immediately frustrated with their father.

"What do you mean, '*anthe*'?" she demanded. "It's not just *anthe*. It's not just *that's that*. This is not just about Deepaavali or—"

"Kashvi, not now," Jaisri murmured, placing a hand on Kash's shoulder with a motherly squeeze.

"*Sarele*," her grandmother said placatingly, offering the start of a goodbye, like she knew their amicable happiness was a thin thread of a facade. "*Meeru chuskondi, memuntamu.*"

"*Sare attha,*" Jaisri answered with a smile. "*Malli matladuthamule.*"

"*Sare, oontamu ayithe,*" both grandparents parted with a twinkling smile and a wave.

They all waved back with plastered smiles until Jaisri ended the call, and their smiles dropped like actors' faces after the curtain call.

"You know, you yell at me for being stubborn," Kash told her father loudly. "You should check where I get it from."

Makrand rolled his eyes at that, taking his tablet and setting back on the coffee table. "You don't get it from me."

"Do you have to be like that even in front of them?" Jaisri admonished all of them. She looked to her husband with a withering glare. "And she gets it from you. They all do."

She ushered them out onto the deck to grab the candles and remaining boxes of fireworks. They left the water bucket of used ones next to the sliding door that led back into the family room.

Inside, there were bowls of freshly cooked curries and *pulihora* rice on the dining table, along with a stack of plates and napkins. The smell carried Kash over into the warmly lit dining room and she started shoveling food onto her plate so she wouldn't let out her anger at her parents.

Red frustration itched at her fingertips. She was frustrated at her father for acting like Rafi was a stranger, at her mother for acting like nothing was wrong at all.

They all ate in heavy silence around the dining table, Kash taking care not to spill anything on her clothes. The decorative stitching dug into the softness of the inside of her arm as she moved to put more rice on her plate.

Rafi, who was sitting next to her, pulled the pot of rice closer for her ease and she thanked him inaudibly.

"My nails are going to be yellow tomorrow," Kishori whined after a moment, breaking the silence.

Rafi cleared his throat and nodded. "So will mine. I'll be teaching guitar with yellow fingers." He wiggled his fingers as he laughed, and the twins joined in after a moment.

Kash smiled to herself.

"You're teaching guitar?" Makrand asked with a raised eyebrow, as if Kash hadn't already told him months ago when Rafi first told her.

"Yeah," Rafi nodded carefully, "yeah, met some people through school. I've got about four students so far. I teach them piano and guitar. It's nice."

"Is that what you wanted to do?" Makrand asked, barely concealing the passive aggressive curiosity in his voice.

Rafi frowned and shrugged. "I don't know, *Nanna.*"

"I thought you didn't want to do music?" Their father persisted.

Kash watched as Rafi clenched his jaw.

"I didn't want to go to school for it, no," he said through his teeth. "Didn't want to make a career of it, no."

"Huh," their father said, grabbing a handful of milled rice *vadiyalu* and crunching down on one, "I thought it was useful to go to school for music if you wanted to teach it. And I thought teaching music was a career."

Rafi scoffed and Kash watched as he quickly finished his food, stood up, and dropped his plate in the sink with a harsh clatter. He washed his hand and wrung it, not bothering to even dry it on the hand towel hung over the oven handle. He ran his fingers through his hair, eyes downcast for a long moment before he looked up at them all with his brows drawn over his eyes in a harsh frown.

"I should leave, then," he said firmly.

Kash shook her head, reaching out to him. "What? Why?"

"He's been ready to leave since he came here, didn't even take off his jacket," their father said off-handedly.

That seemed to be the last straw.

"I've been ready to be *unwelcomed*," Rafi fired back, "and I've been proven right, so I'll go!"

"I was the one who asked you to come!" Makrand yelled.

"I grew up in this house!" Rafi's voice cracked. "I shouldn't need a *damn invitation*!"

"What do you want from me, huh? *Emikaavali neeku*?" Makrand asked, eyes flashing with anger and hurt as he slammed his hands onto the table and stood up with enough force to knock his chair back.

"Nothing, I'm—" Rafi started before cutting himself off brokenly. His fingers twisted together in panicked movements and Kash watched as he further resembled a cornered animal more than he did her older brother.

"I don't want anything from you," he said with glistening, defeated eyes, "I'm not asking for anything."

"Rafi," their mother interjected firmly, "we're afraid. We're not sure where you're going, and we don't want you to make the wrong decisions. We're scared for you. Can you blame us?"

We're scared of you.

"You don't think I'm scared?" he gasped out, gesturing wildly.

"You're the one who wanted to be independent," their father said, his arms folded intimidatingly, food and unwashed hand be damned.

Rafi threw his hands up helplessly. He slumped and sighed heavily before looking down at the ground, jaw locked and hands fisted. "I don't feel independent. I feel disowned."

The breath whooshed out of Kash's mouth, and she felt the tension in the room peak. Everyone stood stock still, taken aback.

Kash looked to her parents and internally crumpled at the utter hurt painted on their faces.

"I should've stayed home," Rafi muttered, guilt evident in his voice and slumped shoulders. He made for the front door and Kash felt the remaining warmth of the room leave with him.

"No, wait," she called out. Everyone looked at her and she froze, suddenly forgetting how to speak.

"What?" Makrand asked in a low, gravelly voice.

"It's just," Kash floundered helplessly, "it's *Deepavali*. It's— we can't—"

Their mother moved then, walking gingerly over to Rafi and pulling him into a slow, motherly hug. She tucked his head tenderly underneath her chin, an awkward gesture considering Rafi stood at least a foot taller than her. But Kash supposed the way Rafi was forced to curl into the embrace and take comfort in it was the intention.

"Stay," Jaisri said softly in a voice that made Kash feel like she was intruding on something private.

Rafi shook his head, a muffled sob escaping him as he resolutely kept his arms at his side.

Kash looked at her father with wide, imploring eyes, and her heart sank at the manufactured indifference in them.

She wondered, as she watched her older brother cling to her mother like a child, how crushing it must be to feel like a stranger in the place where you grew up, to not be able to fall back into who you were before. To be estranged from your old self, when you hadn't really yet found who you are now.

deepavali, late in the night.

Rafi's jacket was slung over the back of Kash's desk chair, which was currently occupied with the messy pile of all the moving parts of Kash's *langa voni* ensemble she'd worn earlier.

"Do you have school tomorrow?" Rafi asked next to her, voice quiet.

"Of course, I have school tomorrow, it's a Friday, dumbass," Kash said, flicking her brother's ear.

He flinched away with a squawk of protest, scooting a minute amount farther away on Kash's somewhat meager full-size bed. They were both lying on their backs above the covers, and Kash was too scared that Rafi would flee at the slightest hint of him staying over for the night.

"Thank you for letting me hide away in your room," Rafi said after a moment. His eyes were focused on a loose thread on Kash's comforter that he was playing with absently.

"I'm sorry you feel the need to hide in the first place," Kash murmured as she glanced at the stoic expression on her brother's face.

Rafi shook his head, mouth curling into the faintest grimace.

"You're not disowned, you know that?" Kash said carefully.

Rafi squeezed his eyes shut, swallowing audibly, before looking at her and saying, "Can we talk about something else?"

Kash opened her mouth to protest but Rafi held out his hand dismissively.

"Please, *ra*," he said, eyes earnest but tired.

After a moment, she conceded and nodded.

"Have you written any good songs recently?"

Rafi scoffed at her, a familiar smirk slowly making its way onto his face. "*All* my songs are good."

Kash rolled her eyes and shoved him with a flat grin.

He shoved her back and, in retaliation, she kicked at him until he was on the edge of the bed, barely hanging on.

"Hey, stop it—*stop!*" Rafi hissed, battling her flailing attacks with his arms. He grabbed her ankle after a moment and yanked it before pinning it down with an elbow.

Kash laughed and rained fire on his back with her hands, slapping as hard as she could until he yelped and let go. She looped an arm around his neck and fell back, accidentally knocking a pillow to the ground in the process.

"Kash—*damnit*—" Rafi spat as she held him in a light chokehold "—I am *not* in shape for this. It's not a fair match."

Kash laughed triumphantly and let go, kicking him lightly in the thigh.

"Yeah, well, the days of you winning just because you're bigger are over. And your sister's a star player on the varsity team, can you imagine that?" she said with mock surprise.

"Jesus," Rafi winced and pressed a hand to the back of his neck, "you should come with a 'warning: do not engage' sign."

Kash grinned at that, theatrically flexing her arms to show off the muscle she'd developed from playing soccer since first grade.

He laughed, shaking his head, and flopped back into the plushness of Kash's bed.

"Missed you, copycat," he said softly, smiling up at her.

She stared at him and gathered herself together, arms coming around to hug her knees to her chest, and cheek resting on her forearm. She watched him with a soft smile, basking in the fact that he was here, in the house, and was smiling back at her.

"How're the boys?" he asked after a moment.

Kash shrugged. "They're fine. We're all just stressed with college apps, nothing new."

She paused then, realizing that the last time she'd properly caught up with her brother was last December, right before everything happened. "Nothing new" was not even remotely true.

"Well," she added with a grin, "as of June, I'm officially taller than Raza."

Rafi laughed loudly at that, raising an eyebrow, and asking, "Seriously?"

Kash nodded smugly, flipping her hair over her shoulder with an air of vanity.

"What about Levi?" Rafi asked.

Kash scoffed. "No but not by much. Only an inch or two."

"Are you taller than *me*?" Rafi asked incredulously.

Kash widened her eyes in anticipation. She hadn't paid attention to it earlier, but it had been a year since, and she'd had that weird growth spurt this past spring.

"Get up, get up," she urged him quickly, pushing him off the bed until he stood up, slightly ruffled and unimpressed.

"I'm actually not keen on figuring out if my kid sister is taller than me," he said flatly.

Kash brushed his words away with a shake of her head. She grabbed him by the arms and positioned him in front of the mirror. She eagerly measured herself up against him, back-to-back and gasped when she realized that she had beat him by at least an inch. She let out a whispered scream, and pumped her arm in celebration, while Rafi held his head in his hands and groaned.

A moment later, after she'd sufficiently rubbed it in his face, they fell back onto her bed in careless disarray. Kash's arm was stuck beneath Rafi's shoulder, and her legs were hanging off the edge, but she felt so warm and familiar that any movement felt like an interruption of a good memory.

"How's Lani?" Rafi asked.

Immediately, Kash felt a flush heat up her cheeks and ears and she unconsciously burrowed further into the mattress beneath her.

"Oh," Rafi sighed out, amusement evident in his voice, "right. It's *Lani.*"

Kash scrunched her nose and looked over at him with a frown.

"What do you—"

"I know you like her," Rafi said with a lopsided grin. "You have since the day she moved here when you were in, what, ninth grade?"

Kash stared at him before relenting with a sigh. She nodded, remembering exactly the day, and moment, she'd first laid eyes on Lani.

"It was two weeks into school," she mumbled, tangling and untangling her fingers together. "I was being nice."

"You were crushing on her," Rafi teased. "It was obvious in your smile. Still is, isn't it? I'd bet money on it."

"Shut up, fuck you."

He laughed quietly, shaking his head as he looked at her through the corner of his eyes before looking back up at the ceiling.

Kash looked over at him and took in the way his hair had grown much longer, covering his eyes and splaying out on the pillow beneath his head.

"Have you not cut your hair since last December?" she asked.

"Nope. Haven't cut my hair since. Been meaning to grow it out long. And there's no one stopping now, is there?" he shrugged, toying with his thumb in the air like he was finger painting a map.

"How're your roommates?" she asked.

Rafi smiled, like he was remembering something funny.

"They're good," he said, "Tommy—you might remember him, you met him when we were in freshman year—he's still at school. But he's been kind of… just, *there* for me after I dropped out last year." Rafi paused before letting out a chuckle and continuing. "He's kind of terrible, though, now that we're really living in our own place with the others, and we have an *oven*. He's got into the habit of baking when he's stressed and he's also in the habit of collecting cheap bottles of wine that he thinks look cool, and so our kitchen is full of fucking *artsy wine* now…"

Kash smiled as he trailed off into a long rambling explanation of how messy and crowded their apartment was and how it was almost entirely Tommy's fault, among the four of them that lived there. Her eyes traveled up the sharp curve of his nose, his prominent cheekbones, the way his face almost glowed while he spoke. She watched him smile, disgustingly fond, in a way she hadn't seen him smile in a *while*.

"You know," she interrupted him, pausing his ranting for a moment. She pursed her lips to hide a smirk before saying, "I think you smile in the same way, too."

"Same way as what?" Rafi asked. His brow furrowed in confusion, and he turned so he was on his side, facing her.

She threw him a knowing look, waiting until realization lit up his eyes and he suddenly looked years younger with a blush saturating his cheeks.

She cooed at him and poked his face where his dimples would be.

"Yeah, well," he said. "Another thing I can do freely now that no one's stopping me."

Kash frowned at that, but a part of her knew what that meant.

And a part of her agreed.

"Nobody was stopping you before," she said meekly.

Rafi's face darkened and he shook his head.

"You know they would if they knew. You know what they would say," he said in a quiet, hard voice. "Or what they *wouldn't*."

Kash squeezed her eyes shut, tensing, before quickly kicking up the covers and slipping underneath. The blankets fluttered above her for a second before they settled gently against her face. The comforter was heavy against the rest of her body, cool and encompassing, and for a moment she felt safe, hidden away from the heavy realizations at large outside the covers.

Until Rafi yanked them away and peered down at her with a quizzical expression.

"What are you doing?" he asked.

Kash looked up at her brother for a moment before asking in a small voice, "Do you think… you'll *ever* tell *Nanna*? Or *Amma*?"

"I haven't entirely figured it out myself, much less telling anyone," Rafi said with a gentle, forlorn smile. "I don't think I would even if I did have it figured out, but. It's not—I wouldn't be able to give a proper answer, so I think I'll be blissfully ignorant about all that stuff for as long as I can. Like you, I guess, with Lani." He chuckled, brightening a bit, before adding, "Copycat."

Kash smiled at that.

"Have you always known, then?"

"Sure," Rafi shrugged, "I knew I wasn't the one in this family to count on for normalcy, at least."

"Do you ever get tired of that?" Kash asked. "Of not being normal?"

Rafi didn't answer for a while, staring up at the ceiling with pensive, distant eyes.

"I think yeah," he said quietly, just above a whisper. "I think it's not necessarily about normal—or maybe it is. It's just fucking difficult to be anything outside of what others want you to be. I think it's fucking difficult, especially within this family, to be anything outside of what's expected, isn't it? Sometimes I think I should shut up and be grateful. Grateful that *Nanna* is someone who pushes me to pursue my passions instead of stability. That he's someone who sees stability in passion. That *Amma* does, too."

He shifted so he was looking at her in that imploring, selfless way he always did before giving her advice.

"But you don't have to make something your everything just because you love it, you know? I don't think—I don't think he gets that and it's—like it's just, I wonder what other things are out there for me to find and be passionate about. Like there has to be something out there that, just, consumes me." He gestured vaguely to the room, like he was indicating the world outside of it.

"Consumes you?" Kash repeated.

Rafi nodded.

"So, music doesn't consume you?" she asked.

He shook his head.

"But you act like it does," she said carefully, not wanting to sound like all the other voices that must be living in his head, all the other voices that must be telling him what to do and yelling at him when he strays.

"It's me, of course it is," he said, "I couldn't live without it, but. I don't know. Maybe I'm always going to feel like there's something more, something just out of reach, and I'm going to spend my life reaching for it. Maybe that's my hubris or whatever they call it."

"It's hamartia," Kash corrected him with a smile. "And I almost forgot how big of a drama queen you are."

Rafi threw her a dirty look. He reached over abruptly and ruffled Kash's hair, digging his knuckles into her scalp.

"Oh, *I'm* the drama queen, drama queen?" he asked mockingly, as he tackled her into a wrestling hold.

She yelped and pushed him away with effort, and for a moment fell into a frustration and begrudging fondness that she felt like a memory. She kicked at her brother, taunting him in hisses and whisper-screams, and for a second the memory swelled in her and then she was hit square in the chest with the ordinary but indwelling familiarity of having a brother, home, again.

* * *

Rafi didn't stay.

At two a.m., he got up with finality and walked over to grab his jacket from Kash's desk chair. Kash asked him if it was because he didn't want to sleep in his bedroom. He nodded and said he never wanted to set foot in that room again. She offered for him to stay in her room, and he'd shook his head. He instead said something that absolutely ripped Kash's heart in two, but also made her light a fuse in anger.

"D'you know the last time I slept in this bed? When you were twelve and made me stay up with you to watch the fucking Perseids." The corner of his mouth lifted as he continued, "You fell asleep well before we would've been able to see anything, and I almost threw a bucket of water on you to wake you up."

"You did throw a bucket of water on me. My bed was drenched for two days."

"Oh," he said with a smug grin. "Right, I did."

She rolled her eyes and sat upright, tense and rigid.

"This is your home," she reminded him, wanting so badly to convince him to stay, to keep up the pretense of normalcy they'd had for the past few hours.

His face darkened and he took a deep breath before throwing the knife with his words. "This isn't my home, not when everyone looks at me like I'm blown glass, ready to crack at any moment. You know who's fucking cracking? Them. *Amma* and *Nanna*, they're the ones that can't fucking—" He paused, hands fisting until his knuckles looked white and smooth. After a deep breath, he relaxed and flexed his fingers as he put on his jacket. "I never want to revisit the childhood, the life, I had in this house. So, I'm going to go home, *proper* home. *My* home. And you're going to go to sleep. It's late, and you've school tomorrow. So. Take care of yourself, Kash."

Kash was too stunned to say anything as her brother left without even a footstep of sound.

He must be so practiced in sneaking in and out like a strange intruder, to not make a sound, to know where the creaks in the floor were. Her chest tightened at that thought and she flopped back into her bed with a heavy whoosh of breath.

She stared up at the ceiling and drew the covers up to her nose. She sniffled once and heard a distant thud of a car door. Light beams tracked across the room from the headlights of Rafi's car as he turned onto the road. He probably had his high beams on, because he'd always had trouble turning them on and off. When she was in the car, he'd make her reach over and turn the knob for the windshield wipers or figure out how to turn the heating on without blasting it. She would always yell at him for not knowing how to use his *own car* and he'd always brush her off.

Underneath the covers, she wrapped her arms around her torso and dug her fingers into her skin. She blinked hard and clenched her teeth to try and dispel the aching anger growing in her. *Anger* at the way things were panning out, at Rafi for not *trying*, at herself for trying too *hard*, at their parents for being so *blind*, so *stubborn*. Hot tears trailed down her temples, soaking her pillowcase, and she swallowed again and again until the lump in her throat was small enough to ignore. Everything was multiplying inside of her, and it hurt, excruciatingly, to carry.

you never know what to do.

The trees were blinding on either side of I-290 as they drove to school. Little sparklings of white whipping past in broken shapes. She closed her eyes and relished the tiny white dots interrupting the dark red of her inner eyelids.

"Did you sleep last night?"

Her eyes snapped open.

"What?" she asked.

"Did you sleep last night?"

"What're you—yeah, why?"

Rafi raised an eyebrow and looked over at her. "You're falling asleep."

"'M not falling asleep."

He gave her a questioning look which she returned with a small shrug.

"I'm seeing the light spots," she explained.

"The what?"

"Like when you look at headlights and then you blink and see them all over."

A small fly buzzed into the corner of the windshield and dropped onto the dashboard, a tiny black dot. She grabbed

the hem of her sweatshirt and pulled it over her knees, bringing her legs up underneath herself.

"Hey!" Rafi shouted, glancing over at her. He pushed her
shoe-clad feet off the seat violently, undoing a tied lace in
the process.

"—Hey!" Kash slapped his hand away.

"Don't put your shoes on my seat," Rafi spit at her.

Kash scoffed at him and turned her body to face the window. They passed under a bridge and for a second she saw his
reflection in the glass. She glanced back at him.

Rafi ran a frustrated hand through his hair and gripped
the steering wheel tightly. He groaned and hit his head back
against the headrest, eyes fixed ahead. Some messy black hair
fell into his face as he glanced over at Kash with a quick, withering glare, without even turning his head in the slightest.

She emboldened herself and glared back at him.

"Why do you care about my sleeping habits anyway?"

"You're in eighth grade," her brother said in a monotone
voice, "you need to take care of yourself and all that shit."

She scoffed and reached a hand out to change tracks on
the CD.

"You don't take care of yourself and *all that shit*, and you're
a senior," she said, sitting back and enjoying the beginning
of the next song.

"Don't say 'shit.'"

"*Shit.*"

Rafi smirked as he watched the road. He turned on the
blinker and changed lanes leisurely. The clicking loud of the
blinker blended slightly into the music until he turned it off.

"I take care of myself," he said firmly.

He hadn't slept well last night. She knew because she
could hear him and their father yelling well past midnight.

He hadn't eaten properly for the past three days—he'd said he wasn't hungry at every meal, but she could see right through that. Their father wasn't much better, either.

"You don't," she said, looking at the side of his face. His nose dipped too much at the bridge, like their mother's.

"I do," he said, more to himself than to her. "And I've got five more months."

"You always talk like it's a sentence," she mumbled, frowning.

"What d'you mean?"

She shrugged and leaned down to fix her shoelaces.

"Like you've got five more months to *serve*. And then you're out of here," she explained. "That's how they talk in prison in the movies."

Rafi stared ahead at the road, hands clenched around the steering wheel. The blinker clicked loudly over the soft music as he drove down an exit ramp and merged onto the highway.

He sighed before saying, "Look, I just—I don't want to do *anything*."

She stared at him.

"But what about college?"

"I don't know," Rafi shook his head softly, glancing out the window before turning left. She shook her head at him.

"You have to go to college," she said gently. "Everyone kind of does, right?"

"That's not true, Kash. I mean, I'm gonna move out, but people sometimes go straight into work, you know?"

"So, a gap year?" Kash asked.

Rafi shook his head.

"Is it because you don't know which college to pick?" she asked. "I know you'll be fine wherever, because you're like—"

"I don't want to go to college, Kash," Rafi declared, voice cutting and raw. "I don't want to pretend like I want to, either."

Kash reached out to grab his elbow or tug his sleeve, but he shot her a sharp glare. She recoiled and hesitated between needling him for answers or fighting back. Instead, she curled up, pulling her feet under herself, and leaned against the cold window.

She could feel him staring at her shoes, and a small part of her triumphed at that.

Rafi sighed after a moment and blindly rummaged through the CDs in his center console box. He glanced down occasionally until he hummed and handed one over to Kash. There was a picture of a lady lounging in a red chair on the cover and Kash immediately smiled to herself in recognition. It was *Over and Over,* by The 88, the album Rafi would play on particularly good days, and the album she held dear to her heart because of all the memories of the two of them singing along to it. Maybe he was hoping for a good day, a good memory, now.

She grudgingly put it in with a fond eye roll, changing tracks to her favorite song just to annoy him a bit more. Jabbing piano chords slowly grew louder and Kash sat back with a satisfied smile, tucking the previous CD back into its sleeve.

Rafi rolled his eyes, a fond exasperation rushing over his face, and they listened to music together like they always did, nodding along and tapping their fingers against whatever surface they could find, sometimes humming and singing the lyrics when that wasn't enough,

Rafi pulled into his usual parking spot a song later, in the senior lot opposite to their school.

Neither made any move to get out of the car.

It remained quiet between them until he took the keys out of ignition with a click. The music cut out midsong and Kash blinked. They always let it finish, no matter what. She looked at her brother.

He was holding his head in his hands and looked so resigned. A weight pulled at her heart, and she took the keys from his hand.

"I'm always here?" she offered.

Rafi laughed.

Kash didn't know if it was a good one or a sad one.

"I'm so…" Rafi trailed off and Kash reached out and fumbled to turn the key in ignition. With a click, the music started playing again, right where they left off, in the middle of the last song on the album.

The almost chromatic notes of the guitar and screaming repetition of the lyrics were imminently apt and hard to ignore.

Kash shook her head, waiting as the confrontational chant of lyrics moved from one accusation to another and she wondered if Rafi knew they'd end up listening to this song, if that was the real reason why he'd handed it to her before.

They sat in silence until the song finished in an abrupt culmination of piano and electric guitar and drums, all at once like a rock cacophony.

The CD clicked in indication of the album's end.

"I'm so scared I'm going to do the wrong thing?" Rafi murmured, more like a question than a confession.

Kash tilted her head. She'd always believed, in the back of her mind, that Rafi could do no wrong. No *harmful* wrongs, at least. How could he, when he was this effortless, creative, wonderful person she tried everything in her might to be.

And it was just college, wasn't it?

"How could you?" she asked genuinely.

Rafi shrugged and hung his head, his chin pressed against his chest. His eyes were barely visible under thick black brows as he looked out the windshield.

"By disappointing people."

i've never been here alone.

Kash walked up to the yellow line, pushing her hands down against the straps of her backpack. The announcement voice repeated the arrival time of the next train into Boston and Kash leaned forward to watch the tracks.

A nervousness twisted in her stomach. She shouldn't be here.

It was still relatively warm out, and she squinted to where the tracks narrowed into distance, willing the train to come faster.

She'd left an hour early, even though the walk to the station was less than a mile from the house. *Nanna* had been out in the front yard, working on some stupid Halloween decorations with her sisters, *Amma* was busy with a work call upstairs in her office, and Kash had snuck out the back door.

The train came with a whoosh of sound and air. Kash's hair flew wildly, and she planted her feet down onto the concrete until the train slowly came to a stop.

Stepping off the platform felt like a final decision, the point of no return.

She tried to pick a row and sit down without thinking too much. The seat felt cold beneath her jeans, and for some reason the air inside the compartment was much cooler than the air outside. Kash shivered a bit and gripped the small purse of money she'd dug out of her piggy bank. She shook her legs up and down, heels tapping against the floor.

The ticketer came down the aisle about ten minutes into the journey and the whole time up until then, Kash practiced the process in her mind.

"Hi, where're you heading?" The ticketer stopped at her seat.

Kash smiled and carefully handed over a previously counted wad of bills and coins. "Back Bay, please," she said, trying her best not to make it sound like a question.

"One way or roundtrip?"

Kash paused and for a split second her heart wavered, and she suddenly had the need to get off the train and run back home. "One way."

The ticketer nodded, handed back some change, and tucked a ticket underneath the flap before moving on.

Kash shoved the change carelessly into the front pocket of her backpack and checked her phone. No notifications yet. She let out a breath and slumped into her seat. Outside the window, trees and houses and railroad tracks flew by, and she eventually pulled out her notebook and, after some digging around, her pen.

It was difficult to write on a train, but her thoughts were flitting about like birds and pecking at her brain. A significant bump caused her pen to streak across the paper uselessly and her head fell back against the seat with a frustrated thud.

The hum of the train lulled her to sleep for most of the journey, but she kept waking up with a jolt at each stop, nervously making sure she hadn't slept through hers. By the time the train arrived at her station, her memory of the ride was hazy and distant, and her muscles ached as she stretched, arms reaching out, before making her way off the train.

The station was filled to the brim with people. Her eyes darted around, as she walked up the stairs, nonchalantly watching for signs pointing the right way out.

A man with a briefcase bypassed her quickly, taking the stairs two steps at a time. He left behind a rush of air that smelled strongly of cologne. She tapped her fingers against her thigh and tucked her hair behind her ear as she quickened her pace.

Her phone rang, abruptly, *loudly*, echoing off the concrete walls and she hurried to the top, cursing under her breath, before stepping aside and pulling out her phone. Embarrassment burned her ears and cheeks.

"*Nanna*" was on the screen in big letters above a picture of her father she'd taken months ago at a restaurant. Her finger hovered over the screen, and she stared, heartbeat quickening more and more with each repetition of her ringtone, until it stopped, and the screen went black.

Her breathing was heavy and ragged, and she opened her phone to find a missed call notification and four text messages from her parents.

Shit.

She shook her head and put her phone away. One thing at a time.

* * *

The sky was getting dark now—almost night—and Kash gripped the straps of her backpack nervously. The first street she was supposed to look for was somewhere around here and she turned slowly in a circle, eyes searching and catching on anything that looked remotely like a street sign.

No luck. The map on her phone showed the blinking dot of her location and she felt idiotic, closely watching the little dot move as she walked.

Failure tugged at her shoulders every time she had to backtrack. It should've been a straight shot from the station, no chance to even get lost, because it should've been almost right in front of her.

How could she think she could do this on her own?

She huffed angrily and pulled up her call log in a frustrated rush. Her finger trembled over her father's name, and she dug her teeth into her bottom lip. The need to cry for help shivered through her and the immediate, instinctual refusal of it pressed down on her throat.

You're so stupid.

She scrolled and tapped. The line rang two times before he picked up.

"Kash?"

Kash's lip wobbled, and she tried to rid her voice of any sign of crying or frustration. She cleared her throat. "*Anna?*"

"Yeah, hey, what's up?"

I'm in Boston.

Kash shrugged, and said as casually as possible, "Not much."

Rafi sighed, the sound crackling through the phone speaker, "Okay. Why're you calling me, then?"

Kash opened her mouth.

I'm lost.

She closed it. "No reason," she said.

"Oh, are you missing me already?" Rafi teased. "It's only been two months, and I came home, like, two weekends ago."

"No," she spit out. After a moment, she let out a sound of frustration and squeezed her eyes shut. "Fine. How do you—like, how would you, *hypothetically*, get to your apartment from, I don't know, Back Bay?"

Silence from the other end of the phone made her heart race and she squeezed her hand into a fist and hit it against her forehead.

"Well," Rafi said matter-of-factly, "I'd, *hypothetically*, already be driving, or I'd take the orange line to Ruggles and then walk."

Kash opened her eyes wide.

Shit.

"The orange line?"

"Yeah. Why?" Rafi asked cautiously, like he already knew what Kash was going to say.

Kash hesitated, wiggling her fingers and toes in embarrassment. "Can I come and visit you?"

"Of course, you can," Rafi said. "Why?"

"How would you, hypothetically, *walk* to your apartment from your school? Or the, like, general Back Bay area?"

She winced when he didn't answer right away.

"Kash. Where… are you right now?"

Kash glanced at the nearest street sign and relayed the name to him quietly. She heard him curse distantly on the other end and winced.

"What the hell, Kash!" Rafi's voice exploded through the speaker. "Are you in Boston?"

"Maybe—"

"Alone?"

Kash nodded, saying a small "yes." She could hear the disappointment from the other end of the line, and it burned.

"Why would you—" Rafi's voice trailed off and she heard him put down the phone.

"Raf?" she called out. He didn't respond and panic swept up from her chest and into her throat. "Rafi?" she called again, squeezing the phone in her hand.

"Yeah, yeah, I'm here," he said, muffled by something. She heard him fumble until his voice came out clear. "I'm guessing *Amma* and *Nanna* don't know?"

Kash stayed silent.

"You're so, incredibly stupid."

Kash bristled. "I'm not—"

"Shit, why would you—it's not—" Rafi groaned before continuing, "Right, okay, I'll tell you where to go and you just confirm and follow, okay?"

Kash nodded, jaw locked in anger.

"Kash?"

"Yeah, yeah. I got it."

She walked diligently, according to her brother's directions. The sky got darker, and she retreated farther into her hoodie, huddling into herself as much as she could as she glanced around at the lit up streets. Couples and groups of friends laughed into each other, and it was like multiple casts of characters were all converging in the same film scene, around glittering bar fronts and restaurant windows. Her brother's voice stayed gentle and instructive the entire way through, grounding her from thoughtlessly continuing on in naive rapture.

If she'd called *Nanna*, he would've yelled at her and then driven into the city to pick her up, but the whole car ride back would've been the trap, the time he'd use to needle into Kash how stupid and selfish she was being.

Her cheeks were cold, and her nose and toes were just shy of frozen by the time she arrived at Rafi's apartment building. She hung up as she saw him waiting behind the glass door, suppressing the relief and excitement twisting her insides. He opened the door for her quickly, beckoning her inside, and she stepped into the warmth with a nervous smile. He was in his pajamas. His hair was messy, and he looked like he hadn't shaved in a month.

"Can I stay with you tonight?" Kash blurted out, before her brother could say anything.

Rafi groaned loudly, head lolling back and then to the side in a semi-circle. He faced her with a terribly inconvenienced expression and stared.

Her heart thudded harder and louder against her chest.

He smiled abruptly and shrugged. "I guess, whatever."

She sighed out in relief, walking up to him and punching his shoulder.

"Hey!" he exclaimed and immediately punched her back. "I'm letting you stay with me, at my expense, and this is how you act." He threw his hands up in theatrical disappointment, and she grinned.

"Nik's staying with his girlfriend for the weekend anyway, so you're lucky," Rafi told her as they approached the elevator.

As soon as the doors closed in front of them, Rafi whacked her upside the head.

"What the hell?" Kash yelped.

Rafi grinned coolly at her. "You know, you could've just asked me, and I would've come and picked you up for the weekend. No need to sneak out behind *Amma* and *Nanna*'s backs. If it hadn't crossed your tiny mind, it's not *safe* for you to just be walking around lost and alone, Kash, *use* the minimal sense that you have. Don't be stupid."

Kash huffed, "I have *sense*."

Rafi laughed and ruffled her hair. "Yeah, okay, copycat, keep on making my life miserable."

The elevator doors opened on the fourth floor and Kash followed her brother down a long hallway of doors to one with flaked paint and a brass 4C that matched the slightly rusted doorknob Rafi twisted to open. The living room was small, almost the size of Kash's bedroom, and it was still minimally furnished. There was a loveseat cushion on the other side of the room, in front of a decent-sized TV, where one of Rafi's roommates was sitting with a guitar in hand.

"Hey, Tommy," Rafi smiled, tilted his chin up and then gestured over to Kash, "'S my little sister. She's just staying for the night, because she has no brain and ran away from home."

Tommy nodded and grinned at Kash. He ran a hand through his hair, brushing it out of his face, before waving and saying, "Hey, name's Tommy."

Kash smiled back awkwardly, hand coming up in a small wave that Tommy acknowledged with a warm laugh.

"I commend you," Tommy said with an indicative nod that brought his hair back over his face, "I only ever wrote down a packing list for running away when I was younger."

Kash laughed at that and looked pointedly at Rafi before saying, "Your roommate's cooler than you."

Tommy whistled at that and leaned against his guitar, his cheek resting against his arm, while grinning at Rafi.

"Your sister is cooler than you, Raf," he said teasingly.

"I know, I know, it kills me inside," Rafi said sarcastically, gesturing his hand out to the rest of the apartment that was visible through the hallway. "Welcome. To our place, so far. It's about 60 percent unpacked. We'll be in better shape by Thanksgiving."

"Suggestions for decorating are welcome, by the way," Tommy said. "We all suck at that."

Kash laughed amicably and nodded, waving at Tommy from over her shoulder as she followed her brother out of the living room. She took in the haphazard posters taped to the walls, and the intermittent mess of belongings littering the floor. A fuzzy winter coat hung from a set of hooks above an ancient-looking side table that had a dinner plate with keys and knickknacks piled together messily.

"Is that a *plate*?" Kash asked in amusement. "You couldn't find, like, a catch-all dish or a box or something?"

Rafi shrugged. "A plate *is* a dish"

Kash scoffed at that.

The hallway opened into a small dining and kitchen area that continued into a second hallway around the corner, which was filled with even more boxes and one of Rafi's suitcases. Another two roommates were sitting in the kitchen area eating takeout food, and Kash thought it was funny how they barely seemed to fit around the small table, in the small space.

"This is Jack and Tenu," Rafi said. "And this is my little sister, Kash."

The two of them greeted her with friendly smiles, mouths still full of food, before going back to their meals.

Rafi regarded them fondly, swiping the back of his hand over his nose and gesturing for Kash to follow as he walked down the second hallway to the last door.

"Your apartment feels bigger than it did in August," she murmured, maneuvering the boxes and almost tripping over Rafi's suitcase that was halfway tucked between two boxes overflowing with books and CDs.

"That's where all the CDs went," Kash laughed softly. "I was wondering where your collection of The 88 was."

"Have you been going through my stuff in my room?" Rafi asked with a grin, setting a hand on the doorknob. "Are you rummaging around now that I'm not there? Never should've trusted you."

Kash rolled her eyes and gestured for him to open the door. There were two unmade beds on opposite sides of the bedroom, and Kash could almost clearly tell which side was her brother's. A guitar was left on the bed on the right, like a persistent afterthought, and there was a perfect shelf of books and notebooks next to his desk, where papers were strewn about in a shuffled clutter.

"Well, that hasn't changed," Kash said, running a finger along the book spines.

"What hasn't changed?" Rafi asked, taking the guitar into his hands.

Kash gestured to his side of the room. "Your messiness."

"Spoken like someone who isn't also messy," Rafi said with a scoff.

"Wonder where I learned it from?" Kash taunted.

"Definitely not me," Rafi mocked, punctuating it with a cacophonous strum of his guitar. "And Nik doesn't think I'm messy."

"He's probably just being nice—"

"Shut up or I'm calling *Amma* and having her pick you up right now," Rafi said, waving his hand in front of Kash's face in warning.

"They've been calling me nonstop," Kash grumbled, taking her phone out of her pocket and looking at the numerous notifications from her parents. "Don't think I can ever go back at this point."

Rafi laughed and reached a hand out to ruffle her hair.

She shied away from him, throwing him a withering glare before turning back to the books on his shelf.

"Don't worry I texted *Nanna* as soon as you called me," Rafi said, smoothing a finger down the fretboard with a smug grin.

"You… told them!" she yelled. She immediately reached over and slapped him upside the head.

He yelped, shielding himself and shying away from her attack. "Well, what did you want me to do? Get in trouble because of you?"

"No." She punctuated each word with a punch to his shoulder. "You. Could. Just. Not. Tell. You *idiot.* You absolute *dick.*"

"And do what? Let them yell at me for hours for being a part of your pathetic escape attempt?"

"I wasn't escaping!" Kash insisted dropping her arms by her side and slumping against the side of the bed. "I just—I just—"

"You just what?" Rafi asked. "Wanted to go for a *walk*?"

"I didn't walk here," Kash spat.

"Oh good, so you have some semblance of common sense," Rafi hissed mockingly.

"I just, I don't know, I—," she groaned and pressed her face into her hands before glaring at her brother through her fingers. At the prompting look on his face, she curled into herself and tucked her chin under the collar of her sweatshirt. "I missed you, okay?" she murmured, tugging on the sleeves of her sweatshirt. "You're so annoying," she added under her breath.

Rafi's face brightened in a self-satisfied grin that made Kash want to throw something heavy at him. He patted the bed, kicking his legs up onto the side table and leaning back against the wall. "C'mon. Relax, it'll be fine."

Kash huffed and used her hands to push up onto the bed.

"They'll just yell at you for a bit and that's it," Rafi said, throwing her a reassuring smile. "I told them you called me before you left and that I picked you up from the train station. And that you were stupid enough to let your phone die, so can't pick up any calls or anything."

"Oh."

"Yeah, happy?"

Kash rolled her eyes and mocked him—"*Yeah, happy?*"—before digging a foot into her brother's ribcage. "Thanks," she said, grinning when Rafi slapped her foot away.

"Of course. That's all I'm there for, aren't I? Just covering for you when you do something stupid." He sighed the words out like a martyr, strumming another cacophonous chord on his guitar.

"Ah, so you're saying whenever I really decide to sneak out or run away I can just say I'm with you," Kash said with a grin.

Rafi frowned at her. "Do you really want to run away?" he asked.

Kash's grin fell, and she shook her head. "No, no, it's just… something we joke about, like Levi and I. You know, normal teenage stuff."

Rafi looked at her like he knew that was a lie and she needed to allay that immediately.

"It's not—" she sighed. "I mean, yeah it'd be nice, but it's not real, you know? None of us would ever."

"Don't worry," Rafi said quietly, "I understand the feeling." He strummed again, louder this time, and Kash jumped, startled.

"What do you mean?" she asked.

Her brother shrugged. "You're fourteen, and you get it," he said. "Try adding to that by another four years."

After a moment, he scoffed and said, "Normal teenage stuff, right."

Kash's eyes wandered, settling on the familiar CD player that used to sit on Rafi's desk at home, and now placed on top of a stack of boxes. She got up to walk over to the player.

"Have you used it yet?" she asked, running a finger across the control buttons along the side. She pressed the eject button and a Bruce Springsteen album slowly came out. "Oh, so you're really in your teenage stuff," she laughed to herself before looking over at her brother. "You always played him whenever you were in your head, I remember, on the rides to school. 'Hungry Heart,' 'Jungleland,' 'Born to Run.' *Nanna*'s been doing that too sometimes, you know? I think he's missing you because he hasn't stopped playing his *Born in the U.S.A.* CD. I mean, really hasn't stopped. It's killing me. And that's my favorite, but there's only so much Springsteen I can take at a time."

"What are you talking about, you love him," Rafi said with a soft, private smile. "*Nanna* played him for you once when you were, like, four, and you've been in love ever since."

"I do love him," Kash said. "But I'm telling you I've heard 'Glory Days' almost every morning before I leave for school."

"Oh. Well, that must be fun for you guys. I bet the twins *love* that."

"Yeah," Kash said, grinning, "Kishori wears her earbuds twenty-four-seven now and won't listen to a single thing happening around her. It's driving *Amma* up the *wall*."

Rafi laughed at that—a loud, fond laugh that filled the room.

"Yeah," Kash continued, "it's hilarious to you, but it's an actual battlefield. And *Nanna* acts like a toddler as usual, so he refuses to turn it off. *That's* also driving *Amma* up the wall."

"Sounds like she's having fun," Rafi chuckled. "And sounds like *Nanna* is having a *blast*."

Kash hummed in agreement, lips twisting into a smirk at the memory of her dad refusing to turn off the speaker they had in the kitchen. He'd been practically petulant, crossing his arms over his chest in a way that would've been intimidating if he hadn't been a grown man pouting like a child.

"He starts every day missing you, I guess," she murmured. "But I think we all do."

At that, Rafi's face fell, and he frowned into the sound hole of his guitar. His fingers squeezed the fretboard, and a few strings sounded softly, before he let go altogether and set the guitar aside. He slumped into himself and covered his face with his hands. His elbows pressed into his knees and his back curved forward. He stilled like that, chest expanding periodically with deep breaths, hair falling over his hands in long black waves. He looked like a sad sculpture come to life.

"I start every day missing home, too," he repeated, voice muffled and quiet. After a moment he sighed out and dragged his hand down his face before looking over at her with a small smile and nodded.

Kash nodded back and pushed the CD back in before walking over to her brother and getting back up onto the bed. She reached over and grabbed the guitar, swinging it slowly around Rafi and gently holding it in her arms. The last time she mishandled his guitar, he'd screamed at her, and didn't let her so much as touch it for a month.

She pressed her fingertips around the first fret, taking care not to touch the wrong strings, and picked in the pattern that Rafi'd taught her a while ago. "How are you, really? How're classes?"

"Oh." Rafi frowned, glancing down at the floor, fingers twisting together. "I just—it's still the beginning. Plenty of time to, like, fit myself in somewhere."

A scramble of words were on the tip of her tongue, but she didn't know how to respond without potentially incurring damage, and any interruption to the pensive look on his face seemed like the wrong thing to do, so she continued to pick softly. Her fingers were a bit clumsy, and a particularly off-key twang made her smile despite herself. She wasn't that partial to playing the guitar, but something about it felt warm and embracing, familiar, like a well of feeling that slowly filled up the cavities in her chest she'd been harboring since her brother first moved out.

"Sometimes," she murmured without thinking, "I feel like, there's this empty space now. Like an empty space that I have to somehow cross over in order to be part of the family."

"Part of the family?"

"Yeah. It's like there's *Amma* and *Nanna,* and then there's the twins, and they all fit, and there's this empty space, and then me, and that wasn't there before."

"Empty space?" Rafi frowned. "Why's there an empty space?"

"I don't know." Kash shrugged. "Maybe it's where you used to be. You know, like your room now, but everywhere. Not just physically, but everywhere, in everything. I just feel alone sometimes."

"What about the boys? And Lani?"

"They're there. Obviously. But I'm talking about at home. It's not—it's a different kind of alone. Home… feels different now."

"I'm sorry," Rafi said, and there was a rawness in his voice that sounded like understanding. "I get it. I know what you're saying, I mean. A distance." He looked up at her with a wistful smile.

"From home?"

"No," he said, "No. Here." He pressed a hand to his chest and trailed it up to his neck. "Feeling it, feeling wrong… I don't know, there's this detachment. In me." He paused between words like he was contemplating exactly what to say.

"To what?" Kash asked.

"To," he sighed out heavily, "to everything that I'm doing here. Everything that I see myself doing here."

Kash hummed in response. She looked down at the guitar and slowly ran her thumb down each string. "You feel wrong here?"

"Yeah," he laughed wistfully, "yeah maybe. Maybe I knew I would and came here anyway."

"Do you feel like you've already made a mistake?" she asked carefully.

She heard him exhale sharply and glanced over to see his eyes squeezed shut.

Oh.

"I don't know," he said in a strained voice. "I—everyone says it's not, it's not a mistake, so maybe it isn't."

"Coming here? Or being here?"

"Yeah, yeah. Just in my teenage stuff, like you said."

"You sound like you're trivializing it."

"I'm not."

"Yeah you are, you're just—"

"Kash," Rafi said suddenly, looking up at her with wide eyes. "I'm not, okay?"

Kash leaned back and shook her head at him. "Okay."

He deflated further and fell to the side, head hitting the pillows with a soft thud.

"Okay," Kash murmured. "So where am I sleeping?"

Rafi looked at her without picking up his head. "Have you eaten anything?"

"Not hungry."

Rafi hummed before grandly gesturing to the floor with a slow smirk. "Then be my guest."

all we're comprised of.

The world was falling on her shoulders, and nobody cared.

"I just don't know! What do you want me to say?" Kash cried out, digging her fork into her noodles.

They all sat around the kitchen island, uncomfortably partaking in some takeout Thai food from their favorite restaurant for dinner.

Rafi was there, too, shoulders hunched slightly like he was ready to make himself disappear at the slightest sign of trouble.

The dinner had been a surprise for Kash, for getting into all of her top choice colleges, and the only reason her brother had showed up too, apparently.

"You're smart and you want to be a writer, Kash," her father said, using his chopsticks to unsuccessfully clamp down on some noodles. "You need to go to a good college if you want to succeed at that."

Kash rolled her eyes. She wanted to point out that maybe her father didn't know everything, or at least wasn't the one to act sensible, if he was twisting his chopsticks like that and eating one miserable noodle at a time.

"Just use a fork," she muttered, rolling her eyes as the clump of noodles he'd managed to pick up promptly dropped back into the container with a messy splat.

"I just don't understand," her mother said. "*Nuvve kaavaalani* apply *chesavu*. I mean, you wanted to go to school for writing. NYU, Middlebury, these are not easy schools to get into, Kashvi. Doesn't that tell you it's something worth pursuing?" Her voice was annoyingly matter-of-fact, her points logical and grating on the increasing chaos of Kash's dilemma.

"Yeah, but that's not the point. Raza got into NYU too, and he's smarter than me, so it's not like I'm special," she insisted.

"We're not talking about Raza, we're talking about you," her mother said, pointing her fork at Kash.

Kash made a sound of grave suffering and speared a piece of chicken with her fork.

"Where do you want to go?" Rafi asked.

Kash shook her head.

I want to go far away.

"So," her father said slowly, "you don't even want to entertain the idea of going to college?"

Kash paused and without thinking, looked at Rafi who was staring back at her with wide eyes, dark and betrayed and shocked. It immediately cut her more than she expected. She gripped her fork tightly and looked down at the tines glinting in the warm light of the kitchen.

"Are you going to?" her father added firmly, clinically. "You applied. So, we all assumed you wanted to. And now suddenly once you get into all the colleges you wanted, you're confused? Do you want to go? Or is there something else you want to do that you're not telling us."

Or do you want to be like your brother?

Her father knew how to get his point across without ever having to say it. She wished she had learned that from him.

"I didn't even know that was a choice," she said, fisting her hands for the smallest sense of bravery. "I was just voicing my thoughts, I didn't—" She cut herself off before she could say anything too incriminating.

Kishori and Kumari started whistling and snapping their fingers, like a pair of avid spectators and it made Kash want to violently wrangle them into a room and lock the door on them forever.

Her mother immediately grabbed their hands and glared at them in a way that made Kash's insides flare briefly with vicious triumph.

Makrand leveled them both with a hard look before turning to Kash and saying, "So?"

Kash stared into her noodles, willing a black hole to open up and pull her in.

"You know we'll support you, Kash," her mother said with manufactured warmth. "Of course. No matter what. And we know you will always make us proud, *ra*."

Is that a threat?

Kash ground her teeth together as hard as she could, felt her head shake with the effort. There was no point in reasoning through this mindset, anyway. She was standing on a precipice they would never understand.

"I know you'll support me, that's not the problem." She fisted her hands and hung her head before looking back up at every single member of her family staring back at her. "I just don't want to—"

Make the same mistakes.

How could she say that, when Rafi was sitting right there, looking at her like he knew exactly what she was thinking.

"—I'm just thinking it through, okay?" she finished.

"Thinking through whether you want to go to college?" her father asked.

Kash resisted the urge to slam her fist against the table, or her thigh, or something. "Thinking through what I want to do," she said firmly, bordering on petulance because she felt like a child, felt ignorant and naive, and she hated being made to feel that way.

"You know what you want to do above all of this," her father said, sincere confusion coloring his voice.

No, I don't fucking know what I want, that's the whole problem isn't it?

Kash held back a scream and looked at Rafi earnestly until he met her eyes. The betrayal still hadn't drained from them. His eyebrows were furrowed, and his jaw was clenched hard enough to accentuate his cheekbones. Or maybe he really had become sallower over the past year and a half, and she was just noticing now.

"I don't know," Kash said through gritted teeth.

Rafi sighed, dark eyes darting down so they were hidden by thick lashes that looked suspiciously clumped together, like he had just been crying. He closed the lid on his noodles and placed them in the fridge.

Kash followed his actions with her eyes, unable to look at anyone else.

"Yeah," he said softly, passing by her chair. He put his hand on her shoulder and looked at their parents as he slowly spoke his next words. "'S hard to know and do what you really want to do. And it doesn't matter where you go, I guess, because it doesn't change anything. It's disastrous to think that you know what you want, when you don't. people can be fickle." He then looked at their parents. "And making others proud should just be a byproduct of what you do, whatever it is that you end up doing."

Kash could feel the atmosphere go frigid, and she shivered out of instinct. A need to escape crawled up her spine and she shivered again. She watched as Rafi left the kitchen and heard his footsteps on the stairs.

"Oh," she exhaled slowly, her breath stuttering with the effort as she looked back at her parents.

The twins were silent, for once, eyes wide and if she didn't know any better, Kash would've thought they were afraid.

"I think—" Kash swallowed and nodded, closing the lid on her noodles as well. "—I'm done, too. Full."

"Kash," her father called.

"I'm full," she reiterated firmly before gracelessly getting up from her chair, shoving it back into place.

A cold silence settled around them, amplifying the cracks of sound as they each shifted to find something to say or do.

"I think I am, too," Kishori said with a clearing of her throat. Next to her, Kumari nodded in agreement and dropped her fork in her rice.

Kash watched as they carefully pressed the lids back onto their containers of fried rice.

"*Nanna*, can we watch a movie maybe?" Kumari asked, expertly offering an out, and Kash felt a surge of warm gratitude rush through her. Trust her sister to be smart enough to know exactly how to handle each of them.

"I'm too tired for a movie," Kash said in a voice that sounded so performed, even she winced. "Have fun."

She shot her sisters a grateful look as she walked out, and she could almost see the smug "you owe us" in their eyes.

The lights were off on the second floor as she made her way upstairs, but Kash knew where Rafi would be. The door to his bedroom was ajar enough for her to see him standing there like a ghost, staring at his bed.

"Raf?" she called out gently, stepping into the room.

He turned around and looked at her with sad eyes, magnified by tears.

"Haven't been in here since…" His voice trailed off as his sight caught on an old Queen poster that used to belong to their dad. "They haven't changed a thing."

"Why would they?"

Rafi shrugged. "Because I'm not coming back. I'm not. And keeping this doesn't—I have a bedroom. One that I can actually sleep in."

"I doubt sleep comes easy to you," Kash said firmly.

"It does when I'm sleeping in a place I *belong*, or I *love*, or *next* to someone I love," he fired back in a sharp voice, turning around again so his back was facing her.

I don't love this place. I don't love any of you.

Kash's breath hitched, and she fisted her hands by her sides as she walked over to him.

"Sorry," Rafi said after a moment, shoulders sagging. "I just mean, I wish they would stop, because this is practically blackmail."

"You know they don't mean it like that," Kash said, grabbing his shoulder gently so he would look at her. "Or at least, not consciously."

"Aren't you tired of their shit?" he said. With a loud, burdensome sigh, he stepped back and fell onto his bed, long black hair splaying out on the clean, unused sheets.

"They're our parents," Kash said, joining him by sitting on the edge. "Of course, I am. I always am."

Rafi snorted at that. "Congratulations on getting into college, by the way. Hopefully you won't fuck it up."

"Thanks," she said dryly.

"Kash. Do you seriously not want to go?" he asked in a strained voice as he sat up laboriously.

"No, I just don't know what I want to do," she murmured, tangling her fingers together. "I don't know what I want."

"I think it's easier to know what you don't want than what you do," he said.

"Maybe."

"Don't do what I did."

Kash squeezed her eyes shut. "I'm not doing what you did," she bit out. "I'm so sick of people saying that."

"Okay," Rafi said, laying back down and throwing an arm over his face. "Okay, sorry."

Kash laid down next to him with a sigh and bumped her fist against his shoulder. "How are lessons going? Any prodigy students?"

"Don't ask me about that."

Kash nodded, a sharp pain shooting through her heart. It took her a moment to muster up the courage, and it hit her that she was being brave around someone she usually relied on for being entirely unguarded. "Okay. How're your roommates?"

"Don't try to fill up the spaces, Kash. It's useless." He lifted his arm and stared up at the ceiling. "They're fine. Nik's moving out this summer, so I'll have my own room again. And Tommy's been visiting his family since last month, so it's been mellow."

"Is that why you came over this time when *Amma* asked? You were bored?"

"Maybe," Rafi sighed. "Maybe I forgot what it was like last time, got caught up in thinking it would be different or better."

"Stop."

"No."

"Rafi," Kash said, hitting her fist against him again, harder this time.

"What," he bit out.

"I'm…" she exhaled slowly, blinking her eyes and swallowing hard, "—scared."

She heard Rafi move, heard the comforter rustle and pull underneath her, and looked over to see him rolling onto his side to look at her, expression suddenly gentle, and experienced, as if he knew exactly what was going on in Kash's mind, because it was going on in his.

"What are you scared of?" he asked softly.

"Isn't it obvious?" she said.

"To whom?"

"Just… in general."

"It's not."

Kash huffed and turned to face the ceiling.

"You're hoping it's obvious to *Amma* and *Nanna,* or to me, or to anyone else but yourself." He said it like a prescription.

Kash swallowed audibly. "I'm hoping they have the right answers, I guess. I certainly don't."

Rafi let out a short, dry laugh and sat up. "Right. Do any of us."

Kash followed his line of sight to his old desk.

"Well," he spoke stiffly, jaw locked, "take it from someone who's already made the mistakes or keeps on making them. They don't know. Nobody does. I mean that."

"You're not just making mistakes. You're figuring things out—"

"I'm trying to find something I have no knowledge of." He looked down at her, his eyes narrow and glittering with tears. "Is that not a mistake?"

Kash stumbled to her feet roughly, fisting her hands and glaring down at her brother.

"You—you're angry," Kash said, digging her nails into her palms. "Or—"

"You are correct, copycat," Rafi said dryly. "That's not all, but you are correct."

Kash watched him slump slightly, like he was tiring from carrying a heavy weight on his shoulders for too long.

"This is wrong," he muttered. "This was all—I shouldn't have come or…" He pressed his palms to his eyes and a raw, shaky sob wrenched from his throat in a way that rendered Kash paralyzed.

The last time she'd seen him cry felt like a lifetime ago.

He inhaled shakily and opened his mouth, but nothing came out for a long moment, and she thought maybe he'd finally broken down, fully lost all function.

"Can I share something?" he asked. "Before I lose my fucking nerve."

She nodded, and he caught the movement with the corner of his eye before nodding back.

"I don't know how else to say this, so."

"Okay," Kash murmured.

Rafi clenched his jaw and fell back into the bed, arms falling on top of his stomach. His chest rose with each breath, and he looked out of place. His legs were long, and his knees were bent higher than the bed, so he looked like a giant, like he was too big for this room. Frayed jean cuffs brushed his ankles, too, and Kash suddenly couldn't stop picturing him as someone who had long outgrown their own body.

He heaved a big sigh, like he was preparing for something vital.

"I'm scared of everything.
You take up everything,
Like some permeating chemical fog.
And more of me,
Counts off every
mistake I'm comprised of."

He barely sang, affording flat, indifferent notes to each syllable and finishing with a coarse clearing of his throat. He dropped his hands into his lap with a scoff. "God, I can't even—the *only* way is just, parsing through the mess with lyrics. Even if it's shitty. I can't—*escape* it."

"You think," Kash began softly, still paralyzed, "that all you're comprised of, are mistakes?"

Rafi stayed silent, teeth grinding, and eyes boring into the ceiling above them. "Yeah," he said, voice raw and resentful.

An immense ocean wave of heartbreak rushed through Kash, and she flinched harshly, bracing a hand against her chest as she doubled over.

"That's what I'm telling you," Rafi continued. "Mistake after mistake after mistake, that's all I am. I just, I can never guess the right thing."

She tried to tamp down the fierce need to refute everything he was saying, but it bubbled up from inside her irrepressibly. "You're not—"

"So, maybe," he interrupted firmly, looking at her like his next words were something she should write down on her arm, "I should just stop guessing. We should all stop *guessing.*"

father's son.

Loud yelling jarred Kash awake, and she sat up quickly, a painful rush of blood to her head made the world spin around erratically. She frowned, trying to understand who was yelling and why. A quick glance at her phone told her it was a little past four in the morning. The sky was still dark outside her window and the air in her room was cold enough to make her shiver as she tossed the warmth of the blankets aside and got up from her bed.

She rubbed her eyes and tucked a loose lock of hair behind her ear as she walked over to her door and leaned against it, listening.

It was her dad. Yelling in Telugu.

She blinked.

Fully slipping back into his mother tongue wasn't a good sign. He only did that during conversations with their family in India, or when he was speaking from heightened emotions. So, right now, he must be *angry*.

She gingerly opened her door, careful not to make any sound loud enough to signal the fact that she was awake. Her hazy mind barely remembered where to step to avoid creaks as she made her way down the hall from her bedroom door.

She passed her sisters' room and noticed light coming out from the opening beneath the door.

It opened slowly and two twin rumpled heads, Kishori and Kumari, peeked out with squinting, tired eyes.

Kash held a finger up to her lips and gestured to her sisters to go back into their room.

Kishori frowned and opened the door wider, letting warm light spill out into the hallway.

Kash shielded her eyes from the painful suddenness and recoiled.

"Turn off the light," she hissed at her sisters as they tiptoed lazily out of their room.

Kishori looked at her with an annoyed frown before lighting up in delayed understanding and leaning back to flick the switch off.

Kash rolled her eyes and threw them a cranky glare while gesturing at them to be silent. She snuck over to the landing and descended the stairs cautiously, looking back at her sisters to make sure they weren't doing anything to give their presence away.

Her father's voice was discernible now, coming from the kitchen, anger and hurt burning through every word.

"*Asalu yemi lekka lekunda yetla chesthavu idhi?*" Makrand yelled.

"You're talking like I did this without thinking!"

Kash froze. That was her brother's voice, sounding just as angry as their father's.

"*Dhengurinchi alochinchavu,* Rafi? *Nee* future *gurinchaa? Nee kosam entha* time spend *chesamu, nee, nee* education *kosam entha dabbulu petemu, dhani gurinchaa?*"

"I didn't—" Rafi's voice broke, "No! It's not that I didn't think about those—I just, I wasn't happy, I—"

"Oh," Makrand's voice was cold and biting, "you weren't *happy*."

What is going on?

A bitter silence filled the space and Kash shivered. Her mind raced with reasons why her father and brother would be in a yelling match this early in the morning. She glanced at the clock that hung on the opposite wall of the foyer, squinting to make out the position of the hands, double-checking the time.

"What time is it?" Kishori whispered behind her.

Kash looked back at her sisters and hushed them before stepping out onto the hardwood floor. She took care to step lightly, wary of telling creaks.

"Look, I thought through this, and I just—" Rafi's voice was helpless and frustrated and Kash could picture the look on his face.

Her feet moved before she realized what she was doing, and she found herself walking down the hall and into the kitchen.

Her parents were standing around the island counter while Rafi was standing a few feet away, backed into a corner of the kitchen, near the entrance to the family room.

"What's wrong? *Emaindhi*?" Kash asked softly, squinting at the onslaught of light from the central fixture.

"Nothing," Rafi responded curtly. His jaw was clenched, mouth set in a tight line, and there was a telltale visual tick of grinding teeth along his jawline.

Kash did the same thing when she was trying not to cry. She instinctively reached over to him but paused at the sound of her father clearing his throat.

"Go back to sleep, Kash," Makrand said firmly.

"Well, I can't if you guys are going to keep yelling," she said sarcastically before thinking.

"Kashvi," her mother warned.

"What—are all of you awake now?" her father said, annoyed, gesturing to where Kash stood.

Kash frowned. She looked behind her and saw both of her sisters sleepily emerge from the darkness of the hallway.

"You woke us up," Kishori explained in a voice barely above a mumble.

"Mickey," their mother said, pressing a hand to her husband's shoulder, "why don't we have this conversation at another time. Let's go back to sleep."

"Jaisri, if he wanted to have this conversation at another time, he wouldn't have brought this up now," Makrand said, almost petulantly.

Rafi spluttered, "I'm not the one who—"

"Okay," her mother held her hand up to silence them, "*inka chaalu*, let's go to bed. We'll talk about this later."

"Talk about what?" Kumari asked loudly behind Kash.

Kash nodded in emphasis, searching her parents' and brother's faces for answers. Her mind raced trying to figure out what was happening.

"Nothing," Makrand and Rafi said at once, voices sharp and forceful.

Kash took a step back instinctually. She folded her arms and watched as her dad and brother exchanged glares and refused to back down.

What happened?

Kash's eyes widened. Had Rafi finally revealed his grades from this past semester, maybe?

After a moment of no budging, her mother sighed and tugged on Makrand's arm.

"*Dha*," Jaisri coaxed, "*nalugu ayindhi.*" She gestured to the clocks on the microwave and stove, where it read 4:12 in bright green numbers.

"*Nuvvu, nenu, Amma, eevale kalisi.*" Makrand pointed heatedly to Rafi. "We're going to sort this out, *aradhamaindha?*"

Rafi nodded.

"You're going to explain everything," Makrand said through his teeth. "And why you think you had the right to do this without talking to us."

Rafi bristled at that.

"The right?" he cried. "It's my life!"

"And it's my money and my time and my life that I have given to you to make sure that you're able to do and be exactly what you want—*nuvve chepavu naaku idhi kaavalani!* I never asked you to do anything more than to succeed in doing what you want. Do you know how much it cost to send you to your piano lessons since you were three years old? *Nee* guitar lessons, *nee* singing lessons—*anni!* How much time and effort *Amma* and I spent taking you to your concerts and programs!" Mikrand roared.

"I'm not ungrateful!" Rafi yelled, tears rolling down his cheeks. "I just can't keep doing something—being someone— on the basis of money or, or someone else! On the basis of you guys!"

"*Idhi* money *gurinchi kaadhu! Idhi mana gurinchi kaadhu!*" Makrand swiped his hand through the air, barely missing Jaisri next to him. "*Idhi nee* future *gurinchi!* Me and *Amma* would give *everything* we have a hundred times over so you can be *successful* and *happy* and have a *good future!*"

"I can take care of my own future! That's what I'm trying to do! I'm trying to be happy, and I'm telling you that I'm *not!*" Rafi threw his hands up helplessly. Tears were falling fast down his cheeks, gathering at his chin and dripping down onto the hardwood floor.

Kash had to fist her hands by her sides to stop herself from going over and hugging him. She hated seeing her brother cry. He rarely ever did, at least in front of her, and it was therefore painfully jarring on the rare occasion when he did.

But crying in front of his entire family was something she never thought she'd see. The gravity of it dropped a weight in her stomach and she bit her lip nervously.

"If you want to 'take care' of your own future, if you think you know better, if you think we're hurting you… then maybe you shouldn't stay here," Makrand said with a calm, sad finality.

Kash's heart dropped past the floor, and her eyes widened.

Her father wasn't irrational, wasn't as strict as he appeared to be. He just had a habit of getting caught up in his emotions and saying or doing things he later regretted. It was something Kash had inherited from him.

But he would never tell one of his own kids to get out of the house. He would never.

What the hell is happening?

"Wait, what?" she cried out. "*Nanna*, why're you—"

"Are you kidding me?" Rafi said, a defeated slump in his shoulder that pulled on Kash's heartstrings. "You asked me what was going on, I—I didn't—"

"Oh, so if I hadn't caught you awake, you would've just kept quiet? Lied about everything?" Makrand's voice exploded, loud and dangerous in a way Kash had never heard before.

"No!" Rafi protested. "No, that's not what I—" his voice broke off before he could finish.

The confusion of why both her brother and father were acting so terribly out of character dug into Kash's chest sharply. She spluttered, eyes darting back and forth between the two of them. Her mother caught her eye and the worry in them made cold run through Kash's body, from her chest down to her fingertips and toes.

She nervously turned to Rafi and whispered, "What did you do?" She knew it must sound like an accusation, but she was getting frustrated being left in the dark.

Rafi looked back at her sadly.

She felt the weight of what he was about to say like the growing pressure of sinking in deep water.

"I dropped out," he said simply with a small shrug. He sniffled and wiped a hand against his cheeks to clear away tear tracks.

What?

Kash's heart beat loudly and erratically in her chest, like a bird bumping around against its cage.

"Oh," she murmured under her breath. She wrapped her arms around herself and walked over to him gingerly. She was still trying to register what this all meant.

"I'm sorry," he sighed out.

She shook her head, looking up at him earnestly. "What happened?"

"Kishu, Kittu," Jaisri called out to the twins.

Kash watched her mother gesture at Kishori and Kumari to follow her as she moved out of the kitchen and down the hall. After a few moments, the muffled sound of footsteps of carpeted stairs signaled that Kash, Rafi, and their father were alone.

"Is everything okay?' Kash asked her brother. Her hand twitched, almost reached up to rest against his shoulder, but she thought the better of it. She was acutely aware of her father a few feet away, and she didn't want to take any sides in a fight she still didn't fully understand and clearly wasn't wanted in.

"How can it be okay?" Makrand asked incredulously.

Kash looked over at him and furrowed her brows at the utter disappointment underneath the anger.

She never understood it. It was so easy to fight between themselves—they were a family of stubborn, quick-tempered imaginaries—and yet every time after the fight, they always ended up having to lick wounds and mend relationships. It was never pain-free, but they did it all the time. Like it was their routine to disagree on everything as a family. Usually, they could mask it under sarcasm and mischievous teasing. But there was no playfulness between the three of them right now.

"Well, why did you drop out?" Kash directed her question at Rafi but maintained eye contact with their father.

"It felt pointless. Like I was doing it for someone else."

For Nanna.

Kash nodded. This notion was familiar. He'd expressed as much to her when he first went to college just over two years ago.

"And that started to overpower how much you love it?" she asked softly.

Rafi nodded.

"What do you mean for someone else?" Makrand interjected hotly. "I didn't ask you to do anything for me. I asked you to follow what you want. You love music, so you pursued music."

Kash shook her head. "No one said you asked Raf for anything."

"But I *was* doing it for you," Rafi blurted out. "You didn't ask me, but. You expected it."

"What?" Makrand's voice was astonished and hurt.

Kash suddenly felt like she shouldn't be standing in the kitchen right now, witnessing this. She already knew what Rafi was going to say. He'd told her how he felt about going to college for music before. But this moment of confrontation between father and son felt painful and private. Her fingers itched and her toes curled and relaxed over and over again as she contemplated leaving, but movement felt like an interruption. She desperately wished to turn invisible, collapse into thin air.

"You wanted me to be a musician, *Nanna*," Rafi said earnestly. "*Meere chepevaaru, naalo—naalo* 'talent' *unte, aa, aa* 'talent' *ni*… that I have to take advantage of it. You told me I can't just put it to the side. You told me that this is my main thing. I believed you."

Kash felt a lump grow in her throat.

I believed you.

She felt her brother's words like a rush of blood from her head to her toes. A memory resurfaced from first grade of her father reading a story from her notebook, while she stood back shyly. She remembered the look on his face when he'd finished and smiled at her.

Chaala baaga raasevu, thalli, he'd praised as he took her into his arms and blew playful raspberries to make her giggle. *Nuvvu o peddha* author *avuchu. Someday. I can see it.*

She blinked out of the memory, returning to the present like a drenching splash of cold water.

"But the more I committed to it, the more I wanted to say no. I want to—I want to do other things, *Nanna*," Rafi said, voice breaking and again tugging painfully at Kash's heart.

Makrand's arms were folded, and his face was unreadable save for a furrowed brow.

"*Nanna*," Kash called out softly to him.

"Kashvi, go upstairs," he said firmly, arms folded so his stance appeared unwavering.

"I'm not tired anymore," she insisted.

"*Poduko*, Kashvi," Makrand said, tone dangerously dipping into a vehemently short temper. His eyes flashed along with his words.

"It's four in the morning!" she cried out.

"Kashvi, this is between me and your brother. Leave."

Kash stood her ground for a few more moments, just long enough to satisfy her defiance but not to disrespect. She huffed out, shoulders moving with the effort, and threw her father a withering glance that he would no doubt admonish for its teenage attitude later.

She glanced at Rafi in what she hoped was reassurance, but her brother just watched her with a resigned, self-deprecating look in his eyes.

Her mouth quivered.

"Okay," she murmured placatingly and turned to walk down the hall, taking care to dig her heels against the hardwood loudly. She fisted her hands at her sides, squeezing her eyes shut as she walked the staircase blindly, having climbed up and down it enough times to know it by muscle memory. She heard soft voices from her sisters' room and opened her eyes to peek at the light peeking out from the thin opening at the bottom of the door. A wave of tiredness melted her residual anger and frustration. Her legs were wobbly as she walked into her room and flopped onto her bed heavily. The covers were cool beneath her, and she lay there for a while, staring at the dark sky through the curtains of her window.

Footsteps sounded past her door, and she wondered what had happened after she left. She hadn't heard yelling, but sometimes quiet voices did the most damage.

She kept her eyes trained on the window as she burrowed beneath her covers and watched until the sun slowly lightened the sky. Her mind was racing too quickly for her to fall back asleep.

She'd always regarded her brother as someone who, if a little indecisive, knew who he was and what he was passionate about. He gave her comfort that her passions, what she liked to do, were who she was. That she didn't need to go searching—but that's exactly what he'd done.

She turned over on her back, looking up at the ceiling, as morning light started to filter into her room softly.

Anxiety seized her chest tightly and tears leaked from the corners of her eyes as she stared up, determined to not blink.

Did *she* have to go searching now?

i don't think we'll come back to this but maybe we can.

They had mispronounced her name when they called it but that wasn't a surprise. And it didn't dampen her excitement about graduating.

She couldn't stop grinning as she descended the stage into the crowd, keeping her eyes out for familiar faces. Her fingers tightened around her diploma like it was the last ticket for the only train to her destination.

"Blue!" Levi came out from between a family in the crowd, catching Kash unexpectedly in a tight, bone-crushing hug.

"Hey, Lovie," Kash laughed, voice straining as Levi squeezed his arms around her before awarding her a blinding grin.

"You did it," he said, knocking his knuckles affectionately against Kash's cheek.

"We did," she agreed, "Where's Raz? The idiot was right next to me until now."

Levi shrugged, scanning the crowd before lighting up and dragging Kash behind him as he quickly maneuvered through the chaos of the crowd.

The gym was buzzing with laughter, voices, and celebration. They smiled amicably at familiar classmates and giggled at the light feeling in their chests.

No more high school. No more dreaming about running away, they didn't *need* to now. No more fighting for independence, they *had* it now.

"Raza!" Kash called loudly as her friend and his family came into view. She laughed and barreled into him, Levi following close behind.

The three of them tangled together in an ecstatic hug and Raza yelped as Levi's arm came up around his neck in a teasing chokehold.

"Congratulations kids," Raza's dad said proudly with crackling laughter. "Didn't think you'd make it, but I guess miracles can happen."

The three of them scoffed at that and Raza shot his father a fond look of exasperation.

"Hi Aunty," Kash greeted Raza's mom, who pulled her into a firm, motherly hug.

"Where're your parents, *nana*?" Selvi asked, pulling back to smile at her.

Kash shrugged. "*Thellidhu,* Aunty. I was looking for them, too. I'm pretty I saw them in the back during the ceremony but—"

"Makrand!" Raza's dad bellowed suddenly with his arms outstretched.

Kash whirled around to find her father making his way over to them with a big smile on his face, calling back in an equally boisterous manner, "Irshad!"

Kash immediately rushed over and wrapped her arms around her father's shoulders. He squeezed her with such a familiar, comforting pride that it made her grin helplessly, unable to feel anything but unequivocally elated. She looked over his shoulder to find her mother and sisters making their way toward them.

"Congratulations, *akka*," the twins chorused and Kash, fueled by her blinding happiness, grabbed each of them with one arm and drew them in for a brief, suffocating hug.

Kash's mother immediately insisted on taking pictures and Selvi started flapping her hands at them, ushering them into various poses.

Kash grinned and went up onto her tiptoes at the last minute every time, so she looked taller, and every time, Levi and Raza grabbed her by the shoulders and pushed her down with varying sounds of protest.

They slowly found Levi's grandparents, exchanging congratulations and thank you's.

The three of them indulged in more photos with reluctant eyerolls, Levi and Raza looping their arms around Kash to make sure she stayed put and giggled together like they were experiencing the highest euphoria of their lives.

Kash felt immense, as if she were both physically there wearing her cap and gown and high above the crowd like an abstract presence, watching herself and her friends glow with giddiness.

We're so close to touching unabashed freedom.

"Kash!" Lani called from behind her and Kash whipped around to see her rushing over with ruddy cheeks and a brilliant smile. She'd taken off her graduation gown, draped it across her arm instead and held her cap and diploma in one hand.

Lani's dress was a slip of soft white fabric that swept across her chest and unfurled from her waist and looked almost ethereal against her dark skin.

"Hey, Lani," Kash said a little breathlessly. She felt a little silly, eyes roving over Lani's appearance like it was something precious.

"Congratulations, babe!" Lani cried out, pulling her in for a brief, affectionate hug.

"You, too, love." Kash caught the eye of Lani's dad and smiled.

"Hey Mr. Kahele," she said, shaking the hand that Lani's dad outstretched cordially.

"Congratulations, Kash," he said with a twinkling smile and then tipped his head to the boys, "Raza, Levi."

The two boys chorused a unison thank you while Kash searched the crowds for just one more person.

"What is it?" Lani leaned toward her ear and asked.

"My brother. I think he's running late," Kash mumbled before rolling her eyes. "Again."

"Oh, he's usually late? Must run in the family," Lani teased and Kash couldn't help the fondly annoyed smirk curling her lips.

"Funny," she said dryly, before turning to her mother and pulling her aside.

"*Entiraa*," Jaisri said, tucking some of Kash's hair over her shoulder with a tender smile.

"Have you seen Rafi?" Kash asked carefully.

Her mother's smile fell instantly.

Oh.

"He texted Kishu since you didn't answer." Her mother leaned in close, voice barely above a whisper. "He said he couldn't make it."

Kash's heart plummeted through her, clawing a tunnel into the ground far enough to hide from the lights of the gym.

"Oh," she croaked. "Why?"

"He said something came up." Jaisri looked guilty, and Kash thought that was quite incriminating of her.

"Oh."

"Sorry, *ra*," her mother said, bringing a hand up to caress Kash's face.

"No, it's fine." Kash smiled tightly, pushing her mother's hand away with light force.

He had said he'd try when she asked, hadn't he? Maybe he had. She imagined, for a split second, Rafi sitting at the tiny kitchen table, car keys in hand, willing himself to enter the fire again, just to attend his sister's graduation. She imagined him losing the courage, hating it, and opening his laptop to watch the livestream instead. Or maybe not even opening the laptop in case he caught sight of them in the audience. "It's not his fault, I guess," Kash concluded.

Her mother's face fell, and Kash hoped she was picturing a similar scene, hoped she was picturing her son struggling, aware of the reason, and hoped it was pulling at her like a thread of wool caught on a fresh cut.

"Kash?" Levi stepped up behind her and rested his chin on her shoulder. "You okay?" he murmured, his warm breath tickling her ear.

She resisted the urge to flinch at the feeling. "Yeah. We just graduated, didn't we?"

"Yeah." Levi grinned. "Yeah, that we did do."

Kash nodded. "Right."

So, what now?

The light, liberating happiness from earlier had drained out of her and she felt like a smiling shell.

"I have no idea what to do now," she muttered, quietly enough to be meant only for Levi's ears.

Levi laughed at that, a full-bodied warm sound that carried through into the crowd and grew distant like setting sunshine. Without warning he turned her around, gripped her forearm like a gentle vice, and looked at her with wild eyes.

"Fancy the castle?" he asked and Kash frowned before realization bloomed across her features.

Now that reality was on cue to crash down on them before the summer was over, Kash felt a strange sense of urgency, like maybe now was the only time they could go back, like if they waited any longer they'd find themselves drifting farther into space in separate directions with no way of moving forward and no tether to follow back.

"Yeah, actually," she said with a slow smile, "I think I would."

* * *

After deciding on the sculpture garden behind Kash's house, it was easy to convince all four families to convene an impromptu dinner party at the Narahari-Blue household. And, just like old times, the three of them immediately ran out to the backyard upon arrival, Lani in tow. They shed their caps and gowns on the grass as quickly as they could before making their way into the woods.

Levi led the way, hollering things into the sticky summer air, like how glad he was that he never had to set foot on school premises again.

Kash laughed and turned her head up to bask in the filtered evening sun. It was heavy and humid out, but the woods offered a fresh coolness that settled softly on her damp skin and eased the slight dehydrated headache she'd had for a while now.

"Is this the castle place you guys talk about?" Lani murmured next to her.

Kash rolled her head to the side and smiled. "Yeah."

"It's about time you took me here, then," Lani said, throwing her frizzing hair behind her shoulder with a flick of her hand. "To your domain," she added in a teasing voice.

Kash laughed and nodded. "Yeah, yeah. We haven't really come here since before you came, so. This is the first time in years."

Lani frowned. "Then why now?"

Kash shrugged. "A bit of nostalgia, I guess. To be a bunch of kids again before we can't anymore."

They approached a familiar warped tree, three large knots combining with a few smaller ones to create an intricate, almost mangled pattern on the old bark. It was framed by a tangle of branches from surrounding trees. Her, Raza, and Levi had tried to carve their names into it when they were in first grade.

"We're here," Kash whispered to Lani, jumping when Levi whooped and ran forward, disappearing around the corner until the castle tower came into view, along with the rest of their childhood hideout.

Lani's breath hitched, scanning the circular clearing, surrounded by occasionally flowering trees, and filled with mismatching objects and monuments. The center was occupied by a dining set up, a thick stone slab sitting on the back of a stone bear, surrounded by carved toadstools and tree stumps. A pair of statue children sat on one of the stumps, a little farther away, reading a book together. Kash felt a wave of nostalgia almost knock her back. This felt like a homecoming.

"Oh," Lani said next to her, amusement coloring her voice. "What is that supposed to be?"

Kash followed her eyes to the ghostly garden statue of an old bearded man in robes framed by a full moon, placed at the edge of the wide clearing like some kind of ominous welcome host. She shrugged. "We thought he was God when we first saw him—"

Lani burst out laughing.

"—but then we came to the conclusion that he's not and settled on him just being an ambiguous old man." Kash grinned at the way Lani leaned forward, like she couldn't support her own laughter, shoulders shaking.

"He's a werewolf!" she said, blue eyes wide and bright and theatrical. She gestured at him. "Full moon and all."

Kash gasped dramatically and snapped her fingers. "You're a genius."

"I am. And what's that?" She pointed to a large, practically life-size, rusted metal skeleton of a raptor.

"Oh, he used to scare the shit out of us," Kash explained, walking toward it and jumping over a mossy log so she could face the skeleton head on. "We'd play out here in the winter, too. The snow would sometimes gather on the bones, and one afternoon we came out here—you know how the sun disappears once it hits two—and we hadn't realized it was dark out since we were sitting up in the tower."

"Oh no," Lani said, a knowing smile curling her lips.

"Yeah. Nearly died of a heart attack. He looked like that T-Rex from Jurassic Park." She ran a finger along the thick pole of its neck. "Now he doesn't seem as terrifyingly big, though. Kind of—kind of sounds silly that we were very much mortally afraid."

Lani giggled. "Would not put it past the boys to still be mortally afraid."

Kash grinned.

"Oi!" Levi called to them from across the clearing, jumping over a patch of overgrown shrubbery to sit on one of the stone toadstools with the air of a monarch. "Hear ye, hear ye!"

They gathered around him, Lani following with distracted eyes darting every which way.

"It's smaller than I remember," Raza mused. "Do you think we'll all still fit up there?"

They all looked up at the constructed tower. It looked ancient, peeling white paint revealing the dark wood underneath. Kash wouldn't be surprised if parts of it were rotting, wouldn't be surprised if she touched it and it crumbled under her fingers, but that thought made her inexplicably sad. She hoped it stayed forever, ever so slowly wasting away from its initial childhood grandeur, yet still standing tall and present.

"Don't think so, no," Kash murmured. "The time's already passed, I guess."

"Maybe," Levi said softly, barely heard above the background of birdsong and rustling leaves.

"We should still meet here," Raza said with a smile. "You know, sometimes. When we're all in town."

Kash was hit with the disheartening notion that perhaps them all being in the same place was going to become rare enough to celebrate.

"Like," Kash began, "I don't know, like, a yearly thing."

Levi hummed noncommittally. "We shouldn't plan it. Planning it means it'll never happen."

Kash frowned. "Since when?"

Levi looked up at her, hazel eyes bright and imploring, and Kash had the sudden feeling that whatever she was failing to discern in those eyes, was something that would haunt her for the rest of her life.

"Since when, Levi?" Kash asked.

Levi shrugged. "I don't know, just a recent realization."

Kash stared at him, even as Lani let out a happy sigh and leaned forward on her forearms and said, "I wish I grew up here with you guys."

Kash's heart skipped a beat at that, imagining falling in love with Lani from the beginning, but it quickly morphed into a reel of every time she had looked into Levi's eyes and made plans for a future together.

"Yeah," Kash said casually, smiling down at Lani with effort. "Yeah, I guess growing up is the only thing we can really guarantee together."

Lani nodded slowly. "It would be nice to guarantee the rest, though."

Raza laughed and leaned his head against Levi's shoulder. "Yeah. Yeah, that would be nice."

Kash nodded, trying her hardest not to catch Levi's gaze, and ultimately failing when she stared at him and watched his lips curl into a foreboding smile.

"Can't, though," he said. "Trying to would make every-thing harder. That's what I mean." He twisted his arm around carefully and brought his hand up to cradle the back of Raza's head. He scrunched his fingers, mussing up his hair a bit.

"Everything will work out perfectly according to you," Raza sighed. "I'll believe in that for a bit."

Levi smiled fondly and leaned his cheek down against the top of Raza's head.

"I'll believe in it, too," Lani murmured.

Kash barely registered the way the toe of Lani's sandals nudged her ankle, entirely too focused on the way Levi seemed to be foreshadowing something that would derail Kash's life.

She wanted to ask him what he was up to. She wanted to shove him away and ask the sky why people kept pulling her out of the cloudy dreamland of graduation, of moving on, ask why they had to bring her down to Earth too quickly, too harshly.

"Okay, Levi," Kash said, eyes not straying from his. "I'll believe in it, too."

you are unforgivable.

Levi's hair was amusingly festive. He'd messily entangled star-spangled ribbons into the red curls along with royal blue little girls' barrettes. A gaudy amount of silver glitter surrounded his eyes. It was smudged slightly, sticking to the baby hairs along his temple and the hollow of his cheek. His lips were red from drinking his grandmother's homemade cherry lemonade.

The two of them were sitting on Levi's front porch, both of their families hollering and laughing inside like a proper party. The sky was cotton candy; pink clouds floating against a fading light blue backdrop of the sunset. The faint smell of campfires drifted through the air, making everything warm and fuzzy and easygoing.

"How long is it going to take you to get that stuff out of your hair?" Kash asked, eyes trained on the slope of his freckled nose. His skin was kissed golden by the setting sunlight.

He shrugged. Two long fingers twirled into his hair, tugging at a ribbon. He frowned and nodded with affirmation. "A while."

She laughed, shaking her head and looking down at her hands. Her mother's old engagement ring glinted from its place on her left middle finger, a thin golden signet with an inset pearl. She'd given it to her as a keepsake offering, a sort of acceptance that Kash was going to be moving out to college soon and her mother would have to act like that was okay. Kash would have to act like that was okay.

"When are the fireworks?" Levi asked with a sigh, looking up at the vibrant sky.

Kash looked down at her phone. "I think in another half hour or so?"

Levi hummed in acknowledgment. His eyes glazed over for a moment, like he was thinking hard about something. "Should tell you this before…" he trailed off. "Kind of late at this point, but now or never, yeah?" He dipped a finger into the rolled up crease of Kash's jeans and pulled at the fold.

"Tell me what, Lovie?"

He started bouncing his right leg, and she resisted the urge to reach out and stop it with a press of her hand. She grabbed his wrist and pulled his hand from her jeans. Their fingers tangled and she looked back up at him. He was nervous. He didn't have to be.

"I, uh, I don't think, I'm gonna go to New York," he said, barely above a whisper.

"What? Did you get a waitlist somewhere else or something?"

"No, I… don't think I'm gonna go to college. I don't think I want to."

Kash paused. "What."

"I'm, uh, moving?" He winced like he had more to say but couldn't.

Kash's frown deepened. "What do you mean?" she asked.

"Like, not right now. In the next month or two. I think, at least," he mumbled, "like, my grandparents, they've got a friend and, well—"

Her heart leaped out of her chest and crash landed onto the grass in the span of a second. "You're running away," she confirmed.

He'd talked about it since the first day of middle school, hadn't he? Only she half-hoped he was talking in cowardly hypotheticals, like her. They weren't leaving yet, they still had so much baggage to get rid of. They still had college and messy personal lives and social inability and useless sentimental attachments and so much *shit* still to learn.

But of course. Levi was the one who didn't care about any of that. She was hesitance and teenage insecurity in an overflowing fishbowl and he was life at its greatest and most reckless.

It *worked* for him, though, didn't it? He could climb the roof of an abandoned apartment complex and take a nap under the stars. He could play a game of chickie run and come out victorious and unscathed. He could jump from the Tower Bridge into the Thames and surface with a wide grin on his face and his hair stuck endearingly to his forehead. He was stupid and infuriatingly lucky, and it was horrible for her heart.

"Well, I'm not—nothing yet," he said.

"Oh."

They met gazes and she could see him looking for a reaction.

"Oh," she repeated blandly.

He deflated, eyes darting back and forth between her eyes. It was dizzying to watch. "Right, okay, yeah," he nodded.

A block of cement fell on her chest as he pulled his hand out from her grasp. "Just thought I'd say something, to you, you know?"

She nodded. "Thanks for the notice. The *courtesy*."

He scoffed at her, looking away with a disappointed shake of his head. "Thanks?"

Her eyes burned. What did he want? What did he expect? What did he imagine? She was not the kind of person who could risk everything and live with it. It didn't work for her. Nothing ever *worked* for her like that.

"So," she said, pressing her thumb against the nail of her index finger. "Where are you running away to?"

"I'm not—" he sighed, his protest fizzling out with a dry smile. "Pops' friend lives somewhere in London, I don't remember exactly, but I would be staying nearby—"

"Four years ago, you wanted to be a lawyer. And then, right after that, you went on and on about going to film school. Three months ago, you decided on New York. You—you and Raz made all those plans. Now you want to run away to *London*?"

He shook his head obstinately and glared. "No. Stop it. I'm not—stop saying I'm running away, I'm not *running away*," he spat.

She stared at him, eyes wide.

He was breathing hard, nostrils flaring in a way she would've found amusing if not for the situation. His face nearly matched his hair, along with the tips of his ears. The nerve of this boy sitting in front of her with blue ribbons and blue barrettes and glitter, huffing like an angry horse.

"You're naive," she told him.

"You're selfish."

"You should go to school for fucking *something*. Go to the top school you got into, for the one thing you've been talking everyone's ear off about for the past three years!"

He paused, scrutinizing her in a way she did not welcome. "You need me to go to college," he said after a while. His voice was incredulous.

She shook her head, livid. "No! But—yes! Of course, I think you should! Like. I think everybody should—it's the smart choice, it's what—I mean, like, where is this coming from? I thought you already accepted, already chose a college, a *path*. You made plans with our best friend, move in together, live in the city. Did you tell Raza about this? Did you tell him that you were *ditching* him?"

"No! I'm not—I'm not ditching anything or anyone—"

"You're leaving."

—me.

She watched him look away and the defeated disappointment on his face, in his body language, hurt her more than she could ever admit.

"I don't understand, Levi, what—"

"I've got a plan, it's different but it's real, but that doesn't matter, does it?"

She shook her head. "No, you don't have a plan. That's not—"

He pressed his hand abruptly against her mouth, curling his fingers around her jaw, and muffling her words. "I don't need to do the stupid things you do," he said harshly. "I'm not running away. I'm just doing what I always said I would. Whatever that is."

He didn't blink for the next minute or so, eyes wide and watery and trained on her face. They turned a tired red before he let his eyelids close, tears falling quick in salty rivulets.

Glitter tracked down his cheeks, all the way down to his chin. Salt and silver shined on his skin.

"And," he exhaled heavily before continuing, "it's not even decided. For all anyone knows, I'm still going to New York in the fall. I just…"

She watched him in painful, confused rapture.

He didn't even bother to attempt hiding everything playing across his face, his mind. It was heartbreaking. It was baffling.

Her chest seized, ribcage collapsing in on itself. She felt her eyes begin to well up. It was nauseating. The salty taste of his hand and the choking lump in her throat stopped her from swallowing properly and a shiver slithered down her neck to the bottom of her spine.

"I was going to ask you, Blue," he said with a heavy, exhausted sigh. He removed his hand, a sign of truce, and looked up at her with breathtakingly earnest eyes.

She nodded after a moment, "You already did once. We already did once. But it was a hypothetical, Levi. It was a childish manifestation."

He nodded as he suddenly turned around, lay down, and settled his head in her lap. He stretched his legs out to the side, long and lean, ankles crossed and dangling off the side of the porch. She hesitated for a moment before settling a hand in his hair and gently massaging his scalp. He sighed and closed his eyes. A couple of more tears escaped down his temples and into his hair. They both ignored them.

She could hear his uneven breathing and smiled softly as she looked down at him.

His eyes were slightly puffy around the lids and orange freckles stood out prominently against his flushed face. The glitter was almost gone, a thin layer of it everywhere from his forehead to his neck. She wiped the wetness away from his temples and chin gently. It was a gesture that comforted them both.

"We're still super young, yeah?" he said suddenly.

She paused her ministrations and looked down at him until he opened his eyes. She nodded and continued to run her fingers across his cheekbones and through his tangled curls. "Yeah. Yeah, we are."

He closed his eyes again and nodded along with her. With a soft sigh, he folded his hands above his stomach and relaxed with a visible shift in his body language. His shoulders pressed into her thighs and the arch of his spine dipped down against the old wood of the porch.

"So, we can still, I mean, I can..." he trailed off, tapping his fingers in arrhythmic patterns.

"Take me with you?" she murmured with a smile, looking out across the yard at the surrounding houses. Levi's neighborhood was quiet, each house decorated with a wraparound porch and shuttered windows. One particular house to the left was covered head to toe in festivities. Red, white, and blue ribbons wrapped around the railings of the porch. Huge bows decorated the windows and doors in gaudy, American glory.

"We've still got time, I mean. To like figure all of this shit out," he said matter-of-factly. His shoulders shifted up, an attempt at a shrug.

"Yeah," she agreed absently, "we've still got time. You've still got time. You don't need to decide anything, you know? And going to New York, going to college isn't a final... decision, right?"

Levi nodded hesitantly. "Right. No final decisions."

A trio of festively dressed people walked out onto the equally festive porch with varying themed goods, laughing with the kind of ease only longtime friends had. They set their trays of food down on a table covered in an American flag cloth, and their voices carried slightly so Kash could just make out the rambunctious bantering dynamic between them. It strangely reminded her of an ideal hypothetical, a sneak peek of something just out of reach.

"I'm going to college, Lovie," Kash said with practiced finality. "I want to."

Levi tensed under her fingers. "I don't think you know what you want."

"And you do?"

He shrugged and looked at her in such a knowing way that she abruptly felt like he had flayed her to the bone and ripped her open to peer at her insides.

"You're a mess," she countered uselessly, eager to get rid of the violent feeling crawling up her spine. She gestured vaguely to his hair and face in explanation and Levi chuckled.

"Yeah," he swiped a finger across his cheek, and it came off with a sheen of silver glitter, "it's gotten all over the place."

"That's not what I meant."

Levi laughed dryly and leaned up, so his nose was barely touching the tip of her ear. "I'm going to go wash off," he murmured before clumsily getting up and pulling her into the house along with him.

She yelped in surprise and stumbled slightly over the raised doorstep as they entered the foyer, glaring at him pointedly until they reached the kitchen sink.

He shot her a smirk before leaning down expectantly, and the utter arrogance in the gesture made Kash's heart skip with fond annoyance. She watched him, unimpressed, until he turned the faucet on with a theatrical sigh and leaned forward, splashing some cold water onto his face.

"That's dish soap," she stated flatly, and watched him reach blindly for the nearest squeeze bottle, face and fringe dripping with water.

He let out a trilling breath and wiped a hand down his face. Glitter still lingered in the crevices of his nose and the tips of his eyebrows. He looked up at her, eyelashes clumped and streaked with silver, eyes standing out in stark clarity beneath the tiny shocks of metallic color.

A sudden, loud boom sounded in the distance.

Kash jumped, heart thudding. The hairs on her arms and neck stood on end and she looked over to find a dangerous look in Levi's eyes.

His lips curled into an almost wolfish grin. "Oh good," he said in a low voice that made terrible shivers run up and down Kash's back.

She murmured, "Fire—"

"Fireworks!" He brought his hands out to frame his face and fluttered his fingers.

Levi's eyes were flying sparks. He looked down at her and tugged on her arm, dragging her out to the backyard.

She wanted to protest, dig her feet into the floor and refuse to be moved about, but some unknown force locked her tongue to the bottom of her mouth.

"Fireworks!" Levi whooped again giddily.

They ran back onto the porch and a small smile teased the corner of her mouth as she watched Levi let go of her to skip into the middle of the yard, hair bouncing and shining in the warm light coming from the open doorway. He threw his head back and grinned at the sky, spreading his arms out in childish abandon, blinking up at the bursts of color lighting up the sky.

"Please tell me. If you go," she implored him, voice soft and private.

Levi watched her, eyes growing more indecipherable by the second. He nodded after a moment.

"You'll try to stop me," he said, like it wasn't a question.

"Maybe," she said, meekly. "If you do run away, I'm assuming you won't come back, so maybe. Yes."

A particularly loud boom jolted the both of them and Kash watched the golden umbrella rain down and swim in Levi's shiny bright irises. Small tears gathered in the corners of his eyes, and she didn't know if it was lingering glitter or the fireworks that made them shimmer sadly.

"It's not—I'm not running *away* or *abandoning*—" He dug his teeth into his bottom lip, cutting himself off, before hanging his head. "—I'm just trying to figure it out, okay? Same as you, same as Raz, same as anyone. Or at least, I know myself well enough to realize that I get bored of things and I'm tired of being here."

"We all are. So go to college. Move out."

He nodded, mouth quirking up in a disappointed curve. "Yeah, yeah, I know." He made an aborted movement, hand outstretched. "Kash."

"Yeah."

He watched her with a soft, nervous smile that twisted her insides. "Don't tell anyone," he said softly. "You—you get it. It's just confusion."

"Hypotheticals."

Levi nodded jerkily. "Right, yeah. Hypotheticals."

She needed him to listen, to promise, to understand. "*Levi.*"

"I'm not going rogue." He huffed out a laugh. "Or maybe all of us are and that's the point."

"Going rogue? What, like, moving to a different country on a whim?" she said mockingly.

"No," he smiled crookedly, "going rogue like, doing whatever I want over…"

"Sense? Job prospects? Reality?"

Levi laughed louder and his eyes darted up as another set of fireworks boomed and lit up the sky. "Yeah. Sense. Or lack thereof, maybe."

Kash hummed, scrunching her nose up in an attempt to hide her smile. "I told Raza that I think he belongs in the city. That I think he'd do really well there. And I believe that about you too."

Levi shook his head, pressing his thumb to the space between his brows. "Oh? How'd you come to that conclusion?"

"I don't know, I just did. And even if I'm wrong," she said, shrugging her shoulders, "I guess we find out the hard way. That's the way it goes, maybe."

Her heart skipped a beat suddenly, an epiphany blooming in her.

"The hard way?" Levi murmured. "Isn't that what I'm trying to avoid?"

I guess the only choice we have, is to just find out. The hard way.

Kash fluttered her fingers by her sides as she watched another burst of gold, red, and blue light up the sky. "So maybe we stop avoiding it."

college: part one.

warmer than i thought.

Iowa was only an hour behind, but time almost seemed irrelevant here. Too much was going on for Kash to even comprehend the minutes passing.

"What floor is this again?" her mother asked, setting down a box of Kash's clothes.

"The fifth," Kash answered, slightly out of breath from carrying all of her stuff up the stairs.

"When's your roommate coming? Shouldn't everyone be checked in by now?"

Kash shrugged, arms akimbo, as she looked around the room she was going to inhabit for the next nine months. She wondered how long it would take for it to look like home, how long it would take to get used to living with a stranger, how long strangers even remained *strangers* after you met them.

"I don't know. She's probably coming later, whenever… she gets here," she said. "I'm still calling the bed on the right, though."

"You don't think you should wait until she comes, maybe," Jaisri said with a raised brow.

Kash shrugged. "But I got here first."

Her mother opened her mouth to speak but just as she did, the door to the dorm opened quickly, and halted against a wooden storage unit they'd just bought yesterday.

"Oh here," Kash muttered as she crouched down to move it over and stumbled to the floor when the door opened fully.

"Ah! Sorry did I hit you?"

There was a girl on the other side who was smiling down at her apologetically. She was wearing a thin blue spring jacket the color of early morning sky, over a loose white t-shirt tucked into a pair of fraying denim shorts.

"No," Kash said, and gestured to the storage unit, "it was just, uh, that."

"Oh," the girl sighed, tucking her long black hair behind her ear. "Well, glad we didn't meet with me swinging the door into you. You're Kashvi right?"

Kash nodded, realizing she was still on the ground, and stood up. She brushed herself off, suddenly aware of the dull black of her jeans, the dirt and scuff marks on her sneakers, and the probable humid mess of her hair.

"Yeah, I'm Kash. Stella Mai?" she asked, and outstretched a hand when Stella nodded.

"In the flesh. Call me by my first name though, I prefer it like that," she said playfully. "It's so nice to finally meet you!" She tugged on Kash's arm and pulled her into a hug without warning.

Kash inhaled sharply before tentatively wrapping her arms around her.

"Yeah," she laughed softly, "very few people've ever pronounced my name correctly on the first try, by the way."

She could feel Stella's breath by her ear, and gasped when Stella squeezed her. It felt foreign, to hug a stranger like this, it felt far too familiar, but Stella apparently had no such qualms and Kash wondered if this was something she'd have to get used to. Probably.

A small part of her cowered in fear of what that might mean, but another part of her was still caught up in the sheer energy her new roommate carried.

"Oh, you smell good," Stella said as she leaned out of the hug, hands lingering on Kash's shoulders like she wanted to get a good look at her.

Kash wrinkled her nose, heart skipping a beat. She was sweaty and tired and had just stopped panting from carrying a box of books up five flights of stairs.

"I do?" she asked.

Stella waved her hand dismissively. She reached behind her and Kash noticed two large suitcases in the hallway.

"Let me help," she murmured as she stepped out and brought in one of Stella's suitcases as Stella dragged the other. They awkwardly shoved them into the first free space they could find, so they could close the door on the noisy hallway full of belongings and freshman and their frantic parents.

"Thank you," Stella said, looking around the room. "Well, looks like you've definitely moved in."

"Trying to," Kash said. She gestured to her mother. "This is my mom, by the way."

Stella immediately brightened and waved. "Hi! Mrs…"

"Call me Jaisri, it's nice to meet you Stella," Jaisri said warmly.

"Likewise," Stella all but laughed out and Kash thought she was probably the happiest person she'd ever met. She abruptly wondered if Stella ever got sad, and what she was like when she was.

"Are you—is this all your stuff?" Kash asked, gesturing to the suitcases pushed haphazardly against each other just by the doorway.

Stella shook her head. "No, I've got another suitcase with my mom, she's just finding parking. We just flew in this morning. I'll probably be getting packages in the mail, though. Couldn't take everything with me on the flight."

"That sounds stressful. We mailed a lot of Kash's stuff early, too. We have family about an hour away, so we picked it all up on the way," Jaisri said, taking some clothes from one of Kash's suitcases and organizing them into the provided closet.

Kash knew she would take them all out and put them back in differently tomorrow.

"It is stressful. When did you guys arrive here?" Stella asked.

"We flew in about a week ago," her mother explained. "We ended up going out to get some snacks and storage for Kash, just to help organize."

Kash nodded to confirm, watching as Stella huffed out a breath and settled into one of the desk chairs.

"That's smart," Stella said. She shrugged off the thin jacket she was wearing and draped it across the back of the chair. "It's warmer here than I expected. Humid, too, isn't it?"

Kash nodded. "It feels like a hundred degrees, I just had to carry those—" she gestured to the boxes of her books "—up the stairs. The elevators were taking forever 'cause everyone's using them."

"No way," Stella said in clear disbelief. "That's impressive. That's *heavy*, isn't it?"

Kash's lips twitched, and she kept herself from grinning.

"She's useful if you've got a jar you can't open," her mother said with a teasing smile.

Kash threw her mother a warning look, widening her eyes in emphasis.

"Noted." Stella laughed and got up laboriously from her chair. "I assume you've claimed that bed?" She pointed to the lofted bed that Kash had called earlier.

"Yeah," Kash nodded sheepishly, "is that okay?"

Her mom shook her head as she placed a folded sweater inside the closet.

"Of course," Stella said.

Kash nodded with a smile and looked down, bumping the toe of her shoe against a brand-new empty storage drawer. She felt tired, drained, like she'd had the effort sucked out of her through her fingertips.

"Do you want some help?" Stella asked. "You guys look like you could take a break, and I've only just gotten here."

Kash immediately shook her head. "No, no. We're good. Do you need help with your stuff?"

"No, thanks!" Stella grinned and then looked at Kash inquisitively. "I'm from New York, you?"

"Boston," Kash replied. She winced and bent down to reach over and open a box of shoes. "Well, uh, about an hour outside of Boston. Little over an hour. Massachusetts."

"Ah. We're both East Coasters, then, are we?" Stella smiled warmly and something in her eyes or in the way her lips curled or in the way her cheeks were just slightly pink from the heat, made Kash's breath hitch.

Should be easy to make home together, then.

"Yeah, I guess we are."

give me a monument.

Stella tumbled in through the door of their dorm as she opened it and Kash sat up quickly.

"Oh," Stella gasped abruptly, eyes wide and apologetic, "did I wake you?"

Kash shook her head, adjusting the pillows behind her and leaning over the railing. "No, no, I'm awake."

Stella nodded exaggeratedly and closed the door with a flourish. She shrugged off her signature Carhartt jacket and slumped into her desk chair. With an expressive sigh, she swiveled around and leveled Kash with an excited grin.

Kash sighed and indulged her. "What is it?"

Stella let out a high-pitched sound and pointed at herself. "There's a restaurant named after me," she said, drawing out the last vowel.

Kash raised an eyebrow. "Really?"

Stella nodded happily. She haphazardly pulled her glossy black hair up into a ponytail as she got up and walked over to her bed. "It's like it was meant to be," she said, climbing up the slats, sighing once she reached the top and sprawled out on her back. After a moment, she tilted her head up and peeked at Kash.

"I'm a little drunk," she said, holding her fingers up in a pinched gesture.

Kash nodded. "I know you are."

Stella's eyes bugged out. "You do?"

Kash laughed and nodded again. She leaned her head to the side and smiled. "Yeah, it's pretty obvious."

Stella laughed and settled back into her bed. "We had some drinks at Laura's apartment, but I saw it as I was walking back. *Stella*. It exists." Stella gestured at Kash. "We'll go there sometime. We have to. I mean, it's like I'm meant to be here. To find my self-titled restaurant. Forget classes. This is self-discovery, I'm here!"

Kash shook her head, laughing softly at Stella's ramblings.

"Wonder if there's something named after you?" Stella asked, twirling her fingers in the air absently.

Kash shrugged. "Not much named after me. I'm the one who's named after someone."

Stella frowned at that. "Who're you named after?"

Kash smiled and pulled the comforter up around her. "My dad named us all after musicians that he liked," she explained. "I'm named after Freddie."

Stella squinted. "Who's Freddie?"

Kash made an affronted sound. "Freddie *Mercury*."

"Oh." Stella drew out the vowel, confusion draining from her face only to come back full force a moment later. "But your name is Kash?"

"Yeah," Kash said, "and my dad decided to make my middle name Mercury."

"Well, that's creative," Stella snorted.

"Yeah, yeah. We don't talk about it." Kash pressed her finger to her lips in a hushing gesture. "But yeah, not much named after Kash."

Stella sat up and looked at her with an earnest expression. "Money? Like, *cash* and coins?" she offered.

Kash stared at her for a moment before slowly grinning. "Yeah," she said, nodding her head. "Okay. Go to sleep, Stella."

Stella groaned as she fell back into her bed. She pulled her sheets over her body haphazardly and let out a heavy sigh.

"There's got to be a restaurant. Some fancy, hipster place that has too much going on at once," she mumbled.

Kash got up with a fond shake of her head and climbed down her bed. She walked over to the door to turn off the lights and looked back up at Stella, leaning against the wall for a moment. She could barely see her through the gaps in the railing, but one of her arms dangled off the side, fingers twitching like she was having a particularly exciting dream.

Meant to be here.

Kash took in a deep breath and exhaled slowly before walking back to her bed, climbing up, and getting in under the covers as cautiously and quietly as she could.

A muffled thud sounded from the room above as she stared up at the ceiling, and for a split second, she imagined it falling onto her.

Stella's breathing became lighter and more even as minutes passed by.

Kash turned over onto her side, facing her roommate. She brought her hand up to nestle further into her pillow and let herself fully sink into the bed, completely lifeless. An intangible heaviness pressed her down, making her bones creak with pain, and she closed her eyes.

I'm not meant to be here.

what are all these parts of me.

"Hold it like this," Lani instructed, gently positioning Kash's arms so her left elbow touched the tip of her right hand.

Kash smiled and watched as Lani demonstrated, gracefully moving her hands in slow rolling repetitions, like long grass in the wind.

"Just the hand?" she asked.

Lani nodded. "Like a forty-five-degree angle," she said, tan fingers fluttering in the air above them.

Kash could feel the grass beneath her, poking through her sweaty jersey and tickling her back. She moved her hands smoothly, tucking them against her elbows, like Lani was doing, and bending them back and forth like the surge of the ocean.

"I'm doing it, I think," Kash said, frowning when she looked over at Lani and realized how graceless her attempt was in comparison. "You move like, something fluid," she said softly.

"Like water?" Lani suggested with a raised eyebrow.

Kash squeezed her eyes shut and dropped her hands onto her stomach.

"Yeah," she laughed. "Yeah, water. Give me a break, I've just finished a game not even two hours ago, 'my brain's all tired.'"

Lani laughed loudly, a bright musical sound that echoed across the field they were lying on. The soccer nets were still up on either side of the spray-painted touch line, and the sky was washed with blues, purples, and oranges.

"Brain all tired from losing, is that it?" Lani teased.

Kash scoffed. "You're supposed to be cheering me up, according to you."

"I am," Lani insisted. "I'm teaching you the hand movements, free hula lessons."

Kash snorted. "Thanks," she said dryly, "I'm *elated*."

Lani threw her a playful glare. Her lips pouted slightly.

"And what does this mean?" Kash asked.

"*Niu*. A coconut tree," Lani said softly, moving her arms again in the same way, and Kash could see the semblance of a swaying tree.

"I don't think I've ever watched you dance, like, properly," Kash murmured.

Lani hummed in agreement and sat up. She looked down over her shoulder at Kash in a way that was so efficacious in turning her inside out, that it took her a moment to register Lani's words.

"Huh?" Kash mumbled dumbly, blinking from fool's vertigo.

"Get up," Lani said with an outstretched hand. Her hair was long and slightly frizzy down her back with bits of grass tangled in the loose blond curls. Though Kash decided that they looked like they belonged there along with the sweat gathering at her hairline, the dirt on her knuckles, and the indented creases in her skin on the backs of her arms.

Kash took her hand and stood up laboriously, groaning under her breath when her muscles felt weak to a point of inability. "Lani," she sighed out, wincing as she bent down to fix her socks.

"Come on," Lani said, hand still gripping Kash's, and led her a few steps away farther infield. The skirt of her dress fluttered slightly with each step and Kash watched with mindless focus as the fabric brushed against Lani's calves.

"Where're we going?"

"Nowhere. Just here."

"Okay."

Lani toed off her shoes and socks and gestured for Kash to do the same.

With another heavy sigh, she complied and wiggled her toes in the cool grass after.

"Ready?" Lani asked.

Kash frowned. "Ready for what?"

Lani answered by smiling and setting her hands on her hips. She bent her knees slightly and stepped to her right with effortless fluidity, her left hip coming up and down like the crest of a wave or the unraveling of a spool.

"Copy me," Lani said, jutting her chin out at Kash.

All Kash wanted to do was *watch*.

She stumbled on her first step, her thighs aching as she bent her knees. She wanted to whine and insist on laying back down in the grass, but she lifted her feet anyway.

"Two steps to the right, and then two steps to the left, and you just move," Lani explained, tilting her head up to the setting sun for a moment before glancing back at Kash.

"Right, simple, just move," Kash mumbled, purposefully keeping her hips as still as possible as she stepped side to side. Her cheeks were warm with embarrassment and awe as she watched Lani dance, ignoring her own graceless movements. "Can I just—" Kash exhaled and dropped back down to the ground in a tired heap. "—I'll just watch you."

Lani grinned at that and took a step forward and then back and brought her hands up level to her shoulders. She moved like drizzling honey, hips swaying, shoulders steady and cheeks flushed with a pleased smile. Her hair was still disheveled with grass and knots, her dress had streaks of green, and her feet were a mess of grass and dirt, but her entire body was washed in the setting sunlight like a spill of watercolors, and Kash decided that Lani was something beyond beautiful.

Distant voices echoed from somewhere, likely a few streets away.

Lani stopped abruptly, hands dropping by her sides. Her eyes darted around the field, and she turned once, surveying their surroundings as if checking to make sure no one was visibly infringing on the two of them. With seeming satisfaction, she twirled back round to face Kash, and her dress swished with the movement.

"So?" she asked, eyes twinkling. "Verdict on my dancing?"

Kash smiled softly. "I wish you hadn't stopped."

A deep red blush bloomed on Lani's face, like a rush of ink just underneath her skin. She sat down in the grass and stretched her legs, so her toes dug into the flesh of Kash's calves.

"My dad has this thing that he says—it's not a belief, but I guess it is, in a way—where he tells me he was destined to have a child who would be a dancer, because it's in our name.

Kahele." Lani uprooted some grass between her fingers as she spoke. "And when I was born, he decided. Ailani Kahele. I was meant to not just be a dancer, but a great one. It's why he put me in *hālau hula* in the first place. It's just who I am, by *divine foretelling*," she adopted a mockingly dramatic tone before smiling and saying, "and my dad's."

Kash nodded. "I think I agree with him."

Lani laughed at that. "Why?"

"You dance like," Kash searched for the words, "you just, you embody it. You dance like it's easy, like it's part of you."

Lani stared at her for a searing moment before nodding and asking, "What were you born to do?"

"Me?"

"Yeah, you."

Kash let out a trilling breath and squinted up at the sky. Still a gradient of blues, purples, and oranges, and maybe some fiery pink now, surrounding the sun.

"I have no idea. What's the use in prophesying?"

"Just indulge me," Lani said with a smile.

A few dark gray wisps inched leisurely across the sky, slow and steady, almost not moving at all. In front of her, Lani was silent and warm, and Kash could hear the sound of her breathing like radio static in her ear. She watched the clouds until they reached the tree line surrounding their field and dropped her eyes down to Lani's.

"My dad has these notions," she said into the quiet evening. "I don't know how he knows or how he decides, but he has these notions of what we're each meant to do."

Lani wiggled her toes against Kash's skin, and they both laughed softly, privately.

"He says my brother is meant to be a musician, someone who lives and breathes music, I guess, and hears it in everything, too. I used to think that was just him projecting, because he was one, too, you know. He was a young, passionate musician, before he had kids, got married, and suddenly needed to move on. Maybe that's—I don't think he wants any of us to have to move on."

Lani hummed, like she understood, and Kash wondered if she really did. She hoped that she really did.

"He says I'm a writer. An author, whatever," she continued. "I was born to write things, I guess, born to own a million notebooks, half a million full of words, and half a million left empty. He says the way I speak is like that, too, which is just another sign of confirmation. But I have no idea what that means."

"I think I do," Lani said.

Kash looked at her, drifted her gaze down the slope of her nose, up across her cheeks, and back to her eyes. If she focused, she could almost see her own reflection in them, like she would if she stood at the edge of a lake and peered over at the rippling surface.

"Tell me, then," she murmured urgently.

"That," Lani said immediately and pointed at Kash's lips, like that was all the explanation she needed.

Kash frowned and shook her head. "What?"

"Every time you speak, almost, you have this habit of cutting through people. You wouldn't know, you're not on the receiving end. You wouldn't understand. Others would. I would."

Kash swallowed with effort and fisted the fabric of her shorts in her hands.

"I… cut through you?" she asked.

Lani nodded with conviction. "You do."

"In a way that hurts?"

"No. It's like you cut a hole and pour yourself in through it. You're very hard to keep out of mind." The words tumbled out of Lani's mouth with a breathless laugh, like an embarrassed confession.

Kash's head hurt. She hurt all over, ached and throbbed from exertion, and all of a sudden she wanted to crawl across the three feet of grass between them and fall into Lani's lap. She wanted to collapse into a shape that fit Lani's body like nothing else ever would.

"I can't imagine," she said instead, blinking slowly before taking Lani's ankle in her hand and settling it on her knee.

"Your fingers are cold," Lani murmured with a small laugh.

Kash looked up at her abruptly. "What?"

"Nothing." Lani shook her head, blond hair rippling down her shoulders. "Continue."

Kash watched her for a moment before glancing down at her fingers wrapped around Lani's ankle, caressing the jut of bone. "I mean, I was saying, I can't imagine I'm—I know what you're saying, I—I get the feeling. You're incredibly hard to keep out of mind, Lani."

Lani's blush spread charmingly down her neck and shoulders, and she nodded with a nonchalant smile. "Yeah, see. You get it. Writer."

you keep me (here).

The elevator was full of people, crowded almost to a point of no space, and Kash felt sick at the idea of squeezing herself in among so many bodies.

It was just the fifth floor.

She sighed and shoved open the door to the stairwell, making her way up with forceful, hasty steps and almost tripping to a halt on the fourth floor. She let out a stuttered breath, the sound echoing and lingering in the air. Her mouth felt dry and too hot, and her eyes burned, the pain only letting up when she squeezed them shut, spilling tears down her cheeks. She crouched down and listened for any sign of echoing movement as she curled in on herself.

It took her five deep breaths to get up again. They were rough and ragged like she'd drawn them from some ancient, decayed cave inside her lungs. It took her five more breaths to make it up onto her floor, and another five to make it to her door. She stumbled as she pushed against it, opening it with a bit too much force and lurching forward with a gasp.

"Hey!" Stella called from her bed, looking down and smiling brightly.

Kash stared for a moment before nodding her head and mumbling, "Hey." She closed the door behind her and exhaled softly in relief. Her feet throbbed in her shoes, and she slipped them off, not even bothering to untie the laces. It took a moment of clumsiness, hopping on one foot for a bit, before stumbling into the wooden supports of her bed.

"Are you good?" Stella asked with a giggle that she quickly doused when Kash didn't answer. "Kash?"

"Yeah," Kash said in a short, strained voice. Her mind was filled with a cacophony of voices, of questions, of absurd answers, of things she wished she could shut off but couldn't.

"What's wrong?"

"Nothing," Kash said immediately. She winced a moment after and threw an apologetic look at Stella.

"You're crying."

"No, I'm not."

"You are," Stella said firmly and Kash wanted to bite at her, snap her teeth in warning, and ask her how she thought she knew Kash well enough to talk like that.

"I'm *not*," Kash reiterated. She dropped her bag carelessly on the ground and took off her jacket, throwing it on the growing pile of clothes on her desk chair.

"Do you want some tea? I'm making some." Stella pointed to the electric kettle on her desk that was still steaming. "Earl Grey."

"That's my favorite," Kash mumbled without thinking. She felt so inexplicably tired, and her feet dragged on the floor as she walked over to Stella's desk.

"Here." Stella climbed down off her bed and grabbed a mug from the cabinet next to the fridge, giving it to Kash like she was giving a toy to a crying child.

Kash offered a thanks and poured herself a cup, relishing in the warmth radiating from the ceramic in her hands. She took the tea bag that Stella offered and dipped it into the water until it bloomed a bright golden brown.

"I'm sorry," she murmured after a moment, bringing the mug up to her face and closing her eyes against the fragrant warmth.

"Pour me a cup, too," Stella said, sliding another mug over and grabbing some milk from their small black fridge.

Kash nodded and did as told and huffed out a grateful laugh when Stella also grabbed four packets of honey from the box they kept stocked on Kash's desk.

"I don't think I've found anyone who drinks tea the way I do," Stella murmured with a smile. "Nor anyone who likes to collect honey packets from coffee shops."

Kash hummed in acknowledgment and suddenly had to swallow back the urge to burst into tears. She closed her eyes, brought her mug of tea close to her face, and inhaled deeply. Her eyes flew open, and she nearly choked when she felt the cool skin of Stella's hand on her forehead.

"What—" Kash cleared her throat with a wince. "—What are you doing."

"You're warm," Stella said with a furrowed brow.

Kash laughed dryly. "You always *comment* on something about me—"

"No." Stella's frown deepened. "I mean, you're temperature."

Kash paused at that and set her tea down. She gingerly brought her own hand up to her forehead in a fickle attempt at confirmation. But maybe the fact that she felt both unbearably hot and cold to her bones meant that Stella was right.

"And I don't mean to *comment*, but I can stop if it's bothering you," Stella said gently, tucking her smooth black hair behind her ear.

Guilt washed over Kash, and she shook her head quickly, but stopped as soon as her vision spun and blurred for a brief, disconcerting moment.

"Hey, woah," Stella said, grabbed Kash's shoulders.

"Sorry," Kash mumbled.

"You're not feeling well."

"No, I'm not," she said and reached for her cup of tea. It was still hot, and the steam felt damp against her skin. She grabbed the milk and poured some into her tea along with two packets of honey. "Inside and out," she added under her breath.

"We've literally only been back for a couple of weeks. How can you be sick?" Stella laughed softly, and there was an unprecedented affection in her eyes that Kash looked away from.

She frowned. She'd only known her for a few months. That was not enough time to grow *affection*.

Or maybe it was, for certain things.

She looked over to the box of honey packets on her desk, and to the haphazard jumble of their shoes by the door and nodded to herself.

Maybe it was.

"Do you wanna lie down?" Stella asked.

"I'm drinking tea," Kash croaked. She lifted her mug in indication.

"Come up here with me," Stella said as she began to climb the wooden slats up to her bed with one arm, the other steadily holding her tea.

"I have a bed, you know."

"I know, just come."

Kash stared up at her and felt a bit dizzy. She swayed back and forth, like a tree in the wind, as she sluggishly contemplated what she was about to do.

"Um." She licked her lips, and grimaced when she realized how chapped they felt. "Okay."

Stella beamed and leaned over to offer her hand. "Give me your tea, I got it."

Kash obeyed and cautiously climbed up the bed. Her height meant it only took about a step and a push upward, but even that felt like a gargantuan task.

"Careful," Stella called out in warning.

"I've got it," Kash all but hissed. "'S a bed not a mountain."

"Oh right, I forgot, you're *strong*," Stella teased and Kash huffed at that as she clumsily crawled onto the mattress.

"Shut up," she grumbled and took her tea from Stella's hand. "I have so much work, I don't have time to sit in your bed with you."

"Ah, same here," Stella said, "I have two projects due in the next three days and I'm stressed."

"Oh, Jesus."

"Yeah, it's fine. I was just about to take a break, take a nap or something."

"It's six in the evening," Kash said flatly.

"Yeah, have some tea and then sleep, why not," Stella said, holding her hand up defensively. "Who says I can't just sleep for a few hours and wake up and get back to work?"

Kash shrugged. "Dunno. I can go work in the lounge if you're sleeping."

Stella stared at her for a moment, eyes deep and scanning. "You don't look like you could handle going to the lounge right now," she said.

Kash flinched and set down her tea on the wooden railing, not caring if it crashed to the floor. "What?"

"You just look tired, that's it," Stella said with a placating smile. "I'm not about to ask you to *leave*."

Then what are you asking me?

Kash stared at her from under her lashes until the burning in her eyes became unbearable and she had to blink.

"Just, lie down with me," Stella said gently, and she set her mug on the convenient jut of the wall just above the railing of her bed, and beckoned her forward. She gestured to the three layers of pillows she kept and pulled one out to sit vertically alongside hers. "Here."

Kash nodded numbly, eyes darting back and forth between Stella's face and her hands pressing into the plush pillows. She squeezed her hands around the sheets and dug her teeth into her lip.

"I really don't feel good. You might catch it," she said.

Stella shook her head and patted the pillow again.

It took everything in Kash not to break down into tears as she slowly crawled over and settled into the space between the railing and Stella's body.

"Sorry if I, well," she started to say, before trailing off and closing her mouth. She watched a smile bloom on Stella's face at the same time she felt a tear fall from her left eye, trail down the bridge of her nose, down her cheek, and soak into the pillowcase.

"Why're you crying?"

Kash shook her head. "Too many emotions. M'head feels heavy. I'm not crying."

Stella laughed. "You are. And you're sick, it's okay."

"No, I'm so…" she turned so she was looking up at the ceiling and felt more tears fall. Her lashes were thick and blurry in the edges of her vision. "It's not just that."

Stella hummed softly at that, and it was placating, the kind of hum you'd offer a babbling baby.

"I think," she said, letting out a great big sigh like she was about to preach something philosophical, "I think I've been feeling even more homesick after going home. If that makes sense. It's easy to feel alienated here. Alienated here and at home. Like we don't fully belong in either place, huh?" Kash's throat constricted painfully, like she'd swallowed a ball of tin foil.

"Yeah," Kash choked out. "Yeah, I… yeah. Sometimes I don't know what I'm doing here. Because I don't feel like I— or everyone says it's normal and I don't know if it's normal or if there's something wrong with me, because everyone says it's temporary, but what if it's not?"

"I might be wrong, but I think a lot of us don't know, if that helps," Stella said.

Kash nodded like it did. She shivered slightly and Stella immediately pulled the comforter up over them.

"Stay warm," she said under her breath, and then, louder, "So maybe there's something wrong with all of us."

Kash laughed at that, a wet, loud laugh that probably sounded terrible.

"And cry a little bit more," Stella said as she snuggled into the covers. "It's easier to sleep after."

"What about the light?" Kash asked.

"Forget about the light, we're not paying the electric bill, it's all good," Stella said, turning so her back was to Kash and she was talking over her shoulder.

Kash laughed again and closed her eyes.

It's all good.

She felt more tears fall and tucked her chin underneath the comforter to hide. It was useless trying to stop them now. Her head throbbed and she pressed it farther into the pillow and leaned into the aches she felt all over. After a moment, she heard Stella rustle around and opened her eyes to see her turning over.

"Hey," Stella said, "sorry, just, you're warm and I'm not."

The corner of Kash's lips twitched up. "I'm usually, always, the cold one," she said through a yawn and then, without thinking too hard about it, she leaned her head to the side until it was resting softly against Stella's shoulder. Her skin was cold against Kash's temple, and it made her shiver.

"Am I making you cold?"

"I think that's good, for a fever," Kash mumbled tiredly. "Meant to be keeping me cold."

Stella laughed softly and the sound was warm and crackly like a smoking fire, drifting up above them and lingering pleasantly in the air. "I'll keep you cold, then."

i wrote you a letter and never sent it.

Lani—

I am likely not as important to you as you are to me. That is okay. I am completely, irrationally okay with that.

I don't know why I am writing this. I was listening to that song I played for you in your room this past January and suddenly I thought of you. The song I want to fall in love to.

And so, I continued to think of you and then I found myself writing down the words I was saying in my mind.

I keep trying to act nonchalant around you. Like I'm not dying to hear your voice, to hear the gentle inflection of every word you say. I always end up staring at my phone for way too long, my thumb hovering over the send button. I always end up agonizing over every single word I write to you, beating myself up because. As much as I try to act like I don't, I care about what you think of me. I care about being someone you like.

That's not to say that you are difficult for me. You're important for me, for my heart. You are not particularly easy, but you are far from difficult. I could never get exhausted of you. You're sunshine.

I have always loved to a point of heartbreak and pain. I don't know how to stop myself from falling off the precipice for someone. Each and every time. It hurt. It still hurts. And I kind of do that with you, but for some reason it's as much easier as it is harder.

Because it's not like we never went through times when I wanted to scream and escape from everything. It's not like there weren't times when I saw your name light up on my phone screen and I just sat there in silent panic because I didn't know how to talk to you. I still felt pain for you in the way I felt pain for others that I loved.

But you're still, lovely. I don't know.

And I miss you. I miss you in the way that I can't help but smile to myself whenever I think of you. I miss you in the way that I can't help but giggle softly, privately, whenever I hear your wonderfully grainy voice over the phone. The static, for some reason, makes you that much more perfect in my mind's eye. I like that I miss you in such a deep, unburdened way. Without the chaos.

I cannot label what you mean to me because I might just be making this all up in my mind. We've been friends for years, and in all that time, I've never figured out whether it's all in my head, or whether it's all true, or both.

But you are everything.

You are everything.

I feel comfortable with you. I act nonchalant, I spend too much time typing out my texts, only because you are every-thing. To me.

Fuck, I'm pretty sure I love you. A lot. I don't even know why or how or what loving someone even means. I don't think

I can do it in the way I'm supposed to. I say I love you not in the way people usually say it, I guess. What I really mean is I need you and you're beautiful and I would never stop looking at you if I could.

But I'm listening to that Tchaikovsky piece. And you once asked me what I picture when I do, and I once said jumping into puddles or running away with someone. When I said someone, I fucking meant you.

However little the time I spent with you feels in comparison to those other people we both know, it's not the same. Not right now. I spend too much time typing out texts and deleting them because I don't know how to speak to them anymore. I don't know if I should pick up the phone and call them because I'm unsure. I'm so unsure. So many things have changed this past almost year, I can't take any more.

But you are not like that to me and I just fucking love that. I never, ever want to change that. I hope you don't either. Because I don't know what I would do without you. I don't know what I would do if you decided not to be in my life anymore.

That sounds silly.

You probably think that's a silly notion as well. It probably is. I used to say that about a lot of people and yet many of them have left, or have lost relevance, and I'm still here. And maybe it's a certainty in our lives; that frailty and ephemeral, constant, change. Maybe people come and go and that's just the nature of how it works.

I honestly don't know what I'm saying.

If you ever read this you might stop calling me or talking to me the same. That would drive a knife in me. You just mean a lot to me. I don't have to be your anything, or anything beyond what I am now, but you're the person I picture when I listen to Tchaikovsky, and maybe that's not particularly romantic, and I'm probably not the best person to expect romance from. But I jump into puddles with you, your hair curls in the rain and it's like strands of pulled glass, and I can't stop watching you, and I think I'll picture you like that for a really long time.

If you'll let me.

And okay, maybe I do miss you a little painfully sometimes. So maybe it's good that the semester's almost done, because that means even if I don't sleep properly until the next time I see you, it won't be for long.

I want to ask you to meet up, but sometimes it's hard, and I wonder if that's because I've never really had to ask you for anything. You just happen, without warning, you happen to me, and I withstand it like the fool that I am, because I relish it. I relish you. I adore you.

But for now, I'll tuck this away in a drawer, and once we share a location again, I'll appear on your doorstep, or you'll appear on mine, and without warning, we'll happen to each other. Just like old times.

Kash.

i didn't know you painted your nails.

Kash hadn't been in Lani's car since they had both been wide-eyed seniors. Almost a year to date. She'd forgotten the worn softness of the nylon seats and the warm browns of the interior. The glove compartment had a black scuff on it, like the ones she'd accidentally leave in the truck, while trying to put on her boots. She hadn't driven the truck in a while either.

They had been parked on Rafi's street for the past hour, lost in conversation, reminiscing on memories and sharing stories from the previous semester.

In the driver's seat, Lani gestured passionately, her red painted fingernails glinting in the meager lighting. Kash was sure Lani preferred not to paint them—and if anything, a lighter lacquer. Something more subtle, more natural.

"Wait, I should probably turn off the headlights, too, right?"

Two empty paper ice cream containers were stuffed into one of the center console cup holders. In the other one, two movie tickets peeked out from under a small pile of change.

Kash smiled softly.

She felt Lani's gaze and blinked. "Yeah, you probably should," she answered, nodding.

With a click the headlights switched off. Everything was suddenly quiet. She could hear the rub of her fingertips against her jeans as she traced the seam along her inner thigh.

"I like your nails, by the way," she murmured, looking down at her own uneven ones.

"Oh, thanks," Lani replied just as softly.

"How are you doing over there? How's Iowa City? Writing anything good?" she asked.

Kash shrugged and looked up to admire the soft pink of Lani's cheeks. "Yeah, I'm all right."

Lani nodded with a smile, seemingly happy with the response.

She knew Kash, didn't she? Knew pressing for more was futile.

After a moment of grasping for courage, Kash added, "Miss you, like—a good amount."

Lani laughed. "Me too."

Kash responded with an uninhibited smile.

I miss you too.

"It's *colder* up *north*," Lani mused.

"Is it?"

"Yeah," she confirmed, nodding vigorously.

Kash felt something in her chest shift, like one of her ribs decided to cave in under the pressure of her throbbing heartbeat. "Does everyone live in igloos, then?" she said in a wry voice.

Lani laughed and shook her head, eyes sparkling.

Kash grinned. "So, you've got your winter gear and everything with you, then."

"Yeah, I do. Bought a new coat, actually."

"Oh," Kash sighed out. "Nice."

"Yeah. It was on sale, too. Thirty bucks."

Kash raised an eyebrow. "Nice."

"Right? And it's, like, the stylish kind. With big brown buttons and deep pockets and it reaches past my knees. You'd like it." Lani flicked her eyebrows upward as she smirked suggestively. "I cut my hair, too."

"I noticed." Kash had noticed the minute she'd opened the car door, on the drive to the movie theater, throughout the movie like a sixth sense, while eating ice cream on the hood, and continuously on the drive back.

She allowed herself to stare at it properly now, letting go of the cautious side glances and shy admiration. Since last summer, Lani's hair had become almost dirty blond—dirty enough to maybe not even classify as blond, but Kash *liked* the idea of Lani being blond—and right now in partial darkness, it glowed, like Lani had shampooed her hair with pure silver.

Moonlight streamed in through the rear window, creating a backlit halo around everything. It was surreal. Conversation stagnated for a brief moment. They breathed in and out in perfect rhythm.

It looks beautiful, like everything extraordinary in the world.

You are everything extraordinary in the world.

"It looks good," Kash offered clumsily and winced.

Lani blushed conspicuously and another of Kash's ribs fell through.

There was a newfound glow in Lani that somehow rendered her more brilliant than before. As if that were possible.

And it wasn't just the moonlight. It was emanating from right underneath her skin. Incandescent.

"You look good, love. You really do." Kash nodded assuredly, reverently.

"You do, too," Lani murmured back, blush fading but still evident. She was looking down at her fingers, her nails.

Kash waited for her to look up, to somehow finish the statement with a reassuring glance.

Please look at me.

"I started painting them. Found this red and tried it out. I liked it more than I thought I would, so… I kept it."

Kash nodded as she watched Lani dance her fingers along her thighs.

Another rib. More painful this time.

Please look at me.

"I think I like it better this way. I think I'll keep it for a while."

Kash felt a lump forming in her throat. "I like them, too."

"So, you've said."

Please look at me.

"Lani," Kash choked out, pressing her hand hard against her chest.

"Yeah?"

"*Lani.*"

There was a pause, a slight hesitance in the turn of her head.

Another rib, gone.

Kash floundered. "I—it's hard to breathe—"

"Yeah, I can understand the feeling."

"I can't *breathe.*"

Lani blinked once, very slowly. It was both alluring and terrifying.

"At all," she calmly confirmed.

Kash stared at her helplessly. "It's like, it's like breathing in against wind."

"Oh," Lani smiled softly, "impossible, then."

They were both silent for the next few moments. Kash's chest hurt more and more with each blinking sweep of Lani's lashes. Neither of them said anything. A familiar longing pulled at her, slowly curling her shoulders forward until she was hunched over.

"You should probably head home soon," Kash said tightly, barely holding the will to not cough and swallow the words back into her throat. She could feel her heartbeat thudding in the junction of her jaw and neck. She felt something break. Like the walls of her chest had finally caved in.

"Right! Right, yeah. Yeah, I—"

"I don't mean to rush you or anything—"

"Oh no! No, of course you're not, it's just, I—"

Kash waited for Lani to finish, but nothing followed. She stayed that way, mouth open and eyes wide. Like a fish caught on the line.

"You?" Kash prompted.

"I um—I kinda want to keep talking. With you."

Kash exhaled slowly. Her skin felt hot now, inside and out. Fluid heat moved slowly in sheets across her body. A molten lava shell. "About what?"

Lani shrugged. "Don't really want to go home yet."

"Okay."

Another silence, shuffling feet and blinking eyes and twiddling fingers.

"What time is it?"

"Oh, uh," Lani glanced at her phone, "12:55."

Kash nodded in response, mind filling with thoughts of Lani driving alone in a darkness occasionally lit up by passing headlights. "So, you should really get going, then," she sighed out under her breath as she sat up straight.

Lani gave her an incredulous look, letting out a scoffing sound of protest. "Do you not—"

"I—" Kash started, immediately regretting her words. She quickly reached out to press her palm against Lani's arm. She continued, voice softer, "—didn't mean it like that."

They unconsciously leaned closer, until Kash could feel Lani's breath against her nose. Kash felt an opportunity come and go. "Talk," she prompted with a half-smile.

Lani had a look of confession on her face and Kash braced herself.

"Okay, well, I might've done some stupid stuff since the last time I saw you," Lani said with an embarrassed smile.

Kash couldn't help the breathy, fond laugh that escaped through her teeth. A few of the baby hairs framing Lani's face danced with the impact.

"I would be surprised if you hadn't."

"Right." Lani smiled.

Kash could feel the warmth of it bleed into her cheeks. *Incandescent.*

"What'd you do, then?"

"Nothing illegal."

"I doubt that."

Lani let out a beautiful laugh that brought back the ebbing pain in Kash's chest full force.

"It's kind of a gray area. I mean, no. Nothing illegal, I promise. Just, like, morally?"

Kash raised an eyebrow and smirked. "Oh?"

Lani hesitated before blurting out, "I might've, kind of, hooked up with someone."

There was a painfully quiet moment when the words registered in Kash's mind before she jerked away instantly. She pressed her head against the passenger window, feeling the coolness from the glass numb the back of her head.

"You what?"

"He was kind of terrifying, too."

"*He* was *what*?"

Lani laughed and the sound felt wrenchingly out of place.

The pain in Kash's chest fell flat and in its place came a fragile chill.

"Not like that. Just in retrospect. He's kind of terrifying. In the weird sense. He's kind of weird. Older and all. I mean, not by much. Like four years. But still."

Kash stared at her. "Then why'd you—*sleep* with him?" she asked hollowly.

Lani shrugged and shamelessly explained, "Because I think I kind of like him. And he was just there. All tall and dark and barely visible under those stupid lights."

Whiplash. Kash's neck ached. Her mind nonsensically leaped back in time to a memory of a doctor's office visit, to her standing on a scale and a friendly nurse bringing the measuring bar down to meet the top of her head. Two numbers, five and seven, written down in a small blue booklet. Kash blinked back to the present, to Lani's beautiful embarrassed smile.

"Yeah. Kind of like in the way that you're weird and terrifying."

"Excuse me?"

"Yeah. You're weird. You only eat grapes in even numbers. You just have to spill tea on yourself every time you drink it—"

"I don't do that purposefully!"

"—You write letters to people on a regular basis—"

"Lots of people write letters!"

"—You still listen to Taylor Swift in that Walkman after every game, even when you win—"

"It's more for memories," Kash grumbled.

"Right. Your middle name's Mercury, like what is that—"

Kash made an affronted sound. "Well, I didn't *name myself.*"

"—And. You're terrifying. You're tall. And you've got cheekbones. And you've got, like, *biceps*—"

Kash blushed and rolled her eyes.

"And you have weirdly long eyelashes. Like spider legs, you know those stupid house spiders? And you always wear your dad's old tour jacket. It's huge on you, but. It's still terrifying."

She was wearing it right now, had it draped across her shoulders. She looked down at the fraying cuffs and traced the metal buttons with her fingers. How could a jacket be terrifying? Much less one from the late eighties.

"What are you talking about," she said softly. She looked up through her eyelashes at the other girl. Her heart was dropping at an exponential rate, and she couldn't do anything about it. She watched the slow, tired blink of Lani's lashes and wondered how it would feel to run her fingertip against them.

"You hooked up with a guy in a club, then?" Kash confirmed softly.

Lani nodded, having the decency to appear bashful. "I knew you'd get all judgey, but I kind of missed that about you. So."

"Right," Kash squinted her eyes at her, "I am judging you."

Lani smiled. "I know."

They sat in silence for the next few minutes. Kash looked at her phone and watched 1:05 turn into 1:06.

"You should probably get home, Lani."

"Yeah, I probably should," she said quietly. Her fingers danced across the center console until they settled in the soft crease of the ditch of Kash's elbow.

Kash held her breath. She met eyes with Lani and sighed out silently. "I'll get out. Just. Gimme a minute," she said.

Lani shook her head and gently answered, "It's no problem. Take your time. Please."

Another few minutes. Kash watched the numbers on her phone change to 1:10 before sitting forward abruptly and settling a hand on the passenger door handle.

"I'll see you around then. Kash?" Lani called out.

Kash paused and looked over her shoulder. "Yeah. Of course."

"Okay." Lani nodded in response. "Talk soon."

Kash nodded stiffly and grabbed her phone from the center console. The car door slammed, trembling through her body and ringing terribly loud against the softness of the night. Her throat felt thick and dry, and her fingers tapped anxiously against the sides of her thighs as she made her way up to the front door. She turned around when she heard the engine start, finger hovering over the doorbell. She watched as headlights switched on. They tracked across the street as Lani pulled out of her spot, washing every detail in invasive white light. She could see slight movement from the driver's seat and instinctively waved back until the red taillights disappeared around the street corner.

She quickly entered the code to the building and climbed up the stairs two at a time. She pressed the doorbell once, and a moment later Rafi was standing in front of her in horrible old pajamas.

He leaned smugly against the doorjamb and gave her an amused once-over. "It's one a.m.," he said.

Kash nodded. "I know."

"I'm mad. You've woken everybody up."

She shook her head, smirking. "I doubt that."

"You were spending quite a lot of time in that car. Was worried you'd never come out. What were you doing for that long?"

"Nothing," Kash said.

He grinned at her for a moment before stepping aside and jutting his chin out. She shoved him away as she kicked off her shoes and picked them up by the heel cuffs. She walked in, shrugging off her jacket as she made her way inside.

"You weren't making out were you?" he asked in a mockingly hushed tone.

Kash spun around and shoved him back with all the force she could muster.

"No!" she snapped at him, eyes flashing dangerously, wishing she could turn him to ash right then and there as he stumbled into the couch.

"Shit, okay," he cursed under his breath as he steadied himself. "Did you eat?" he grumbled a moment later.

Kash gave him an unimpressed look. "It's one a.m., Raf."

Rafi threw his hands up in the air. "I don't know! I don't know enough about you these days. I just assume you're like every other teenager who doesn't take care of themselves properly."

Kash rolled her eyes.

They made their way into the small kitchen, and she slumped into a chair at the table. A groan escaped her lips, and she hid her face in her arms.

"Hey, what's wrong?" Rafi sat down next to her and draped himself across her back.

"Nothing," she mumbled.

She felt three long fingers worm their way under her arms and she jerked away.

"Don't tickle me!" she shouted.

Rafi cursed and immediately slapped a hand against her mouth. He gave her a warning look that was softened by a spark of amusement. "Everyone's asleep you idiot," he chuckled. "You're going to wake my roommates up."

He slung an arm around her shoulders and brought her in close until her head was pressed against his neck. She felt him run his fingers through her hair, tucking a stray lock behind her ear.

"What's up, copycat?" he asked softly, squeezing his arms around her. It comforted her more than she let on.

She shrugged and burrowed deeper into his side, sinking into his warmth. It had been a while since she last hugged him like this. She'd missed him before and a part of her still missed him now even as she wrapped her arms clumsily around his torso and squeezed. He grunted comically and a smile broke onto her face before she could stop it.

"Are you trying to break me?" he asked in a strained voice.

Kash shrugged and relented her embrace. "Worth a try."

Rafi snorted. "But really. Kash. What's wrong?"

Kash paused and twiddled her fingers for a few moments before answering. "Just tired is all. Been hanging out too much," she lied. Half lie. She *was* tired out, and she did urgently need a couple of hours of alone time, but that wasn't enough to push her over the edge. Her trigger was Lani, she knew it, didn't have the strength to deny it at the moment. But Rafi would sneak it out of her and into the open air if they kept talking.

She looked over at him and took in his familiar face. There was a moment of comfortable silence and she basked in it gratefully.

"Is the air mattress still there?" she asked. "Know it takes up space."

"What kind of question is that, of course it is. You can stay here as long as you want."

"Okay. Gonna go sleep," she murmured, making a gesture to get up. She schooled her features, closing her eyes slowly and rubbing at her cheek in a lazy manner. Attempting a yawn would give the charade away, so instead she stretched and let out a satisfied sigh.

"Hey." He stopped her with a large, warm hand on her shoulder. She paused mid-stretch and glanced at him with wide eyes.

"Kash," he continued, voice toe-dipped in gentle persuasion, "I know you're not going to sleep until three. I know you're going to sit in bed overthinking things and watching *Adventure Time* on your phone until the birds start singing." He ended the sentence with a knowing chuckle.

She shrugged. Lying in bed alone for hours watching childhood shows sounded like a much, much better option than staying and talking. Even if it was an air mattress in her brother's room.

"I don't think I'm sleeping anytime soon either, to be honest," Rafi continued, and a sense of impending doom settled in her chest.

Kash watched him, watched as a small smile grew danger-ously on his face and his eyes crinkled slightly at the corners.

"Want to watch something? We've got ice cream in the freezer, I'm pretty sure."

There it was.

"I already ate."

"Ice cream?"

"Yeah. We got some after the movie."

Rafi shrugged and pouted mockingly. "But what's wrong with more?"

She shook her head.

His pout deepened. "Please?"

"No." She let out a laugh as he hung his head and assumed a crestfallen stance.

He looked up at her after a moment, like a child, check-ing to see if she was budging and she offered him a laugh of refusal.

His mock pout faded, and he watched her with an adoring, wistful gaze that made her skin feel suddenly cold. Brittle like thin ice hardening the surface of snow in the winter.

"I miss you, copycat. You're right here but I miss you, too much," Rafi explained in an unbearably gentle voice.

She did not need this right now. A painful compression wrapped around her chest and her eyes burned. A need to sob out everything spinning in her mind jerked her forward and she grabbed onto Rafi's outstretched arms.

"Okay. It's one in the morning so all the feelings are creep-ing out," she warned him, "I mean teenage angst in fucking buckets, okay?"

Rafi nodded attentively.

"Brace yourself," she warned tiredly. "Undeclared love declarations and stupid mental chaos. Just. I'm not in the mood for advice, okay? I mean it."

"Okay. Nothing I haven't seen or heard before," Rafi assured her.

Kash regarded him with narrowed eyes before sighing out dramatically, "Fuck—*fine*."

He awarded her a wide grin and jumped up to go over to the fridge. He opened the freezer drawer and turned back to look at her over his shoulder, "Cookie dough?"

She waved her hand dismissively. "Yeah, whatever. I'm going into your room and putting on *Adventure Time*."

* * *

Rafi yelped loudly as Kash tucked her toes underneath his calf with a premeditated grin.

"You're freezing," he hissed at her.

"Yeah, I'm cooling you down," she said instructively.

"I don't need cooling down," Rafi grumbled and raised an eyebrow when Kash laughed. "Feeling better now, are you?"

"I think it's the graveyard hour craziness," she said. "Always get weird after two."

Rafi raised his brow. "Only after two?"

Kash slapped him upside the head and stole a spoonful of ice cream from his pint.

"Hey, stop it—that's mine." Rafi rolled his eyes before shifting down the couch away from her. "Calm down. Now tell me about all this angst."

Kash's grin fell. "Oh. Right." She was drained, absolutely not in the mood to put in effort in divulging her secrets. "Nothing much."

"Tell. Me."

Kash groaned. "I just, sometimes, feel… paranoid, I don't know."

"Why?"

Kash shrugged, eating another spoonful of ice cream. "I think. Things are fleeting, maybe. Or just not permanent, and I have trouble with that."

"Why?"

"Because," she sighed, looking up at the ceiling, "I have these… good things in my life, things that *keep* me alive, I think. And I want those good things to stay. But then sometimes I feel like an idiot for wanting that."

"Why?"

Kash narrowed her eyes at her brother. "Is that all you're gonna do the whole time, just sit there asking 'why'?" she hissed.

Rafi frowned. "I'm just trying to understand."

Kash wanted to tell him that he never needed to ask before. He used to understand her rambling confessions like they were his own. He used to know just what to say or do, used to know everything she needed to feel okay. But maybe that was mean.

"You tell me your angst, then," she said. "I know for a fact you have no shortage of it."

Rafi shook his head. "I'm fine."

Kash felt suddenly vindictive, an aftertaste of her failed deflection. "Are you? I'm the only person in our family you even talk to."

Rafi hardened, jaw clenching and eyes turning to stone. "And?"

"Don't you think that's wrong?"

"Why would it be wrong? They don't want anything to do with me."

"You know that's not true," Kash murmured.

"Oh?" Rafi sneered. "It's not the truth?"

Kash glared, resisting the urge to scream at him about every time she saw her dad pass by Rafi's old room, lingering at the doorway like it would open to reveal her brother sitting on the bed, writing a song.

"It's *not*," she said. "And sometimes I get the feeling you might cut me off, too."

Rafi stared at her, hurt disbelief saturating his features. "No, I don't think that'll happen."

Kash scoffed. *Think?*

"You don't—you don't make me feel like I've failed, I mean. I don't feel less, and they make me feel like I, like all I've ever done is, is not be who I'm supposed to be. You don't. Or you haven't." Rafi cleared his throat.

"You're not a failure. Stop saying that."

Rafi shrugged. "Maybe I am, maybe I'm not. Doesn't matter anymore."

Kash sighed and slumped back, hanging her head off the back of the couch. "I think maybe I know why."

"Huh?"

Kash laughed dryly. "I think, maybe, we're both kind of failures. I think I've been feeling out of place for a while now, too. I just don't have the guts like you."

Rafi snorted. "What guts?"

"I don't know. You're here, aren't you? You're not playing a part for someone."

"What makes you think that?"

Kash ate another spoon of ice cream, slowly, letting it fully melt in her mouth before swallowing. "You just, you always seem incapable of doing so. Or at least, you always seem to refuse to."

Rafi hummed, barely a tune. "I can send you a song I wrote a few days ago. You might like it, might understand it. Mutual failures and all."

Kash lolled her head to the side to look at him. "I always do. Send it."

Rafi nodded. "I will. Look out for it. I expect a full constructive analysis." He threw her a sly smile.

Kash chuckled softly and nodded. "Noted. I'll absolutely tear it apart. Mutual failures and all."

i'll never send this, and you'll never answer.

Lani—

Fuck it. I'm writing you another letter. Or confession. Or apology. Or request.

Because it's 2:30 in the morning again. There's this new song that I found that hurts me in the best way, and it has started playing softly, and it's snowing outside, and my mind has decided to think of you.

I don't know why.

We haven't talked in months, which I guess isn't strange, but it's strange that it feels like longer. Like I haven't talked to you for years, or many lifetimes. And it's strange that I feel both cut to the core and perfectly normal. Or, as normal as I can.

I'm sorry, I guess, I just have this overwhelming ache in my chest like I want to call you suddenly and just hear your smile through the phone.

If you smile when we talk. I do. I did. I don't know if you do, but if you do, I think I want to hear the sound of it again. Right now.

I haven't stayed up this late in a while. And it never ends well, staying up past two. I always end up feeling like this. Like a pit of inexplicable emotion is weighing on top of my chest and all of a sudden I can't breathe. Or I can, but I can't get enough.

It's snowing here, is all. And I'm thinking of asking you if you want to meet up when I come back home for break, but I think you might not answer. Still, I imagine doing another drive at night, no need for a movie or ice cream, this time we're just putting on wonderful music and talking into the night until we forget where we are, even though you never really knew in the first place which means I am the only one who forgot.

I want to keep driving, I wish that were a thing, just floating in space, not needing to have a purpose (I don't know my purpose). I wish it were physically possible and I wish you wanted it too because I have no idea what goes on in your mind or how you feel or how much I should show you or how much you actually show me. I know nothing.

I wish you went here for school. I wish I could put on a thick jacket and meet you somewhere right now, maybe on the doorstep of your dorm. Or maybe you met me on the doorstep of mine and I could just hug you and smile and ignore the cold swirling snow and just know that you were here, you were my friend no matter what, and I could think about you painfully at 2:30 a.m. and be fine because I could talk to you in person the next day or that next moment.

I want to keep being your friend so badly, but I also want to be your someone. And I want you to be that someone because I think you're one of the few people I have left who gets me.

I don't talk to many people anymore. The last time I talked to my brother is the night you dropped me off at his apartment, and the morning after. He told me he'd send me a song. I miss hearing him sing almost the same way I miss hearing your smile. And I don't talk to Levi, I make it a habit of not thinking about him, even though all bets are off during the graveyard hours. The others don't seem to understand why, why I don't want to think of him, why I wish I could tear him fully out of my life the way he did me. He talks to Raz, you know? I don't know why. He doesn't talk to me. I'm starting to think that there are just people we're meant to talk to, and people we're meant to be friends with, and people we're meant to know, and sometimes those things don't coincide. Maybe history has nothing to do with it, and maybe that's why I have this sudden, desperate need for you to be here, in the snow, with me, because I'm holding you like sand in my fist, and I'm scared.

I won't send this, so you won't hear me beg you to answer me. You won't hear me wish you were something you're not. You won't hear me make a fool of myself just to keep you with me.

You won't hear me tell you how much I miss you, and how much that is affecting me, and you won't hear me wonder if it's affecting you the same way. I know it's likely not.

But I'm going to fall asleep thinking of you. I hope that's not at all creepy. I don't think I can help it.

Kash.

college: part two.

i think you're something else.

"All right, you can switch now with the next person, if you're done. Finish up your last thoughts, if you're not! And make sure you're really adding to what the last person wrote and not just writing what you want, otherwise you're missing the point," the professor called out, nodding emphatically.

Kash groaned inwardly and rushed to scribble the rest of her sentence down before sliding it to her right, over to the nearest person three seats down. She hated free-write exercises as much as she hated icebreakers, so a combination of the two was a genuine nightmare.

"Here," the boy to her left murmured, handing over a sloppily ripped piece of notebook paper.

Kash blinked down at the unintelligible handwriting, trying to make out what he'd written. She glanced over at him before quickly looking back down and squinting.

"Sorry, I know my writing's terrible," the boy murmured, and she whipped her head to the left, startling slightly when she found him staring directly at her.

"It's fine," she whispered back before adding, "but I can't read a thing."

He laughed softly and leaned closer, just enough so his voice wouldn't carry farther than it needed to. "Sorry. I can." He turned the paper slightly so he could read it. "It crept like an insect, tiny little chills running up from the rough pads of his toes to the soft space between his—" he stopped reading with a small hitch of breath. "Uh, well I literally meant, like, his upper thigh, inner thigh, you know, how, skin is soft… there? But it kinda comes across as something else?"

He looked sheepish and there was a slight red tint to his face.

Kash cleared her throat and nodded. "No, I get what you mean. I didn't… think it was something else."

The boy smiled. "Ah. You totally did."

Kash shook her head. "No, I didn't. Technically, I couldn't even *read* it."

He laughed at that, a laugh that brought his head forward so his unruly dark hair fell down over his face. "Right, right. Well, I wrote leg, but feel free to improve upon that."

Kash nodded and put her pencil to paper, pretending to have something to write down. In what felt like less than a minute, the professor called out the timer and prompted them all to switch again.

"I'll be proactive and just read this one right off the bat," the boy whispered, and she resisted the urge to roll her eyes.

"Or you could just make an effort to write better," she murmured.

He grinned at her, in a way that made her pause and take in his features.

"I'll be sure to," he said softly, his eyes bright and gray and larger than life. He slid the paper toward her slightly with two long fingers, and drew in a breath before speaking, "Every pulse that the mark gave out felt as if it was trying to compete with the pulse of their hearts."

Kash wrinkled her nose. "What," she said flatly.

"I don't know," he said with a defensive shrug, "I just went off of what the last person wrote."

Kash laughed and shook her head. "What did the last person write?" she said under her breath.

The boy hummed and slid the paper farther over to her. "Their handwriting is decent. Have fun."

* * *

"So, what did you write?"

Kash looked over her shoulder to see the boy walking up to her.

His hair was slightly messier, like he'd run his fingers through it, and in the harsh lights of the hallway, it looked lighter, the color of star anise.

"Hey," she said, hoping he didn't stick around long enough to take the elevator with her.

"Hey," he smiled. "So, what did you write?"

"Nothing," she said instinctively.

"Oh, that's a lie," he said.

"Nothing of note," she countered.

"I doubt that, too," he said, swaying a bit to the side so his shoulder lined up with hers, barely a foot of space between them. "I'm Evan, by the way. Sorry for *my* less than adequate writing skills."

"Kash. And your writing skills are fine."

"I'm glad," Evan laughed.

Kash nodded, not knowing what else to do, and looked down at her toes as he continued to speak. "You look like someone who's good at it. Writing. You look like a, you know, a real, fully-fledged writer."

Kash wrinkled her nose. "How so?"

Evan shrugged and practically beamed at her. His teeth were perfect, straight and white, and Kash swore they sparkled. "I don't know," he said, "you just do."

Kash blinked and averted her eyes, suddenly hit with the unbearable radiance of Evan's visage.

"Are you a writer?" she asked, praying to every deity she knew that the elevator would arrive before their conversation was done.

"I'm in this class, aren't I?"

Kash cleared her throat before laughing and nodding. Her chest squeezed suddenly, in a distantly familiar way that caught her off guard and she pressed her hand against her sternum. Her fingers were cool through the fabric of her T-shirt and it sent a shiver through her body, right down to her toes. She looked over to the small window of numbers beside the elevator controls and bit her lip.

Next to her, Evan hummed quietly, a tune that was unrecognizable to her, and she glanced down to see his fingers tapping lightly against the black denim of his ripped jeans.

"Do you—" she exhaled quickly and flashed a quick smile, deciding to give in, even if it felt somewhat predestined for ruin "—want to just take the stairs?"

Evan twisted his lips in mock thought before grinning and nodding. "Yeah, okay."

liar, liar, liar.

Evan's hands were soft and for a split second Kash felt embarrassed at the probable roughness of hers, but the thought blew away in a breathless rush as she ran faster.

"Hey!" Evan called breathlessly, tugging her back by the hand so she fell into pace with him again. "I already know I'm nowhere near as in shape as you are, so, at least pretend to let me impress you, yeah?"

Kash smiled. "Please, it's not worth trying."

Evan made a squawking sound of betrayal, and it made a warm, syrupy feeling drip down Kash's insides into her fingers and toes and of some unknown new volition, she squeezed Evan's hand and laughed.

"What, did you—" a gasp of air "—run track in high school, or something?" Evan asked.

Kash shook her head. "No, I, uh, played soccer, though. For a while actually."

"Oh, don't tell me," Evan said, exhaling sharply before coughing and laughing. "*Jesus*—you were one of those little kids who played in those town leagues, weren't you? Cute little five-year-old Kash, barely the size of a real soccer ball."

Kash threw him a withering look, quickly overtaken by a smirk. "I wasn't *little*."

"Oh?"

"No," Kash continued. "I was tall and had a bowl cut and they almost always mistook me for a boy."

Evan laughed brightly, breathlessly, like the picture of reckless happiness. There was a trail of sweat inching down his temple, sticking his baby hairs to his skin, and it was strangely—alluring.

Kash tripped over her feet, tugging Evan down with her by accident, and they both yelped and came to a halt. By some miracle, they didn't end up face down on the ground, and Kash looked to Evan with a sheepish smile.

It took one small inhale before the two of them descended into laughter, echoing into the warm night. Kash leaned into Evan, her chin fitting perfectly in the juncture of his neck and shoulder.

"I can't imagine you with short hair," Evan said.

Kash leaned away and flicked her hair over her shoulder with a smile, letting it fall flat down her back in a theatrical flourish.

With another, softer laugh, Evan nodded and brushed his finger along the ends of her hair, his knuckles just barely brushing against her lower back.

Kash held her breath. "It's probably tangled. It always is," she murmured.

Evan hummed, like he agreed, and looked back up at her with a soft smile. "It is."

The trickle of sweat had disappeared into the thick dark fringe framing his face, damp along his crown, and it made his hair curlier somehow. His eyes were gray and luminous like headlights in morning mist, and Kash thought maybe she could spend hours staring into them.

"Do you—" Evan cut himself off with a breath of laughter and ran his fingers through his hair, catching on curls, in a way that was suddenly, uncomfortably familiar to Kash.

Before she could think, she grabbed his hand by the wrist and tugged it down so his fingers were inches away from her chin, hand hovering in limbo between them.

"What?" she asked. It was night, so the air outside was warm and heavy, but not as hot as it would be during the day, and yet Kash felt like she was a human furnace.

"Why have you kidnapped my hand?" Evan asked with a wide, fond smile, wiggling his fingers.

"What were you gonna say before?"

His smile vanished, like some eclipsed sun, and his eyes darted around Kash's face before landing on her mouth.

A feeling of anxious anticipation effloresced inside her, crystallizing on her bones and rendering her immobile as she watched Evan lean forward slightly until she couldn't look at him without crossing her eyes.

Just lean in.

She clenched her jaw, grinding her teeth and unwittingly squeezing around Evan's wrist until he winced.

"Oh," she exhaled, letting go like she'd just touched poison, "sorry, I—"

Evan's hand came up around her jaw, cradling her face, and looking at her with more intensity than she could possibly withstand.

She was acutely aware of the sound of insects and the occasional distant voices of other students, and it all jumbled in her head like a white noise cacophony.

"I think," Kash blurted, "you're pretty much the only person I talk to here other than my roommate."

Evan laughed at that, his breath hot and calm against her skin like she was leaning over a mug of freshly boiled tea.

"I am pretty sure that's a lie," he said.

Kash shook her head slightly, acutely aware of Evan's fingers tracing small indistinct patterns on her neck, just under her ear.

"It's not. 'I'm not very good at socializing," she said. "I wouldn't have even talked to you if you didn't talk to me first."

Evan leaned back, looking up at her questioningly from under his lashes with a small smile.

"I don't—I'm not good at, you know." Kash stumbled over a million words in her mind, trying to find the ones she meant. "I can't *pretend* to be good at—"

"No, I get it," Evan said softly, his hands falling down Kash's neck and shoulders and arms until his fingers tangled with her own.

Kash was almost sure that he didn't, but she nodded in belief anyway.

"So," he said, quirking his lips, "were you any good?"

Kash frowned. "What?"

"Soccer," Evan said, taking a step back and throwing her a smirk. "I'm wondering if you were as effectively successful on the field as you are at socializing?"

Kash laughed. "I, uh, was in varsity throughout high school. And we—" she called up a theatrically haughty expression "—definitely won more than we lost, so."

Evan raised an eyebrow. "So why aren't you playing now?"

"Oh." Kash looked down at her feet and shrugged. "I guess, I feel like I outgrew it."

"Outgrew... soccer?"

Kash exhaled roughly, looking out . "Or maybe I, maybe, I don't know, I just. Wasn't keen on bringing too much of me here. And soccer seemed like, you know, surgically possible to remove without too much damage to the rest of me."

"Who were you before?"

Kash winced. "No, it's not—I don't mean I'm a different person or something. I mean, maybe I am, I guess I am—"

"We…" Evan started, saving her from further digging herself in a mess of words. "Okay, given, I don't know anything but. We all leave pieces of ourselves along the way, as we go."

Kash nodded earnestly. "Yeah, that's. Yeah."

Evan laughed. "It's like some morbid, constant form of metamorphosis, isn't it?"

Kash stared at him and watched in a momentary lapse of all function, as his eyes flashed and widened like soft crepuscular sun rays.

"Oh," he murmured before looking away and scratching absently at his nose. "And by that I mean, I'm almost unbearably curious to know all those pieces of you."

Kash inhaled sharply and nodded, looking out at the green trees and grass and red brick buildings.

"To be fair, you can be curious too," Evan said.

Kash nodded again, eyes still darting around, anywhere but to her left. "What makes you think I want to be?"

"Oh jeez, is that—is that a total shut-down on your part, then?" he asked in a mockingly taken aback tone.

Kash smiled. "No. Tell me. I'm totally, overwhelmingly curious."

Evan stared at her, brow raised. "That," he emphasized with a pointed finger, "I can almost guarantee, is another lie."

Kash rolled her eyes and dodged Evan's arm as it came up around her shoulders.

"Lies!" He laughed loudly, the sound echoing around them, bouncing off the grass and foliage and brick walls and pavement.

Lies? She felt fundamentally composed of lies, head to toe, all throughout her insides, all around her like a weak exoskeleton, constantly shedding her self-distortion with each step she took.

you started it.

They were cuddled together in the vast comforter, sprawled on the large sectional couch in Levi's basement, wide eyes glued to the TV, where a movie was playing. Levi's grandparents were upstairs, and occasionally the ceiling creaked along with muffled thumps of feet.

"There's some cake in the fridge," Levi announced.

Kash blinked and looked at him. They hadn't spoken for the past half hour of the movie.

"It's from Pop's birthday," he explained. "Mamo said that it was too much to eat at once."

"Oh."

He leaned in and whispered, "So, like, obviously, we can't tell them."

Kash grinned.

They both scrambled off the couch, rushing to detangle themselves from the comforter. Kash reached for the remote and paused the movie on screen. She followed Levi into the corner kitchen area behind the couch.

He grinned at her conspiratorially as he opened the fridge. "We can just eat from the box, yeah?" he said.

"Really?"

Levi nodded. "'Cause then there's less evidence."

Kash snorted and grabbed two forks. She giddily followed Levi back to the couch where they repositioned themselves comfortably among the pillows and comforter. She grabbed the remote and resumed the movie. She handed Levi a fork and he opened the lid of the box.

"Oh my *god*," she gasped. "This is why I like you."

Levi laughed and triumphantly dug his fork into glorious chocolate cake.

Kash took a swipe of chocolate frosting on her finger and hummed at the taste.

"Stop eating all the icing!" Levi swatted her hand away as she went for more.

Kash glared at him and emphatically dragged her fork across the top of the cake, collecting as much chocolate frosting as she could, and shoved it into her mouth before Levi could stop her.

He pouted dramatically and she rolled her eyes at him before instinctually glancing down at his lips. They were a bit chapped, small spots of red indicating his biting habit. But they were still pink and full.

She envied them. The shape. The color. Hers were an odd shade between mauve and brown and they curled thin when she smiled. She had a large cupid's bow, and her top lip was just full enough, but her bottom lip folded weird at the center and had a natural dark outline around the corners.

Hers weren't pink like his. Hers weren't nice like his.

"Why're you staring at my mouth," Levi asked through a mouthful of chocolate cake.

Kash grimaced. "What?"

"Why. Are. You." Levi enunciated each word, showing off the chewed contents in his mouth. "Star-ing. At. My. Mouth."

Kash looked at him plainly. "Can you repeat that? I didn't hear—"

"You're staring at my mouth, *stupid*."

"Because you're lips are nice, *stupid*."

Wait.

Her eyes widened. The words had just poured out of her, like overheated honey, creating a runny mess from her chin onto her fingers.

"What?" Levi's voice was blunt but not at all accusatory like she'd expected. Her jaw dropped open, and she watched a spark of amusement light up the boy's face.

"Kash," his tone was cajoling, he pouted his lips teasingly and fluttered his eyelashes in a mockingly coy manner, "I mean—thanks, I guess."

She shoved him away and grimaced when he giggled at her reaction. Her face burned and she yanked the comforter harshly toward herself.

Levi yelped as his bare shins were suddenly exposed to the cool air of the basement. His bright green pajama pants had ridden up slightly and his socks had sagged and bunched around his ankles.

Kash watched the hairs stand up on his skin before he growled with the anger of a lion cub and yanked the comforter back.

"Unfair," he grumbled at her. "You *drag* me down here. It's *cold*. I give you *cake*. And you hog the comforter."

"You make fun of me," she countered.

"You like my lips."

Her mouth twitched. "I don't *like* them. I never said that."

Levi shrugged. "Yeah but you think they're nice. Don't you usually *like* stuff that's nice?"

"Just pay attention to the movie."

His lips curled into a knowing smile, and she glanced at him, thoroughly annoyed.

"I've kissed girls and you haven't kissed anyone. Is that it?" he asked in a stupid, self-satisfied voice.

She rolled her eyes and scoffed at him excessively. She held up two fingers emphatically and said, "You kissed *two* girls, Levi. And it was during truth or dare. That doesn't *count*."

"Yeah, but it counts." He turned his chin up, voice all breathy and lofty. "Because it means my lips are *nice*," he added, pouting his lips in an exaggerated way.

She made a face at him that he only took as fuel to the fire.

"And yours aren't," he continued in his stupid, smug, teasing tone.

"Shut up!" she exclaimed, shoving him off the couch violently and pulling all of the comforter to herself. He tumbled onto the floor with a surprised squawk, his lanky limbs sprawled in weird angles.

"I didn't deserve that," Levi said sagely as he got up. He winced slightly and massaged his knee for a moment. His hair was mussed and curled messily in every direction. His eyes were lidded, and his lashes glinted in the dim lighting. His sweatshirt rode up his hip, revealing an expanse of bare skin along his waist.

He looked kind of—

nice.

"No, I'm pretty sure you did," Kash corrected with a firm nod. She watched in badly hidden rapture as the boy in front of her fixed himself, ran a hand through his hair and flopped back down onto the couch.

Suddenly, in the blink of an eye, the comforter was tugged out from under her, and she fell onto her elbows against the hard curved arm of the couch.

Levi got onto his knees, wrapping the thick fabric around his body before he sat back down with a muffled thud.

"Shall we watch the rest of it?" he asked primly, head barely peeking out from the lumps and folds of comforter as he nodded toward the TV.

She threw him a mocking look before purposefully concentrating on the movie, eyebrows raised, and chin turned down to signal her focus. She could hear soft giggles coming from beside her and her jaw clenched at the sound. There was some rustling and she saw Levi shuffle closer out of the corner of her eye.

Soft, warm breaths tickled her ear, and she instinctively shrugged her shoulder up, pressing it against the side of her head.

"Stop," she murmured.

He remained perched with his face inches away from hers. His breath brushed past her cheek. She could feel warmth against her nose, and she scrunched it.

"You want to try?" Levi asked softly after a few moments, drawing out the last vowel.

She glanced over and found him smacking his lips and wiggling his eyebrows suggestively. "What're you doing?" she deadpanned.

He gave a one-shouldered shrug that was more flirtatious than anything. "Do you want to give it a try?"

She stared at him. Stared at his freckled nose and pink cheeks and hazel eyes. She blinked and watched him reflect the movement. His eyelashes were a golden strawberry color, and his eyes were a warm hazel underneath. His hair was the color of burnt copper and he was covered in storied patterns of freckles, from his shoulders to his toes to the tips of his ears.

Nodding, she said, "Yeah. Okay, yeah."

The grin on Levi's face vanished and she watched him swallow slowly. He nodded back, face suddenly serious and contemplative. "Oh, okay."

"How do I—like, how do I start?" Kash mumbled out. Her eyes trailed down to his lips. She watched them move as he spoke.

"Like, just lean in, I guess."

She wrinkled her nose in response. "Isn't the guy supposed to lean in first?"

"Who said that? You lean in."

"You lean in."

"*You* lean in."

"You—"

He leaned in. She stayed where she was and squeezed her eyes shut. Her lips were pursed to a point of numbness, and she jutted her chin out to press back into Levi's mouth.

He leaned away after a few seconds, eyes wide open.

"That was terrible," he said plainly.

Her heart stopped and she hit him in the side of the head. "You weren't that great, either!" she exclaimed, arms flailing.

"Don't be nervous," he said, finger pointed upward like he was a politician giving a speech.

She screeched out an unintelligible word and tackled him. "I'm not nervous! I'm not nervous, you're just terrible at it," she declared, pulling on his hair and jabbing her hip into his side as she sat down on his chest.

"*I'm* not terrible at it," Levi insisted as he met her assault with a strong grip and grabbed a hold of her forearms. He forced them together and brought them down between their bodies. His fingers were bony as they dug into the flesh of her inner arms.

"Don't pull at my hair, it *hurts*," he spit out.

She glared and glanced down at his lips purposefully. It was a careless warning before she leaned in and kissed him again.

He mumbled protesting words against her mouth but she refused and pressed harder.

She could feel his teeth against hers and both of their lips in between. It hurt. Was kissing supposed to hurt? Did the people who did it all the time—did they get used to it? Was it something you had to break into?

He pulled away from her harshly and ran his tongue along his teeth. "This isn't working," he stated with a slightly frustrated tone. He was looking at her, scrutinizing her, with a thoroughly unimpressed frown.

Kash rolled her eyes at him. Her heart was beating at a choppy, quick rhythm and it was making her vision go slightly blurry at the edges. She watched Levi fold his arms, an arrogant air around his movements and a part of her seethed at that.

He looked down to the side with a frown, eyes glazing over, the gears in his head turning with some rusty squeaks. "Oh wait. Imagine I'm someone you have a crush on, someone you like," he blurted out, grinning wide.

She recoiled instantly. "I don't *like* anyone."

Levi gave her an unimpressed look and she sighed in defeat. She placed a hand gently on his shoulder and leaned in slowly until she could feel Levi's breath on her nose. She nodded and closed her eyes.

"Ready?" Levi asked softly, voice just above a whisper. She nodded again and after a moment she felt him lean in. Their lips met and she immediately tensed. A hand wrapped around her forearm, grounding her. Bony fingers in soft flesh.

She pulled away, a weird feeling pulling her heart into her stomach. "I don't," she began in a hesitant mumble, "I don't like trying to imagine someone else when you're… stuck with me."

Levi shrugged and the gesture was so casual, it made something under her skin itch.

"I don't really like anyone, though," he said.

Kash considered him and found the blush dusting his cheeks too suspicious to believe.

"Yeah, you do," she teased him, poking her finger into the place where his dimples appeared every now and then.

Levi brushed her away with a small smile. "Fine, if it's that important to you, I'll pretend you're someone else, just calm down."

"Who're you going to imagine?" she asked curiously. He withheld an answer for a few seconds before shaking his head and smiling.

"None of your business."

They held gazes, a silent duel with their eyes. She dared him but he didn't relent, instead shallowing out his emotions with a flat smile.

"Is it someone from class?" she asked.

"Shut up."

"Do I know them?"

"Now, here's the deal," he began to narrate.

Kash quieted her amusement and tilted her head to the side, listening but only to indulge him.

"You've got this thing, like, you scrunch up. Like this," he demonstrated by fisting his hands, squeezing his eyes shut, pursing his lips, and arching his shoulders into himself. After a silent second, he popped one eye open to check up on her reaction.

She nodded studiously.

"Right, like, stop that. It's weird. And I don't know. Don't be a brick wall. I *want* to kiss you—"

He wants to kiss her.

"—and you want to kiss me."

She wants to kiss him.

"What?" she blurted out.

Levi smiled softly. "Like, we're both doing it," he explained gently. "So, we'll both lean in this time?"

She nodded after a moment of consideration. "Okay, yeah, makes sense. On the count of three?" Her heart was beating faster now, fingers twitching.

Levi nodded.

"One."

Their voices were in perfect unison.

"Two."

She felt her breathing become erratic, and assumed Levi felt it too. Without thinking, she licked her lips in anticipation and a flicker of eye movement told her he noticed. She paused for a moment. That was gross. She shouldn't have done that. He wouldn't want to taste her spit when they—

"Three."

Is this what Levi's spit tasted like? Or his whole mouth. Did it have one encompassing flavor? Both of their lips were uncharacteristically soft this time. She stopped herself from squeezing and let her hands fall limp in between their bodies relaxing entirely. Her lips went slack, and she felt Levi's slowly push against hers.

"Wait," she said, pulling away. Her right hand instinctively pressed against his shoulder.

"What?" Levi asked, voice slightly breathless.

"Like, what's next?"

Levi frowned. He tilted his head to the side in question.

"Like." Kash licked her lips again. She wrung her hands a bit and began to fidget with her fingers. "Is this it? Is, like, is that it?"

He shrugged nonchalantly and it made her want to suddenly strangle him.

"Well?" she questioned him further, voice sharp like broken shards of hard candy.

"I don't know," he mumbled, scratching his head bashfully, "I mean, that's as far as I've gone."

Kash stared at him for a moment before a grin creeped onto her face. "That's it?" She asked, laughing.

He threw her a wounded glare and she giggled louder, hand coming up to cover her mouth in a false attempt at pacifying the hurt look on the other boy's face, like a kicked puppy. Her gaze darted distractedly back at the TV for a moment. She felt a weight on her lap and looked down to find Levi curled up around her. His head rested on her thigh, and he wrapped his arms loosely around her body. His legs were folded in, and he turned his face into her stomach.

"Why aren't you watching?" she demanded. He opened one eye and looked at her. There was an earnest look in his eyes.

His lips were shiny. "I hadn't kissed anyone before, you know," she reminded him. "So, like, you're still one up on me."

"Well now you've kissed someone too."

"Yeah, but it doesn't really count. Like, you kissed girls from school. I just kissed… *you*."

Levi shrugged, unable to keep the grin from growing on his lips. "Yeah, okay. My lips are nicer than yours."

She scoffed as he burrowed into her, moving his head like an affectionate dog, and shoved him away at the tickling sensation.

Her mouth felt different. Her face felt different. Like it was stuck. She quirked her lips and felt it like saran wrap, pulling from her cheekbones. She stopped swallowing, letting the saliva gather, and suddenly she didn't have the stomach to swallow her own spit. She had a sudden urge to run to the bathroom and brush her teeth. And maybe gargle. And floss.

The rest of the movie carried on, and she forced herself to sit still, with Levi's head heavy on her leg. Telltale tingles began to prickle under her skin and by the end credits, she could no longer move her foot without severe discomfort.

"Ow," she breathed out as she tried to hit feeling back into her leg without disturbing the now sleeping boy. After a few unsuccessful attempts to move out from underneath him, she sighed out and lolled her head back against the couch. She carded her hand absentmindedly through Levi's hair. There was a string of fuzz dangling from the ceiling, and she watched it tremble from side to side.

After a few moments, she closed her eyes.

you're still a child, like me.

'levi's here already'

A deep breath brought Kash out of her truck, as she stared at Raza's text. For a second, she regretted ever agreeing to a reunion. She regretted finding out that Levi was visiting and regretted that desperate moment when she wanted to see him more than anything.

Raza had called her about it a week ago, and it had taken her a whole day to even process what he'd said. And after, she'd driven over to his house and cried in his room and he let an old Bollywood film play in the background because he knew her better than anyone she still spoke to, even if it was at a pace of two phone calls per year.

'it's only for a bit. and you can always leave. he'll be gone again in two days'

It had taken Kash a few hours' worth of crying into Raza's sheets to come to terms with the fact that he'd messaged *Raza* and not *her.* Because how could he? When she'd reached out to him for so long, and he'd refused to acknowledge any of it?

'be there in a minute'

She shut the truck door behind her after hitting send and walked down the street to where Levi and Raza were hanging around in the playground. A stab of nostalgia made her stumble and her heart thudded in her chest as they came into view. She'd known him for ages. She hadn't seen him in ages.

He was sitting with his knees bent, feet hanging off the jungle gym platform he was lounging on, boyish and brilliant. The cherry of his cigarette glowed red, casting the faintest blush on his skin. It matched the shining red mess of curls overflowing from atop his head. His hair was much longer now, ending just below his newly defined jaw. He looked like a horrible cliché, and she hated it.

Levi's eyes shifted to her, and she had to exercise all of her willpower not to crumble into dust.

"When did you start smoking?" she blurted.

Raza quickly turned around from where he was perched on the highest ladder rung leading up to the monkey bars.

Levi gazed at her for a moment before shrugging. "When my roommate gave me one."

She watched him look up and sigh out white-gray smoke like he'd been doing it his entire life. "It's stupid," she announced.

His eyes met hers sharply.

"Thanks." He grinned flatly at her, a drop of malice on his lips.

Raza watched them cautiously with wide, prying eyes. "Hey, Kash," Raza said softly.

Without breaking her gaze on Levi, Kash answered back, "Hey."

"What took you so long?" Levi asked.

Kash shrugged and stepped forward. "Traffic."

Levi hummed in acknowledgment, tapping his cigarette so the ashes fell away to the ground. He appeared to contemplate his next words before opening his mouth to speak in a deep, heartbreakingly foreign voice. "Traffic's worse in London, you know? Wouldn't think anywhere could beat Massachusetts until you leave it."

There was a hint of an accent in his pronunciation, and a performative vanity that was so characteristic of him, it sent a spike of unwanted familiarity through Kash's chest.

Kash rolled her eyes and settled down on the platform next to him, taking care to leave a conspicuous amount of space between them. She sat forward with her hands tucked underneath her thighs and faced Raza who was kicking his legs like a child. She noticed his left arm was strapped to his chest in a sling and frowned.

"Yeah, man, New York's the same. Takes hours to drive, like, ten miles," he laughed jovially.

"What happened to your arm?" she asked him.

"Oh yeah," he lit up like he just remembered, "it's a long story, I—" His phone rang loudly in the quiet night and Kash watched as Raza cursed out of surprise and fished his phone out of his pocket. "Oh wait." Raza glanced down at his phone and beamed brighter than sunshine before looking back up and offering a sheepish apology. "Sorry, I'll be right back."

He leaped up and headed off toward the tree line, far enough away that his words became a blur of sound.

Kash looked at Levi. They met gazes for a split second, and she raised her eyebrows. He tipped his head back, the gesture highlighting the newfound cut of his jaw.

She could hear Raza talking animatedly about something and wondered for a second who he was on the phone with. Someone who made his heart race, no doubt, if the look in his eyes when his phone rang had anything to do with it.

The sound of Levi breathing moved to the aural foreground and Kash squeezed her eyes shut. It sounded particularly warm against the slight breeze around them.

A ringing laughter from Raza startled her eyes open and she instinctually looked over at her friend.

He had grown a bit of facial hair since last August, and it suited him handsomely, awarded him a subtle sense of maturity and complimented his warm playfulness. His hair was longer now, just shy of shaggy as it fell over his face and just brushed the tops of his brows. He was pacing, feet stumbling, and face tucked down into his T-shirt with shy infatuation.

She admired him for a moment, catching his gaze and sharing a pure, friendly smile that briefly calmed the angry unease inside her. He hadn't changed much over the past few years, she thought. It was refreshing.

"One of my flatmates reminds me of you, actually," Levi mused out loud, blowing smoke up to the sky.

Kash looked over at him. "Does she?"

"Uh uh." He clicked his tongue and shook his head. "*He* does."

"Oh."

He laughed and unconsciously leaned into her. She glared at him and pushed him away. "Is he the one that gave you a cigarette?" she asked.

He looked at her and nodded minutely, eyes trained on hers and she felt trapped. His curls danced a bit, brushing across his eyes and the nape of his neck. He looked wonderful, hair messy and boyish and cheeks flushed from smoke and laughter.

She thought she could remember being caught up in that look, a while ago. A lifetime ago.

Don't fall back into it.

"You look like you're trying too hard," she said to him bluntly.

His mouth turned down slightly at her words. He stared at the now short stub of the cigarette and took one more drag before putting it out near his thigh, twisting it into the uneven surface of the old peeling metal. "You look like you're a blink away from self-destruction," he countered, rubbing his hands together.

Her heart skipped a beat. "I am not," she stated.

A smirk tugged at the corner of his mouth, and he pressed his hands against his cheeks, shoulders shrugging up like he was cold. He raised an eyebrow and nodded. "Yeah, sure," he said dryly.

She wanted to tug at his hair and unbutton the stupid semi-sheer shirt he was wearing. She could see the tattoo he had on his ribcage in plain sight, only slightly hidden by the thin black fabric. It upset her in a way she couldn't explain. Everything about him was making her feel simultaneously claustrophobic and lost in space. It was a suffocating kind of infuriating.

"Are you cold?" she asked, poisonously sweet.

Levi scoffed. "It's nearly eighty degrees, Kash."

She nodded. "Yeah, but you look cold."

There was a tense silence, a brief pause in a restless fencing match. After a few moments, he laughed out loud and shook his head knowingly. "I got it at a thrift store."

"Got what?"

He gave her a deadpan look and she couldn't for the life of her stop the coy smirk that creeped onto her face.

"Right. It's nice on you," she said patronizingly.

He rolled his eyes at her, a fond smile widening his full lips. "It's my favorite shirt at the moment, so I'd appreciate it if—"

"It's fucking pretentious."

He rolled his eyes at her again and she responded with a dry smile.

Raza began laughing loudly and they both looked over at him as he nearly toppled down to the ground in his amusement.

"Oi, what's so funny?" Levi called out, shifting so that his arm slung over his folded knee.

Kash watched him lean back, all loud confidence and charm.

"Nothing, shut up," Raza shouted back, swiping his hand as if to tell the both of them to go away.

"I wonder who he's talking to," Kash mused.

"Don't tell me it's someone he *likes*," Levi said, smiling. "*That's* how you speak to someone you *like*."

After a moment, Raza jogged back over to them with his phone in hand and settled back on the ladder rung with a flushed glow on his face.

Kash and Levi stared at him, eyebrows raised, until he leaned to the side and let out a heavy, fond sigh. He stretched his right arm out, fingers flexing, and smiled goofily as he spoke. "I fell into a fountain."

"What?" Kash asked, eyebrows furrowed in confusion, glancing at his injured arm. She looked to her side at Levi and rolled her eyes at the barely restrained amusement curling his lips into a knowing smirk.

"You… fell?" Levi asked in a voice that was shaky with hidden laughter.

Raza sighed out loud, like he was suddenly exhausted with the two of them. Similar to a mother's sigh after dealing with rowdy children. "We were in Central Park for a date, and it was, you know, that super famous one in Gossip Girl," he explained, running a hand through his hair. "And she laughed but it was fine. Had to ride the subway dripping wet, and my arm hurt like hell, but, you know, new experiences and whatnot."

Levi let out a sudden bellow of laughter, loud and spontaneous. It pressed into the warm evening air like ink blooming in a glass of water. "How did you fall into a *fountain*?" he asked breathlessly.

Raza shrugged. "I just did," he said. "We were taking pictures and I was leaning, like acting all cool, you know? And I have shit balance—you know this—and I mean, I didn't even stop it from happening, I just ended up halfway in the water. I didn't realize how much it hurt until we were on the subway, and I was just, like, sitting there with my ass drenched. Turns out I bruised the bone. Very romantic."

Levi scratched absently at his knee as he spoke. "And she laughed at you?" he asked, a playful teasing tone coloring his voice. He was grinning ear to ear like a child and Kash barely had the energy to look away from it.

Raza nodded solemnly. "Yeah. But we were on a date, and she thought it was cute, so it's fine. Still agreed to go out with me again despite it, so. I still win."

They all paused.

"Wait, you're actually going out with her?" Kash asked loudly, voice a bit dumb from surprise.

Raza nodded triumphantly and Kash watched him fold his arms with a touch of childish arrogance. He looked like a little boy who had just snitched on their older sibling for a crime they committed. It was absolutely endearing.

"What's her name?" she asked with a smirk, getting into position to grill him about his supposed girlfriend.

He broke out into a wide smile, genuine and wholehearted, all traces of immature arrogance gone from his face. It was abruptly sweet.

"Naia."

They cooed at him.

"What's she like?" Kash asked.

"She's…" his voice trailed off and his eyes briefly glazed over before he spoke, "she's hilarious. Makes me feel more normal, which is hard to feel in the city. *Mashallah*, she's something different. In the best way."

Kash's smile grew, and she got up to go and pull Raza into a tight hug. She took care to avoid his arm and nuzzled her face into his hair, making adoring noises and tickling him wherever she could.

Levi followed and pulled up some grass to shower over Raza in mock reverence.

Raza cursed and pushed them both away, dancing around to get rid of stray grass clinging to his clothes and hair.

Kash laughed and watched as Levi ruffled Raza's hair, ridding it of grass and mussing it up as much as he could.

Raza shrieked, undeniably girlish, and paused in shock. Dark locks fell over his eyes, and he zeroed in on Levi who was bent over in uncontrollable laughter. There was a brief moment, a slight pause in action, when the look in Raza's eyes shifted from dramatic offense to careless mischief.

Kash smiled knowingly as she watched him grab a hold of Levi's collar with his uninjured arm, before reaching up and aggressively tousling his hair as well.

It was like old times. Kash shivered and laughed with a shake of her head. It'd been a while since she'd seen Raza. A year, since they'd gotten together. Even longer without Levi.

When Raza screeched in pain, Kash yelled out at them to stop. She worked her way between them, halting the hair-tousling fight for just long enough to grab Levi and haul him back to his seat on the jungle gym platform. He sat back down with a huff, warmth returning to Kash's side now that there was an obstruction to the soft summer breeze.

Raza fixed his hair and leaned back against the ladder rungs, suddenly cool and smooth, like nothing had happened. In his pocket, his phone lit up, showing through the fabric of his shorts, and he quickly slipped it out and looked down at it eagerly.

Next to her, Levi coughed and she looked over at him suddenly. He caught the movement and met her gaze with hidden intensity. She gently hit her fist against his thigh. He was firm underneath her touch. She splayed her hand out, fingers just long enough to halfway encircle his leg.

"I forgot about your freakishly warm hands. You've got the body temperature of, like, a fucking star in space," he said, breath distantly warm against her cheek.

"That's a strangely poetic thing to say," she squeezed his thigh before releasing her grip to pull at the rip on his knee.

"Yes, a big bright ball of hot gas you are—hey," he nudged her hand away gently, "stop it."

She smiled. "No."

They sat in comfortable silence, watching Raza text something, fingers typing hurriedly. His phone dinged again, and he paused before laughing to himself.

"When did he get like this? All… smitten," Kash murmured.

Levi laughed softly. "Dunno."

She nodded distantly and pondered how much Raza seemingly hadn't changed and how much he actually had. A feeling of being left behind crept up her neck.

"So, are you with anyone? Is it also a surprise?" Levi asked casually, voice drawling a bit too much to go unnoticed.

Kash stared at him. "No," she said, shaking her head, trying to keep the lie out of her voice. "Are you?"

Levi nodded.

Her heart plummeted at lightspeed, all the way down to the bottom of the ocean somewhere. She skipped a breath, lungs expanding for longer than they should've, before she let the breath out in a quick burst.

"Oh? Who?" Her attempt at nonchalance was feeble.

"My flatmate."

"*What.*"

Levi smirked at her. His lips curled up deliciously in the corners.

"Yeah, cause he reminds me of you."

Her growing panic deflated in a millisecond. A wave of relief and embarrassment washed over her, dripping into her lungs uncomfortably.

"Right, yeah," she let out a breathy laugh that deviated into a cough.

"No, no. I'm serious," Levi said with a solemn face.

"Shut up," she said, shoving him away with a shake of her head. She ignored the hurt still pricking at her in favor of the far easier option of falling back into familiarity with the boy next to her.

"Oi!" Levi snapped his fingers, and when that wasn't successful, he clapped loudly, the sound echoing in the night air around them. "Raz!"

Raza looked up like he just remembered where he was and Kash couldn't help the burst of laughter that escaped her at his unawareness.

Something inside her tilted precariously, like the nausea that fluttered deep inside her every time she tried for a goal in a game. It was likely they wouldn't exist like this again for an indefinite amount of time that she refused to quantify.

She laughed it away for now, filling it in with the current moment instead; the three of them coming together like they used to, when they were younger, when things were simpler, when there were less people between them, less distance. Less *change*.

sometimes we just stop.

Kash stared down at her phone, thumbs hovering over the keyboard. She debated sending the text, almost pressing the blue arrow, before deleting everything and starting a new message.

"Oh!" Stella stood up abruptly from her desk and Kash looked over at her, startled.

"What? What is it?"

"I'll be right back," Stella announced, holding up a finger before rushing out the door.

Kash stared after her, utterly confused. She looked back down at her phone, watching the cursor blink before backspacing and setting her phone on her desk. No need to add one more text to the continuously growing thread of unanswered ones.

It took a foreign amount of effort to climb up to her bed and she draped herself over the railing with a sigh, letting her head hang upside down. The wood cut into her upper back, but it wasn't uncomfortable enough to warrant moving.

She startled and cursed when her phone started ringing. Out of the corner of her eye, she caught Evan's name in white across the top of the screen and weighed the pros and cons of letting him go unanswered.

After a few moments, the ringtone ceased, and a bright notification lit up her lockscreen. She closed her eyes to feign plausible deniability and wondered what their dynamic would be, the three of them. She wondered how different she might be, faced with two people she acted completely different around.

Above her, a thud sounded and she tried to ignore the following heavy ruckus from the upper floor dorm.

"I found a tall person," Stella declared as she barreled through the door and Kash whipped her head up instinctively, immediately letting out a cry of pain when her neck twinged.

"Are you okay?" Stella asked, looking up at her with unbearably concerned eyes lined in thick black. An equally concerned Evan stood next to her.

"I'm fine," Kash said, carefully climbing down without moving her head too much. "You just startled me."

"I'll make it up to you with this." Stella zealously brandished a white package in her hand and Kash looked at her expectantly. "And this." She gestured to Evan who smiled and waved like a nervous new kid on the first day of school. "He can help."

"With what?" Kash asked plainly. "Hi," she added softly to him.

"Lights." Stella was practically vibrating with energy, and it was endearing as much as it was annoying. Kash felt a pocket of warmth burst in her chest.

It took about ten minutes for her and Evan to hang up a section of string lights across one corner of the room, with Stella on the ground, managing the process.

"Should we maybe put them up higher? And then drape them like that—" Stella made a wide sweeping gesture across the length of Kash's bed "—stick them to the ceiling and then let them fall naturally and frame them around—" she gestured to Kash's desk and then to the door "—and we bring them back around to my desk and that's where the plug is."

Kash and Evan stared, nodding diligently like they understood until Stella turned around to look at them with an expectant smile.

"Um," Kash started intelligently, "what?"

Beside her, Evan giggled quietly, and she shot him an unamused look.

It took them another ten minutes to follow Stella's instructions, and it was when the three of them were crowded onto Kash's bed that Kash finally fell back with a frustrated groan. She frowned when Stella's socked foot slipped under her pillows.

"This feels harder than it should be," Kash grumbled.

Stella winced as she reached up to press a thumbtack into the ceiling.

"Here." Kash nudged her gently to the side and firmly pushed the thumbtack into place between the wires of the lights, wiggling it to make sure it was secure.

"Is it bad that I'm already kind of tired?" Evan asked, arms draped over the side railing and head lolled back, his Adam's apple jutting out and moving as he spoke.

Kash shook her head. "I am too. Dinner?" she asked, lifting her foot to poke Evan's thigh. "Have you not eaten anything either?"

He shook his head and grabbed her foot with one hand, the other one coming up around her calf, and yanked gently until Kash was halfway across the bed, practically draped across him.

She yelped and kicked slightly until his arms came down around her waist and held her tight, his chest pressed firmly against her back. She withheld the urge to wriggle out of his arms and, instead, placed her hands on his. "Evan."

He rested his chin on her shoulder. "Yes?"

"I don't—" Kash cleared her throat and looked over at Stella without thinking.

Stella shrugged, a smile quivering her lips, like she could read Kash's mind. Kash highly doubted it, more out of denial than anything. "We might collapse the bed if we stay up here any longer," Stella said, moving to get down.

Kash nodded and watched her slowly climb down, messy ponytail disappearing under the frame. "Yeah, yeah."

"Oh," Evan murmured, his voice loud but gentle next to her ear. "It's you." He gestured to one of the pictures she'd taped on the wall above her bed. "You're a *baby*."

It was from her childhood. Her in a light pink dress with bow-tied straps, Raza wearing his blue baseball cap that was streaked with dirt, and Levi with his hair hanging over his wide, almost green eyes.

"Who're the other two?"

"They're family friends." Kash looked down to pick at a small rip in her jeans.

Evan hummed in acknowledgment. "You've never told me about them."

"I—" Kash paused. "I have." She looked over at him with a frown.

He shook his head, face open and curious and sincere. "No."

Kash blanched. "Then, I definitely—"

"Tell me about them now," Evan said softly.

Kash opened her mouth to oblige and shuddered at a sudden wave of nausea. "I don't—"

I don't know how.

"How long have you known them?" Evan asked.

"Oh. Practically our entire lives."

"Who's your favorite?"

Kash nearly blurted an answer before stalling herself with guilt. "That's unfair."

"What're their names?"

"Raza. On the left. And Levi."

"You seem close."

Kash smiled weakly. "Yeah I guess we are. Or were, I don't know, I haven't talked to them in a while."

Evan leaned into her, his cheek against the nape of her neck, and murmured, "You don't have to talk every day to be close."

"Yeah, but," Kash said softly, partially covering her mouth with a sweater sleeve covered palm, "you'd have to know things others don't, right?"

Evan shrugged, the fabric of his shirt rustling loudly as he moved.

"You do," she said. "Some sort of bond you don't have with just anybody. I'm not sure we have that anymore."

"That's a lie."

Lies, lies, lies.

She wanted to ask what merit, what qualifications, he had to say so. "It's *not* a—"

"You've known each other your whole lives haven't you?"

"That doesn't—"

"Why haven't you talked to them in a while?"

Kash inhaled sharply and maneuvered out of Evan's arms. "I don't know. You just… stop sometimes and it's hard to start again."

Evan hummed in acknowledgment and nodded like he was contemplating an anecdote.

"Okay, we—" Kash paused on a deep breath and looked over the side of her bed, catching Stella's gaze and blinking.

"Dinner?" Stella offered helpfully and the rush of gratitude that swelled in Kash nearly doubled her over.

"Yes," she choked out, nodding enthusiastically, and glancing back at Evan who was still staring at the photograph. "Dinner?"

He startled, like he was entranced, and nodded. "Yeah, yeah. Sounds good." He pointed to another photograph, folded slightly in the corner. "Is this your brother? You look like each other."

Kash looked at the photograph, heart panging a bit at the unbridled joy of Rafi's smile shining clear even through the faded film grain. It was Kash's first day of junior high, in the same building as her brother, the first time she could ride with him to school, the first time they spent their morning yelling together to their favorite album Rafi had on CD.

"Yeah," Kash sighed out. "He used to call me copycat 'cause everyone said we were almost carbon copies of each other. And I tried so hard to be like him."

Evan laughed softly at that. "That sounds nice."

Kash nodded her head. "I was closer to him than I was my sisters or even my parents."

Evan hummed, tracing a finger along the outer edge of another photograph, this time one of Kash as a teenager grinning in front of a goal with her arm around a laughing Lani.

Kash's heart squeezed momentarily before her mind caught up to her heart.

Evan shot her a questioning frown and she indulged him with a small, fond tilt of her lips.

"That's Lani. From high school."

"You liked her," Evan murmured and Kash immediately flushed and reached over to slap his hand away from the wall.

"Excuse me?"

He shot her a playful look and grabbed her head, hands on either side of her jaw. He leaned in until their noses were touching. "You *liked* her."

Kash rolled her eyes and leaned away as far as she could with Evan pulling her in closer. "What do you want for dinner?"

Evan's laugh practically echoed off the thin walls of her dorm room. Somewhere to the right below them, Stella laughed along too.

"You have to tell her about me, next time you talk, I have to be there so I can defend myself," Evan teased between giggles, pressing his nose into the apple of Kash's cheek.

"Stop it," she hissed, pushing him away and froze when Evan's face morphed into the most painful picture of adoration.

She dug her fingers into his cheeks and pulled until his features were distorted, but he still glowed so much so she had to avert her eyes. She tried to smile and laugh it off, let go of him with a flourish and moved to climb down the bed with an exaggerated pout, flipped her hair dramatically. Anything to get that much too lovely, much too empathetic look off his face.

"Evan," she prompted earnestly, setting her foot on the bottom most rung of her bed frame.

He blinked like he was coming back down to Earth from a lucid dream. "Sorry," he said softly. "I was just teasing."

She grimaced and ducked her head to will the heat away from her cheeks before looking back up at him. "I know."

Evan smiled in the gentlest of ways, his head leaning back against the wall, so his hair was tousled and messy behind his head, and his Adam's apple bobbed more prominently when he spoke. "I like you."

From her not at all nonchalant seat at her desk, Stella snorted before immediately slapping a hand to her face and looking up at Kash in wide-eyed apology.

The room went silent, not in an entirely uncomfortable way, but not entirely in comfort either.

Kash rolled her eyes and leaned her forehead against the railing of her bed, looking up at Evan through the lines of wood.

His head was still pressed against the wall, sincere smile still curling his lips, dark lashes low over his silver lining eyes as he looked down at her.

He was almost blinding.

[december 16th, '18]

i want to fall into something.

The low steady hum of the flight coaxed Kash's eyes to blink heavier and heavier with each passing moment. She ducked her head to look out the cabin window and stared reverently at the pretty, fiery colors of the sunrise layered in between a blue and gray expanse of sky and clouds.

She'd taken the red-eye, so she'd be home just in time for her father to drop the twins off at their Carnatic singing lessons in the city and pick her up from the airport along the way.

A restlessness had squeezed her chest since the moment she'd left her dorm with a large suitcase. She hadn't even had the motivation to pack, carelessly throwing in clothes and belongings she'd thought she might want later.

Her phone lit up on the tray table, a soft rectangle of light in the otherwise dark cabin.

You have a new memory
Iowa City—2018

Kash frowned and opened the notification to an album of photos from a lifetime ago. She scrolled through, longing increasing with each swipe of her finger.

It was weird to be nostalgic for a past self. It was weird to want to go back in time while wanting to fast forward. It was weird to both mourn and feel indifference for a devitalizing loss of self.

A photograph of her and Evan made her pause.

They were lying on an air mattress covered in blankets with twin bottles of beer and a platter of fried food in front of them. Both of them were suspended in laughter, Evan sprawled halfway in her lap, like the perfect picture of college romance. Like a movie poster or album cover.

A part of Kash wished she could exist only in that picture. Nothing else. Just that static moment where they both looked happy and young and completely enamored with life and each other. It looked like a nice feeling. Shallow and warm, without any commitments or fears pulling her down from the depths. The girl in the picture wasn't fighting to keep her head above water.

A wave of regret seized Kash's heart, and she continued scrolling with a thick swallow, painfully audible over the soft hum and living silence of the plane cabin. Memories of junior year blinked by, and she shook her head at some of them. A picture of her and Stella putting up lights in their dorm room made her smile, but the fondness was quickly replaced by embarrassment as she realized she looked at her college roommate with more adoration than she ever did Evan.

You're such a creep.

Kash bit her lip and turned her phone off, the screen going black with a clicking sound.

It was easier to pine than to be with someone, wasn't it? There was a habitual comfort in wanting, in just existing in that want. No need for the daunting reality in actually letting someone want you too. In letting someone be with you any more than they already were. No need for the photograph to become motion, to be real life.

Kash took out her notebook, reaching under her seat and into her backpack to retrieve a pen as well. Her chest swelled painfully as she flipped to the next open page and stared down at it.

Her pen hovered over the paper shakily and she blinked back a sudden need to cry.

The dim light from the cabin window washed everything in a softness she could sink into and so she closed her eyes to bask in it for a bit. The feeling clouding her mind, growing in her chest and curling her stomach, slowly took the form of words that she wrote down in emotional, scratchy handwriting.

I'm a masochist. I must be. I like the way it feels to care so deeply about something, and then just lose it. That overwhelming emotion, that pain, it's easy to fall into and just—feel. It might be my comfort zone, to be in that pain. I don't know why.

Her eyes burned as she stared at the words to read them over and over again until she scribbled over everything but the first sentence.

I'm a masochist.

She hadn't slept at all for the past twelve hours and the exhaustion heightened the ache in her chest. When she first boarded she'd been relieved that the seat next to hers was empty. But now it pulled at her uncomfortably. Her eyes occasionally darted down to the seat, trying to imagine someone sitting there, what that person would look like, what their physical ticks would be, how they might react to her. She wondered if they'd turn out to be someone she could confide in, a stranger she'd been inherently looking for in any public place she found herself in. Loneliness soaked through her now, and suddenly she wished there was someone next to her, any annoying or disgusting habits be damned.

She thought maybe it was better to have someone than to not have anyone at all.

keep passing the open windows.

Her bedroom was colder than she remembered, and her mind insisted on getting under the covers, but she remained immobile on her bed, hands by her sides and splayed on the comforter. She hadn't changed out of her jeans and jacket.

A knock on the door startled her and she turned her head to the left to see it slowly open.

"Hey." Her father peeked in and leaned against the doorway once he saw her. "*Emchestunaavu?*"

Kash shrugged and shook her head. "Not doing anything," she answered.

"Can I come in?"

"Yeah, why're you asking like that?" Kash frowned. "It's your house."

Makrand laughed at that. "*Oho*, so when it's convenient, when you want to hang out with friends and come back in the middle of the night, it's your house. *Kaani* when we ask you to clean your room or unload the dishwasher, it's not."

Kash bit back a smile and shrugged.

"*Jarugu*, move over." He tilted his head as he drew the door closed behind him. He walked over to her and jutted his chin out at her. "Scoot."

"No."

Her father made a sound of protest and pushed her over until she rolled to the other side with a yelp.

"Oh my *god, Nanna,* sto-*op*," she groaned, dragging her hands down her face before throwing her father a withering glare. She attempted to push him away, off the bed, but he refused to budge.

Makrand grinned. He lifted the covers with flourish and promptly snuggled under them, pulling the comforter up to his chin like he was a little boy and not a grown man with four kids.

Kash watched him with a mixture of awestruck annoyance and fondness. She had half a mind to push him off the bed or whine until he left.

"*Nanna*—"

"*Dha*," her father said. He patted a spot on the bed beside him and smiled. It was the same smile he would give her when she was little, and she would crawl into her parents' bed during a late night thunderstorm. "Kash, I miss you *ra*."

Kash rolled her eyes as she begrudgingly got under the sheets, purposefully yanking the comforter up harshly so she got the majority of it. "I'm right *here*."

"How is Raza doing?"

"He's good, I think. Or he seems to be. He stayed in the city for break to be with Naia."

"And Lani?"

"Oh," Kash blanched, "I haven't really—haven't talked to her all that much since freshman year summer. Haven't talked to her at all, actually."

"Oh. *Yenthukani?*"

"I don't know why. I guess we just. Stopped somewhere along the way and now, I don't know how to start again. Which is weird because I always thought we would—" Kash cut herself off, digging her teeth into her bottom lip.

"You would what?" Makrand asked.

Kash sighed heavily, breath stuttering, and she squeezed her eyes shut, wishing he would just get it, somehow understand without her having to tell him.

"You thought you would stay in touch?" her father prompted.

Kash winced. "I thought we would stay in touch without having to try because. Because I thought…"

"Of course, you'd have to try."

"No, I know. I *know*, I just. I thought." She hesitated and grabbed the comforter with her fists, hiked it up farther until it covered her nose. The comforter quickly turned hot and damp, and she hated breathing under the sheets, always felt suffocated, but it was either this or scream into a pillow and she figured this would raise fewer *questions*.

Her father hummed in understanding and nodded to himself like he'd just fit in the final piece of a puzzle. "I had a feeling you liked her like that," he said.

Kash paused at that.

I had a feeling you liked her.

She wanted to tell him it was more than *liking*. It was so much more, and it was why she thought it would've stayed, and why she was floundering in the face of it being gone. She shoved the comforter back down and turned harshly to look at him. "And you didn't—you didn't say anything?" she said, trying not to sound as shocked as she was.

Her father shrugged, tucking his arms under his head like a cushion. "I didn't know what to say."

Oh.

He knew. And didn't say anything. Because what would he say?

"So," he murmured in a carefully gentle voice, like he was walking over a thinly frozen lake, "you're gay?"

"No," Kash immediately blurted. "No. I mean, I did willingly date a guy." She dug her fingers into her palm and resisted the urge to get up from the bed, open the window, and scream out into the cold evening air.

"But you said you didn't like it," her father pointed out.

Kash groaned again and spoke through clenched teeth. "No, it wasn't—I didn't like the *relationship*." How was she supposed to explain something she didn't understand? "It had nothing to do with Evan."

Her father hummed like he would when Kash would tell him about a book she liked or a song she found. It infuriated her, made her teeth grind together, and suddenly she didn't want to talk at all.

"So, you don't like anyone… period," he concluded.

I like more than I should, I like to a point of destruction, don't I.

"No," Kash winced and dug her nails into her temples as she quelled the scream that was crawling up her throat, "I do."

Again, Makrand hummed and Kash wrapped her hands around her throat, cradling just under her jaw in a way she hoped was nonchalant, and squeezed slightly.

"So, you like… boys and girls?" Makrand asked.

Kash squeezed tighter. She felt her lips tingle from it, like they were about to go numb. "I don't know, I don't know," she said, "I don't know if it's about boys and girls. I don't know if it's about being in a relationship at all. I don't *know*. And I don't think I want to talk about this with you of all people."

"If you don't know, then how can you be sure you liked Lani?" Makrand asked.

Kash huffed and hit her head back against the pillow. "Because I *did*."

Her father raised an eyebrow at her and she rolled her eyes and looked away.

"It was like," she began. She looked up at the ceiling as if the words she needed were written in the plaster patterns. She began to gesture animatedly with her hands as she spoke. "It was just this constant ache, I couldn't get rid of it until it faded on its own. It still, it still smarts sometimes though, whenever I, when I think of—whenever I reminisce or just, think. I don't know, *Nanna*, I just know that I did."

"Okay, okay. But you don't like that?"

"I think I look back on myself—and I just feel like someone pathetic. Like a creep."

"Why were you a creep?" Makrand slowly shifted so he was on his side, arms folded underneath his head and again, he looked more like a child than he did a man in his early fifties, and it baffled Kash as much as it endeared her.

Kash sighed and covered her face with her hands before finding the courage to speak. "Because I felt things so… ardently and I took that out on everyone. Like I wasn't even discreet about it."

I'm still not discreet about it.

"You should never be discreet about your feelings, Kashvi. And you should never be ashamed to 'feel things ardently,' or feel things at all. You're not a creep."

Kash could've broken down completely at those words. She'd heard them so many times and wished every single time that she could fall into them and believe they were true.

"Everyone keeps telling me that," she murmured. "But it fucking hurts."

"Excuse me?"

Kash froze before wincing and looking at her father sheepishly. "It freaking hurts. It *hurts*."

Makrand grinned at that and waved a hand dismissively at her. "Come here, *dhegarikiraa*."

"No."

"*Raa*." He pouted at her and opened his arms. After a moment, she rolled her eyes and grabbed one of his outstretched arms to wrap around and hold. She tucked her head against his upper arm and sighed.

One of his hands came up to tuck a few stray strands behind her ear and she relished the feeling as he carded his fingers through her hair. He began humming a song that she soon recognized as their favorite song from *The Works,* and she smiled despite herself. He switched repeatedly from the vocals to the melody of the piano, throwing in a few lyrics here and there.

He drew out the vowels, enunciating the words as theatrically as he could. The effort toward lightening the air didn't go unnoticed, but it was almost impossible to resist. She missed this simplicity, missed the music they listened to together, missed when they were in sync with each other because they definitely weren't anymore.

"… windo-*oow*," her father sang as he nuzzled his nose against the top of her head until she shied away in soft laughter.

"You're clearly out of practice, you sound terrible," she said dryly, grinning as her father frowned at her and rolled his eyes.

"You don't know," he said grandly, "I'm incredible. People used to fall all over each other just to come to our shows. Twenty-year-old prodigy, I was."

"You sure they weren't falling all over each other just to *leave* as quickly as possible?"

Makrand laughed at that and shook his head. His stubble rubbed against the fabric of the pillow with an oddly soothing swishing sound, and she curled up farther into the warmth.

"Kash," he murmured slowly.

Kash hummed in response.

"Feeling like that, it does hurt. And it always will hurt. *Andhuke...* being in *love* with someone is the most painful, happy, terrifying, and rewarding thing you will ever do."

"You sound like a Hallmark movie," Kash mumbled.

At that her father swatted her head and scoffed. "*Ehe undu,* hear me out," he said, and Kash could hear the amusement in his voice, "I'm not as poetic as you, don't *blame* me for that."

Kash turned her head, so the warmth of her cheek was pressing against the cool fabric of her pillow and smiled.

"But it is. It is probably one of the hardest things, too, falling in love with someone," her father continued.

Kash's smile faded, and she ran a finger across a loose thread on the hem of the comforter. "And what if I never will?" she asked softly.

"Well," her father sighed out, "I guess, we don't need people to fall in love. Everything you like, everything you've collected as part of yourself, your life, everything you've said is yours, is a form of love. A form of being in love. You can be in love with writing. And maybe that's sufficient."

Kash nodded diligently, trying to keep the lump in her throat at bay.

"I hope," her father continued, in a more gentle voice, "you do fall in love with someone, though. I hope you fall in love with someone to a point of complete exhaustion. But if it's not a person, I hope you feel that way about *something*."

Kash felt a tear slowly fall down her nose toward the pillow and she turned into the fabric.

"And if I don't feel at all?" she said shakily.

"How's that possible?"

"If I want to, like, turn it all off?"

"Kashvi, *ittu choodu*. Look at me," her father coaxed her.

She shook her head and pressed further into the pillow until he relented.

"Why would you want to 'turn it off'? That's stupid."

You're stupid.

"It's not stupid," she cried out, muffled. After a moment, she turned her head to the right, so she didn't have to see her father's face, and he couldn't see hers. Not that it would hide anything.

"Kashvi—"

"It's not stupid to want to stop *hurting*."

Her father sighed and gently resumed his ministrations, carding his fingers through her hair and twisting his hand to catch her wrist and rub his thumb reassuringly against the protruding bones under her skin. "Have you ever thought," he said quietly, firmly, like he was about to reminisce on one of his childhood memories, "Kash, have you ever thought that maybe all this… *hurting* is leading you somewhere? That maybe it's a sign, it's telling you that you haven't found yet what you need to find? Have you ever thought that maybe the reason you're hurting, this much, is because you've been unknowingly going down the wrong path for a while?"

Kash wanted to say that she'd been going down the path he'd told her to go down, the path he'd told her was the right one. The need to blame bubbled up inside her and for a split second she thought she would blurt it out, scream that it was all his fault, their fault, him and *Amma*. But maybe that wasn't fair anymore.

"And how do I get on the right path?"

"I think… your pain knows. Listen to it."

Kash exhaled shakily. "Did your pain lead you here?" she asked.

Makrand took a moment to answer. Downstairs, voices traveled from the kitchen to the family room, growing fainter and then louder, and if she strained to hear the bounding footsteps, she could almost tell who was who.

"*Emo*, I don't know," her father said, looking up at the ceiling contemplatively, "I don't think I ever fully listened to it. I don't think any of us do, we're so adamant to follow our own insignificant attachments."

"Am I an insignificant attachment?"

"No. You, Kishori, Kumari," Makrand paused before saying, with raw emotion, "Rafi."

The name sounded almost foreign. Like reading an old piece of writing from childhood, after years of growing up.

Kash's heart tugged at the mention of her brother, and she swallowed harder to keep the need to cry at bay.

"I haven't talked to him, either. Haven't been able to," she offered.

"No. He doesn't pick up," her father murmured brokenly. "And I haven't had the courage to go to him."

"Neither have I."

"No," her father said in a voice that made Kash's chest squeeze painfully, "none of us have. *Thellidhu endhuko*. I don't know why. I'm like you, I guess. I don't know what I'd say, what I'd do. What *could* I do? *Naavallegaa, idhanthaa. Naavallegaa*. It's my fault. I don't know what I'm doing with any of you." He laughed wetly. "I messed you all up, didn't I?"

"No, you didn't."

"I did. I did. *Naavalle, kaani*, you are all always a part of me. You could never, never be insignificant, okay? No matter what. Nothing could ever change that, how could it?"

Kash nodded, letting the tears fall from her eyes quietly now. She looked up to see her father doing the same, watched as a tear slowly trailed down from the corner of his eye and disappeared into his long, graying hair.

"I love you, *thalli*."

"I love you, too, *Nanna*."

"I make mistakes, and you all may have to bear the brunt of them sometimes. That's not fair, I know."

Kash wanted to tell him it was okay. Or as okay as it was ever going to be. She wanted to tell him that they were all just moving parts, making mistakes one after another, and her brother was the first to break away because that was his nature. He had the guts to, at least, unlike her. Or maybe he'd just reached the end of his rope earlier. Maybe she would reach her own breaking point someday. Maybe her father would too.

"And, I hope you'll forgive me for my mistakes, and their consequences," he whispered.

"I will," Kash said, "I do. I'm not the only one, though. I'm not the only one who's bearing the brunt of them."

"I know," her father nodded up at the ceiling, "I know. How—he's my son."

"Is he, if you don't ever talk to him again?"

Makrand stiffened and immediately the hand in Kash's hair retracted, along with the warmth around them.

She didn't say anything more as her father moved out from under the comforter and stood up. She burrowed farther into her bed and watched as he turned around with a manufactured smile on his face.

"He was doing the same, I think. Following his pain," Kash said.

"*Amma* is making *bhajis*," her father told her.

"No. I'll come down in a bit," Kash answered, pulling the comforter over herself like a cocoon. After she felt securely wrapped up, she added, "I think you pushed him away as much as he did you."

"Okay," Makrand said softly, voice taking on a rambling tone. "Don't be too late or there won't be any. *Unteyile—ante kaavalante Amma*'ll make more, *mirapakayulu inka unayi.* The chilies aren't as spicy this time. *Ginjaalu theesesindhi,* she took out the seeds. I came upstairs on a mission to bring you downstairs before the twins ate them all. They've gotten worse, you know? Worse than—"

Rafi.

Her father was talking quickly, like he was trying to take up all the spaces Rafi might inhabit.

"I'll come down," she assured him flatly, "I just need to… I just, I need a few minutes."

Her father's eyes looked both distant and unraveling, like he could see right through her but didn't know how to make sense of it.

"*Sare*, all right. Don't be too late…" His voice trailed off before he nodded resolutely and said more firmly, "Whenever you want, *kunsepu ayinaka raa kaavalante*. If you don't want any, then you don't have to come down."

Don't come down.

Kash choked back a small sob and blinked, pressing a hand against her chest.

"Yeah," she said in as even a voice as she could muster.

"All right, see you downstairs?" Makrand said, grabbing the doorknob and twisting to open.

Kash nodded until he gave her a smile and walked out of the room.

She felt cracks spider out from somewhere inside her chest, all the way up her neck, through to her fingertips, down to her ankles, and wondered when they would just absolutely shatter her. She thought maybe they already had shattered for her father. Because he acted like he was defeated when no one else had won. Rafi wasn't a victor, he was gone. Because he spoke to her like he understood, like he had the answers, when he had none. All he had were questions, like Kash didn't have enough. Because he was another person she couldn't live without, but he didn't *get it*.

No one did.

i need to be another person to be in love.

It always took a while for the covers to warm up around her body, but Evan's body alongside hers helped a little.

"My feet always end up hanging off the end," he mused, wiggling his socked toes that were peeking out from under the covers.

Kash smiled. "It's 'cause I like pillows."

Evan shrugged. He wrapped an arm around her and snuggled farther into the covers, his body pressing against hers.

She stared at him for a moment before blinking into action and nuzzling her face in the crook of his neck. She closed her eyes and tried to ignore the friction of their bodies, their syncopated breaths, the rise and fall of his chest against hers. She shallowed her movements as she searched for something characteristic to say, to stifle the increasing *noise*.

"You're always cold," she said softly, tracing her finger against his collarbone.

Evan laughed. "Sorry."

"No, no," Kash said, shaking her head slightly, "I mean, I am too. We're both cold. When we get under the comforters. Or when we hold hands, there's no difference. Must mean we're like the same temperature, I guess."

Evan hummed. He stared up at the ceiling of Kash's dorm room.

The string lights he'd helped her and Stella hang, traced chaotic patterns all across the ceiling. It was like a web of stars above their heads.

"Whoever helped with that is a master decorator. That's professional work," Evan said teasingly, pointing up at the mess of lights. He looked down at her with a dimpled smirk, his dark lashes appearing even longer with the angle. "Do you ever actually turn them on?"

Kash shook her head. "No, I guess we don't. We did the other night, though. It sort of looked like outer space."

Evan raised an eyebrow and gestured indicatively.

Kash sighed and rolled her eyes as she reluctantly got out from under the covers. She climbed down and walked over to where Stella's loft bed was and turned on the lights.

Immediately the room lit up in a soft, warm glow, like candles burning in a castle window. The thought struck Kash like a branch to her face. "Makes this shitty dorm room feel sort of magical," she murmured.

"Come here," Evan said with an intimate softness that made Kash's stomach flutter.

She looked up at him steadily with wide eyes, as he draped himself over the railing with an expectant smile.

"What's up?" she asked awkwardly, as she climbed up and carefully got back under the covers. A sense of foreboding rose from her stomach into her throat.

Evan only nodded, expression both unreadable and open at the same time. He tucked a piece of hair behind her ear and suddenly Kash had an urge to laugh.

"What are you doing?" she asked in a shaky voice.

"Can I…" Evan's voice trailed off as he leaned in until his lips were almost on hers. His breath was hot, like the air in her truck when she parked it in the sun for too long.

"Um, yeah," Kash said, shrugging, playing at nonchalance. "We have—"

"No," Evan all but whispered, "not that." His voice was deep and gentle, but it still prickled at Kash's neck and back in the same way the buzz of a nearby fly did.

She inwardly took a deep breath, preparing, before settling into a coy smile, and lifting her shoulder a bit.

"You want to," she cleared her throat and started again when her voice came out heavier than she intended, "you want to—"

Almost like he sensed she wouldn't stop stuttering unless he made her, Evan jutted his chin forward, and tilted down to meet her lips.

Kash made a surprised sound and closed her eyes. Her hands hovered in the air stiffly in indecision as she zeroed in on kissing Evan, focused on giving her best. After a moment, she carelessly rested her hands on his shoulders and tilted her head in tandem with his, mirroring his movements as best as she could. She felt a smile creep onto his lips, pausing for a moment. She leaned away, looking up at him with the same practiced romance as every other time.

He pressed his forehead against hers and she smiled back at him, closing her eyes and basking in the proximity. Warmth and shivering uncertainty roiled inside her as she felt his breath quiver slightly against her chin.

"Hi," she said breathlessly, *awkwardly*, coaxing a laugh out of him.

He had a gravelly, spirited laugh that left his darkly tanned skin flushed. His nickel gray eyes sometimes disappeared if he laughed hard enough, eyebrows arching animatedly.

Right now, his eyes were wide and focused, even as his Adam's apple bobbed slightly with his laughter and his cheeks lifted with a brilliant, flushed smile.

She could almost see her reflection in his eyes, dotted by the constellation of tiny white bulbs above them.

"What do you want?" Evan asked firmly, indicating his meaning with a soft, adoring trace of his fingers across her collarbone and up her neck.

Kash froze. "What do I want?" she repeated with a frown.

Evan nodded imploringly.

What do I want?

She tilted her head to the side, for the sake of appearing like she was genuinely thinking. Her mind scrambled for an answer, screaming at her.

An anchor of unease dropped into the ground below her, dragging her heart down in a panicked instant.

I don't know what I want.

"I don't," she shook her head, trying to voice her thoughts without sounding dumb or insensitive. The last thing she wanted to do was be rude, when he was lying beside her, in her bed, in her room, on a completely different floor than his.

"I don't think I—you—" she stumbled, couldn't come up with the words to just tell him to decide for her, like he did everything else. Her legs involuntarily kicked, trying to find a physical reprieve.

"What is it?"

"It's not," she groaned and pressed her face into the pillow.

"Hey." Evan ran a hand through her hair, his voice lovely and kind. He cupped a hand around her jaw and coaxed her to look up at him. It made Kash's chest split open, Evan unknowingly wielding an axe straight into her sternum.

"Do you not—is this *not* what you want?" he asked, searching her face for answers and seemingly coming up with nothing but false conclusions.

"No!" Kash said, holding her hands out placatingly, nearly falling out of the bed if not for the railing, "No, I want you! I—I want to sleep with you, I want to—"

Who says that?

"—I want to enjoy it," she finished clumsily. Her eyes widened.

Fuck, what is wrong with me.

"You don't enjoy this?" Evan asked, gesturing between them. The look on his face was open and betrayed and it ripped at Kash's being.

"No, I do," she assured.

He gave her a callous, questioning look, his dark eyebrows coming low over his eyes, hiding the brilliance of their color.

"You just," she started, "you always seem to know. Why'd you ask me now?"

She looked at him lamely, hating the disappointed look in his eyes.

"I do?" he asked.

Kash nodded eagerly.

Evan paused, leveling her with an imploring look. "I don't—Do you? Kash—" He shifted so he could hold her better, arm coming around her shoulder to place his hand against the nape of her neck and his other hand lacing with hers. He opened his mouth soundlessly a few times before speaking. "Do you want this?"

Kash stuttered, fishmouthing while trying to find a way to explain herself. "I do, I—I want everything that—that comes with being in a relationship—"

He murmured, "Then what—"

"—I just, every time I actually—"

Evan's thumb brushed her hairline and it melted her in the worst way.

"—every time I go about doing anything, I feel like—" Kash swallowed down a panicked sob "—like an impostor."

Evan stared at her with wide, confused eyes.

"Why?" he asked. "I'm not asking you to be some experienced—"

"No! It's not about experience, I mean, yeah, but no, this is not about—" Kash cut herself off and made a helpless sound. She raked her hands shakily through her hair.

Evan sniffled and rubbed a hand against his nose, looking off to the side. His eyes glinted from the string lights above them and he looked—he looked so beautifully, painfully *sad*.

Don't cry. Kash almost whispered the words out loud. She was the most despicable person in the world. How could she make him cry when he was so good? When it was her fault she couldn't do things with him like a normal person, couldn't be with him like a normal person?

"You're not," Kash started before backtracking and saying in a broken voice, "I'm the one who—I feel like I have to be a completely different person in order to be—to be—and, and I liked that person, until I didn't. Until I got tired because I want—I want to be able to be myself with the person I have a—with the person I like, you know?"

Evan faced away from her the entire time she sat there blubbering out her heart.

"Evan," she called out, panic rising in her voice.

He shook his head, shoulders hunching up with tension.

"And you don't feel that?" he asked.

Kash recoiled at the disappointment in his voice. She sighed out and hunched over into herself.

"I don't know," she said.

"Kash, please just be honest with me," Evan asked softly.

"I don't," she said tiredly, "I don't know, I don't think I do. I'm sorry, I don't. I hate it, I don't know why, I don't know why."

"Have you always felt like you had to act around me?"

Kash looked up in shock. "No," she said shakily. "No, no."

She tried to take a breath, inhaling deeply to calm herself down, but something stopped her halfway, like there was a block in the middle of her chest. She hungered for more air.

Evan turned around to look at her, his hand held out like he was about to make a point, and Kash looked up at him quickly. It took him a moment before his eyes met Kash's and his hand fell to his side as he got up.

"So, you want to just be friends?"

Kash desperately fought the urge to scream, but she couldn't stop trying to inhale. She could breathe but she couldn't get enough air. She was suffocating without actually suffocating.

I don't know, I don't know, I don't know.

"I'm sorry, I'm sorry," she murmured. She wrapped her arms around herself, curling her fingers into the flesh of her upper arms. There was something so inherently wrong with her. She couldn't think of what or why, but it was the only reason for the guilty cramp in her stomach. She doubled over, trying to ease the discomfort and dug her hand into her sternum, but it was fruitless.

"I don't know what I want, and I don't know how to know," Kash said through lips swollen and wet from tears. She gasped again, shoulders rising with the effort and the muscle between her shoulders and collarbone straining painfully.

"Are you okay?" Evan asked, eyeing the way she was breathing heavily with substantial effort. He quickly pushed aside the tangled covers and held her tightly.

Kash nodded instinctually. She nonchalantly arched her back in hopes of opening her lungs.

I can't breathe.

"Kash, if you don't want to, to do anything, that's okay. If you don't want to be with me anymore, that's—" Evan hesitated, jaw clenching, before he continued. "I mean, that's fine. Just. *Tell* me."

I'm trying.

Kash tried to settle for shallow breaths, ignoring her growing need for deeper, longer breaths. She tried not to think much of it, but she frantically wondered if her lungs were failing. Had her body finally caught up with the stupid misfortune of her mind and similarly started to fade into a mess of emotional lawlessness?

She tried to take another breath, but it stopped before she could reach that last distance into her chest. Rogue, panicked tears fell down her cheeks and she coughed for some form of relief.

"I don't want to force you as much as I don't want to lose you, Kash. But I'm not asking you to be anyone. I don't understand why you need to," Evan continued earnestly.

Kash looked up at him and tried to inhale again.

"I don't understand either," she cried, "I don't understand why, I don't."

Evan carded a hand through her hair, holding her head against the crook of his neck.

Kash sighed at the welcome notion of not having to look at him while she spoke. "I'm terrified of, of being with—but I fucking want to, I want to, I want to be wanted as much as I *want*—" she cut herself off, pressing into his skin.

Evan traced a finger across her jaw as he fit his hand against the side of her face like a puzzle piece.

"I want you," he said firmly, beautifully, honestly.

Kash sobbed, breath raw and serrated.

He immediately wrapped his arms around her shoulders and squeezed, unyielding and warm.

She assumed he meant it reassuringly, but it restricted what limited circulation she had and her hunger for air descended into fully-fledged panic. She pushed out of his embrace, holding her hands in front of her defensively. She took ragged, starved breaths in and exhaled loudly with frustration.

"I can't breathe," she said. She quickly wiped a tear from her face and leveled Evan with an honest expression before repeating herself louder, "I can't breathe."

Evan's eyes widened in alarm and for the first time since she'd met him months ago, he appeared at a loss for what to do.

"Just breathe," he said immediately, pushing his hands up and down, palms to the ceiling and then to the floor.

Kash swallowed her scream and groaned loudly.

I'm fucking trying.

She mimicked his hand movements and tried to breathe in time to them but huffed when the block in her chest only intensified.

"Kash, it's okay," Evan said gently. "It's okay."

A sob escaped her lips and she resigned herself to breathing without the satisfaction of air.

Can't do anything right, can't even breathe right.

"Can I be alone?" she asked desperately, fisting her hands in the fabric of her sweatpants.

Evan threw her a crestfallen look, hands flexing at his sides.

"Like, now?" he asked warily. He looked like a small kid, wide-eyed and unsure, hands flexing at his sides.

Kash nodded jerkily, wiping her face to rid her cheeks of any dampness and swiped under her chin to wipe away the droplet of tears gathering there.

"Yeah," she said meekly, moving to climb down her bed. "I'm sorry, I—am sorry."

Evan followed her after a moment, barely taking his eyes off here even as he climbed down the slats.

"I'll see you in class?" Kash asked, eyes darting anywhere but the boy in front of her. "Day after tomorrow?"

Evan set his mouth in a line and gave a minute nod before grabbing his jacket from her chair and turning to leave.

"Can you…" he said, pausing just at the door. "Can you just text me before you fall asleep? Just," he took a deep breath and twisted the unlocked handle before continuing in a soft, sad voice, "just tell me you're okay. Or if you're not. Just. I don't—*shit*—I don't want to be with you if this is how it's making you feel?"

I don't want to be with you.

Kash recoiled. She'd put him off with her bullshit, with her blubbering nescience.

"Okay," she said, nodding quickly. "Yeah."

Evan nodded, glancing back at her over his shoulder once more with sad, confused gray eyes, and left. The door clicked behind him sharply and as soon as his footsteps fully faded, she let out a long, shaky sigh.

She wanted to scream, wanted to take back everything she'd said, take back the moment Evan had come up to her with a question and the moment she'd said yes for whatever reason had allowed her to.

With slow, dejected movements, she climbed up and tucked herself underneath the haphazard covers, burrowing as much as she could into the plushness.

"Fuck!" she yelled into the mattress, a self-deprecating sob escaping her throat. She dug her nails into her scalp until the angry sharpness pulling at her skin like thorns, eased into a dull aching itch. She gasped for breath again but came up short with infuriating consistency.

She cried out again, tears quickly dampening the sheets in wet blotches. Uselessness clenched her stomach and she curled into herself, folding her arms against her legs and trying hard to disappear into the disarray of blankets and pillows around her.

She was so tired, like she'd spent a lifetime being pulled in every direction but the one she wanted. A lifetime of playing a part, of failing to play a part, tired of the way she hurt everything.

She felt unhinged, in a dorm room that wasn't home, in a bed that wasn't hers months ago and wouldn't be hers months in the future. A bed that would recycle its sleepers every year. A room that would recycle its inhabitants every year. The impermanence of it all stung acutely, a feeling she was desperate to escape.

She needed to escape, to *stop.*

you can't just disappear, too.

The long list of blue texts on the right made her want to throw her phone against the wall across the room and break her skull open with her fingers.

It was happening all over again. It was happening just like she told him it would.

She shouldn't have told him.

'happy birthday anna!'

She called him again.

The answering machine voice told her he was out of service, just like the last two times, and she barely held back a scream as the tone beeped, indicating that all of her panic was now being recorded.

"I wish I could talk to you right now," she confessed with a shaky exhale. "You wouldn't—you'd get it, and I wouldn't even have to say anything."

She picked at a patch of pilling on her sweater and squeezed her eyes shut, tears falling fast and warm down her cheeks, gathering below her chin, and falling with the softest of noises onto her jeans.

Her feet were tucked uncomfortably under the legs of her desk chair, and she rocked back just enough to feel like she couldn't catch herself if she were to fall.

"You can't just—look I'm with you if you never talk to *Amma* and *Nanna* ever again but I've never—I haven't—" Kash inhaled raggedly and pressed a fist to her mouth, teeth grinding with as much force as she can muster, until they feel numb and like they might fall out.

"Fuck, forget that, you're an asshole," she spat out as she balanced the phone on her knee. "You can't just do shit like this, Rafi, it's your birthday, I want to *talk* to you."

Her fingers tapped aggressively against any surface they could find. Her thighs, the back of her phone, the desk, her ankles, the nearest post of her loft bed. She flexed them, reaching out in ten different directions with the kind of blind hope that immediately gets dashed.

"*Anna*," she said, "I hope you're…" she pressed the heels of her palms to her eyes and withheld a sob. "You're alive, right? You're just being an asshole to me, too, 'cause you're stupid. It's nothing else."

She brought her knees up, folding her arms around them and ignoring her phone as it clattered down on the floor. "I want you to just—," she pressed her face into the bony ridges of her kneecap, until the bridge of her nose dug in painfully, "—pick *up*. Pick up, Rafi. If you hear this rambling, *desperate* attempt to get you to just *call back*, and you still don't fucking *call back*, I swear to god I will never talk to you ever again, I don't care."

Kash grabbed her face and groaned, hitting her chin into the flesh of her lower thigh again and again until her jaw ached.

"You know, you never sent me that song. You told me you'd send me one of your songs to listen to and I said I'd tear it apart, and I really will now. I'll stomp it into the ground, I swear."

She waited with bated breath, stupidly, as if her brother would magically answer from the other end.

"Rafi, please, I'm sorry, I don't know what to—" A loud, sharp beep interrupted her, and she dug her teeth into her bottom lip like plaster on a broken water tank.

"No," she muttered under her breath, a low whine tumbling out of her like she was a wounded animal. She felt stupid, like she wanted to disappear into a hole in the ground and never emerge, but she also felt belligerent, like she wanted to gather all the memories she could remember and weaponize them.

Her burgeoning CD collection, stacked above her desk, seemed to vibrate with the need for attention and she scanned the titles until she settled on a newly acquired copy of *Come of Age* that she'd been waiting to send her brother a picture of, just to shove it in his face smugly that he could continue keeping his copy to himself, instead of giving it to her like she'd begged him. She'd wanted to take away whatever sense of satisfaction she imagined him to have, devalue his collection with the growth of hers, show off her taste in a show of just how much he'd shaped it—and how much she treasured that.

"Kash?"

Kash froze and looked over to the doorway where Stella was standing, surprised concern painting her face, hand still on the door handle.

"Oh," Kash said, voice wet and meek. "Hi. Sorry I'm—" she gestured to the definitive mess her face must appear like.

Stella shook her head. "It's okay. Are you... okay?"

Kash hummed, nodding her head in thought and looking back at her fingers, digging her nails into her kneecaps. She shrugged and curled her lips in an expression of neutrality.

"Kash," Stella said softly, closing the door behind her and setting her backpack down on her chair. She tucked her hair behind her ear before bending down and wrapping her arms around Kash with a sigh.

"Sorry, I'm sorry, I'm sorry," Kash whispered, squeezing her eyes shut and turning her face into the warmth of Stella's shoulder.

"No, I'm sorry," Stella said, running her thumb across Kash's hairline in a frighteningly apt gesture of comfort. "Did I tell you that one of my professors called me out in front of the whole class and told me my project was the worst?"

Kash laughed sympathetically, the sound wet and pitiful and punching the air from her chest. "Let's go punch them."

Stella hummed in agreement. "Maybe we should. Take her down a notch."

Kash laughed again and nodded. She pressed herself farther into the embrace, arms still around her knees but neck craned so that it curled the slightest bit around the firm muscle just above Stella's collarbone. "Are you okay?"

Stella laughed, her chest rumbling with the sound. "Yeah, yeah. Not all the time, but yeah." She ducked her head down to level with Kash and tilted to one side so her hair fell over her face a bit and the flesh of her cheek stretched the tiniest amount. "Want to be not okay together?"

Kash stiffened. That sounded too similar to someone else she had a long line of unanswered blue messages with. She nodded gingerly. "I want to bake a cake."

Stella frowned. "You can't bake."

"Let's buy one, then."

"From where?"

Kash shrugged.

Stella nodded. "Okay, okay. We'll figure it out. For now, we can welcome our mutual not-okayness with…" Her outlined eyes scanned the room before lighting up. "Honey packets!"

Kash thought that Stella was the kind of person that seemed incapable of sadness.

"My brother won't talk to me," Kash blurted out. "A lot of people won't talk to me."

"I talk to you," Stella countered immediately.

Kash scoffed and looked away. "I'm not—you don't need to do that."

"Do what?"

Kash gestured vaguely to where Stella stood.

Stella hummed like she understood what Kash was saying and took two honey packets out of the box on Kash's desk. "Here," she offered them to her before leaning over and taking two more for herself.

"Do what?" Stella asked again, sitting down on the ground in front of Kash.

"Don't sit on the ground."

"Come join me."

Kash stared at her, ripping the packet of honey and holding it between her ring and middle finger. She squeezed and sucked the honey as her fingers flattened the packet to ensure there were no substantial remnants of honey left inside the plastic. "Okay," she murmured after swallowing and tossing the empty packet on her desk. She clumsily slid down from her chair onto the floor, legs crooked and tangled but comfortable enough not to require repositioning.

"You know," Stella said, eyes trained on Kash's in a way that made it impossible to look away from.

Kash tilted her head in answer. "What?" she mumbled. A rogue tear fell down her cheek and she immediately wiped it away with little care for subtlety.

"You don't need to feel like I'm here because of any reason except wanting to be," Stella said, licking her lips.

Kash blinked. "I don't. I don't feel that way."

Stella narrowed her eyes at her and curled her lips into something resembling a smirk.

"What?" Kash asked numbly.

"Nothing," Stella shrugged. "Just that nothing beats honey."

Nothing beats you.

"Just tell me when I'm too much."

Stella smiled at that. "In what way?"

"Like too much honey."

Stella frowned, smile still wide and brilliant, before descending into incredulous laughter. "That's what I'm saying," Stella said, sucking some honey from her thumb through giggles. "Even if you are, it doesn't matter."

Kash swallowed, throat constricting painfully enough for more tears to well up and blur her vision.

"Okay," she croaked.

Stella nodded and licked more honey from her fingertips. "Okay."

Kash watched her get up and throw her trash away before crouching down in front of her. Some of her hair slipped back over her shoulder, partially curtaining her face.

"What do you want to do?" she asked. "Other than cake?"

Kash shrugged. She closed her eyes, jaw clenching and unclenching. "I don't know."

"That's the problem with you, isn't it?"

The words themselves were caustic, but Kash could hear the smile in Stella's voice, and she spoke in such a sweet, genuine way that Kash nearly registered it as reassurance.

"Yeah," she said barely above a breath, eyes still closed to the world. The sound of Stella's breathing was the only indication of anything beyond the black loudness of her mind. "Yeah, it is."

after: two years.

i've become the pretender.

The foil fabric of Kash's top was bunching uncomfortably in her armpits. For the umpteenth time, she tugged the hem down, stretching it properly over her chest and stomach, and tucked it into the waistband of her pants. The air was cold outside, like early winter, but her clothes were stuffy enough to keep it at bay.

She wasn't wearing a costume. At least not a character, or anything. Her hair was tangled and covered in sticky glitter. She ran a hand across the top of her head and winced at the matted mess. One swipe of her finger confirmed that the generous helping of black makeup around her eyes was smudged across her cheekbones and temples. She imagined she looked like a sweaty demon—with long fangs and ugly yellow eyes from the Indian epics her father used to read to her a lifetime ago.

A part of her itched to go to the bathroom and fix herself up. She felt suffocatingly strung up and grimy. Instead, she leaned against the cool railing of the fire escape and tucked her legs in through the window, so her body was partially inside. She lazily gazed around the room.

Warm bodies moved in a chaotic tandem to loud music. Some stupid dance remix of a stupid pop song that Stella'd picked out for their house party playlist. A few people she recognized were huddled around each other in the corner, seemingly in deep conversation. One of them, a girl from Kash and Stella's vague friend group here in the city, caught Kash's eyes and offered a pretty smile.

Kash barely mustered the effort to smile back and wave until the girl looked away, once again engrossed in conversation with the others. Kash sighed and moved her shoulder up and down as she rolled her neck, closing her eyes and wincing at the stretch in her muscles.

A shattering crash sounded somewhere in the direction of the kitchen, followed by a loud thud and muffled shout.

Kash groaned and got down from her perch. That was probably something important. She made her way through the crowd, smiling at the few familiar faces she saw along the way, and into the kitchen, where she froze.

Stella was crouched on the ground, surrounded by ceramic broken shards and picking them up with shivering hands.

Kash wrinkled her nose in disapproving confusion. She looked up and saw that the shelf holding their mugs had fallen, now sitting at an angle on top of the empty plates shelf below. Her heart sank, in a distant way that felt like she was a million miles away from the insides of her own chest. She swallowed the feeling.

"I told you we had too many mugs," she said stoically.

Stella looked up at Kash, startling a bit. "Oh, hey," she said softly before she rolled her eyes and tucked a stray strand of black hair behind her ear. "And shut up. It's not the mugs.

Shelf broke. It's the perfect time, isn't it? Right when there's a bunch of people in our living room that we have to entertain."

Kash bent down and started picking pieces up carefully. "Hardly a proper living room when it's less than fifty square feet."

Stella laughed wistfully. "Right."

Kash reached over and opened the cabinet under the sink. She grabbed the dustpan and they both cleaned up the broken mess quickly.

Stella insisted on keeping larger remnants of certain mugs, claiming sentimental value and Kash smiled fondly before setting them aside on the counter.

"You terrible social butterfly," Kash said. "It's your fault there's a fourth of the millennial population of New York in our apartment."

Stella shrugged. "One of us has to be. And you've already taken the role of the dramatic introvert."

"I hate parties."

"I know. I'm sorry," Stella said softly, leaning her head against Kash's upper arm. "Thank you."

Kash made a face and shook her head.

They stood there, leaning against the counter, Stella's head on Kash's arm and her hands wrapped around her elbow.

"I hate Halloween, too," Kash added, looking down at Stella's black painted nails that contrasted prettily against her pale skin.

"And I still don't get why."

Kash sniffled and glanced down at her feet. It'd taken some getting used to wearing shoes inside the apartment. Stella convinced her that it would motivate them to clean more often but that never happened.

"I really don't want to go back into the inferno," Kash said in a lightly joking voice.

"I closed our rooms, so nobody's going into them."

Kash looked down at Stella. "I'll hideout, then. You keep entertaining like the extrovert you are."

Stella rolled her eyes. "You say that like it's an insult."

Kash shrugged her off gently, grabbed the keys from on top of the fridge, and started walking out into the narrow hallway that connected their bedrooms to the common area. She bypassed a few people before reaching her room, closing the door quickly behind her, and locking it again.

She let out a long, shaky sigh.

"Fuck," she said under her breath, pressing her palms briefly against her eyes. She walked over to her desk and grabbed a piece of paper from her stationary set. She grabbed her fountain pen—it was old and worn enough to have faded marks along the grip—and stared at the paper.

A heavy tear welled in her left eye. She resisted the urge to blink and let it fall from her lower lid. It landed on the paper with a heavy splatter, and she quickly brought the sleeve of her top over her hand to blot it.

I wish you'd taken me with you when you ran away.

She wrote messily in the margin and stared at the words.

A minute later she found herself sprawled out on her back on the floor, the rug beneath her digging into her naked back. She'd taken her stupid top off, finally. The air was cool against her sweaty skin and goosebumps erupted across her stomach and arms.

Her insides twisted painfully, like a tightly wrung fabric of guilt and anxiety, and she had an aching need to travel into a forest and scream until her lungs gave out, fall into the ground, and disappear beneath the brush and roots and earth.

There was a gentle knock at the door and Kash blinked her eyes open.

"Kash?"

"Yeah?" Kash answered, getting up on her elbows.

The lock clicked and Stella opened the door, peeking out from behind it. Her eyes were wide and tired. "Why'd you lock it?" she tilted her head and asked.

Kash gestured for her to come in and laid back down.

"Everyone's left."

Kash blinked. "Oh."

How long had she been lying on the floor?

"Did you fall asleep or something?" Stella asked as she lay down right next to her, body perfectly aligned.

Kash closed her eyes. "I don't know," she said.

"Did'ya have too much to drink?" Stella asked.

Kash could hear the teasing smirk in her voice. "Yeah. Tried to make things go faster." She waved her hand in the air. "'S hitting me now, I guess."

Stella hummed. She didn't move, didn't talk. They both lay there in silence, the city outside bleeding in through the windows.

A lump grew in Kash's throat. She couldn't swallow. Her breath started coming out all shallow and she drew in a wheezing gulp of air.

"Was the party really that bad?" Stella asked softly.

Kash let out a choked, wet laugh and shook her head. She needed to swallow, spit was gathering up in her mouth, but she *couldn't*. Tears welled up and fell from the corners of her eyes, down into her hair.

"Kash? Love?"

Kash turned her head and looked at Stella, who was staring right back at her.

Her eyes were outlined in smudged Halloween face paint, her hairline was damp, and her lips were covered in a fading black. She looked disheveled in the most intimate way.

"I feel like a criminal," Kash admitted quietly. Tears leaked faster from her eyes.

"How so?"

"Like I'm intruding on—like I'm doing something illegal just by being here."

"Like an impostor?"

Kash nodded. "Like a creep."

"You're not a *creep.*"

Kash squeezed her eyes and brought her hands up to her face. She pressed her palms against her eyes and choked out a cry. The lump in her throat was more than painful now, cutting off her breath and voice, forcing her to let it out and ease the pain. She cried in short bursts, trying hard to stop every time. The fuzziness in her head made it so easy to, just, succumb to it, though.

"You belong here," Stella said matter-of-factly, as if Kash wasn't rapidly descending into hysterics right next to her.

"I can't even get through a party," Kash blurted out loudly. *You're so stupid.*

Stella wrapped herself around Kash's body. Her arms came around Kash's torso and her left leg hooked over her hips while the other tangled with Kash's legs.

Kash froze, not daring to move, even to cry. She held her breath.

"I love you, Kash," Stella said with a sigh.

Kash whimpered and let out another, smaller sob. "I feel like a complete idiot, sometimes," she said.

"Why's that?"

"Like something's wrong with me."

Stella looked up at her. "Why?"

Kash shook her head. "I don't know. I don't know I just feel so, so angry and sad. I don't have a fucking reason."

"You don't have to justify how you're feeling, love," Stella insisted. "You just feel. That's okay."

Kash made a whimpering, wet noise and squeezed her eyes shut. Warm tears trailed down her temples into her hairline. "I wish I could tell you it's because of something that's happened to me, but I've had a great fucking life. I've no excuse but I just—I can't stop from wanting to just fucking scream and breathe fire at everything."

"Okay," Stella nodded, "is that what you want to do right now? Breathe fire at everything?"

Kash laughed dryly. "I think I've been burning things down for a while, actually."

"That's natural, I think," Stella said. She squeezed her arms and legs around Kash.

Kash looked down at her and stared for a moment. She took in the girl wrapped around her, in all her disheveled glory, and inwardly sighed at the familiarity.

"Can I—can I sleep with you?" Kash asked quietly.

Stella watched her for a moment, eyes darting back and forth between Kash's.

"Okay," she said softly, nodding. "My room or yours?"

"Here?"

"Okay."

Kash offered her a watery smile and burrowed her head in the junction of Stella's neck and shoulder. She exhaled and watched the damp hairs around Stella's neck dance.

"Thank you," Kash whispered.

i'm surrounded by strangers; i am a stranger.

The tea was too bitter. She'd left the pot on the stove for too long, found it boiling at half of the amount she'd filled it with.

She sighed as she poured in the milk, watching it bloom just under the surface of the dark Earl Grey tea, a cool creamy brown. She added two more than the average spoonful of honey and stared at the swirling liquid with the kind of existential focus she usually had before a breakdown.

"All right, love?" Stella asked, coming into the kitchen. "G'morning."

There was still a residual mess here and there from their less than casual New Years' celebrations.

"Yeah," Kash said blankly, eyes landing on an empty plastic tray that once held an entire cheesecake. They'd eaten the whole thing at two in the morning, the both of them, sitting on the old couch, laughing nonsensically at the TV. The memory felt incredibly distant, like it had been a lifetime instead of a week.

"No, you aren't," Stella said.

"Astute observation, I'm not," Kash snapped before thinking. She squeezed her eyes shut immediately, regret slicing through her. "No, I'm just—it's a bad day."

"Why?"

Kash looked at her roommate—her friend. She'd never really understood how to grow out of calling Stella her roommate. That's how they met so that's how she introduced her to everyone. But they were more than that. And yet Kash had to second-guess it every time.

"You always ask why," Kash said softly. "Everyone else just leaves me alone when I say that. They know better."

Stella shrugged, like that was a compliment.

Kash wanted to tell her it wasn't.

"How do you introduce me to your friends?" she asked instead.

Stella frowned. "What? I mean, like, with your name?"

Kash made a face, lips curling in and lifting in a slight, fond smile. "No, I mean," she said, "what am I to you?"

Stella thought for a bit, eyes darting up to the ceiling and body twisting side to side.

Kash watched her move and realized she was wearing a thick sweater and had her coat in her arms. She watched as Stella put it on distractedly.

"Are you going out?" Kash asked.

"Yeah, just to get some quick groceries. Milk and whatnot. You want to come?"

Kash shook her head, feeling a little guilty at not helping, but the thought of going outside into the world made her feel sick.

"I think I…" Stella started before pausing and looking to Kash meaningfully, "You're my closest friend here in the city. I do love you, if that's what you're worried about. Swear

I won't run off and live with someone else. Couldn't live here without you."

Kash nodded, familiar with the sentiment.

Stella shrugged before adding, "You're my—lifeline, I guess."

Kash cleared her throat. "Because I'm a friend from college?"

Stella tilted her head before nodding and saying, "Yeah. Like you ground me, keep me connected to who I was before the real world fully set in. Now we've got jobs and stuff, it's *terrible*."

Kash laughed, leaning forward against the counter.

Stella smiled back warmly. "I'll be off, then. Do you want anything specific?"

Kash shook her head and watched as Stella squeezed her arm meaningfully before turning around and heading out the door. It closed behind her with a loud click.

The warmth that had started to rise in Kash fell flat. She felt the emptiness creep in again, swiping out everything in its way as it settled heavily inside her. Her lip trembled and she stared unblinking until hot, heavy tears gathered on her bottom lashes.

The sun gradually came out a little more, dark blue slowly turning into a dull winter gray.

A confused hurt bit like shards in her throat and she tried to swallow fruitlessly. Instead, she slumped defeated, let the spit gather in her mouth uncomfortably, until she felt like she had to throw up. Noise grew loud in her mind, static and scratchy, disembodied words from raked up memories.

The apartment was silent, but in her head it was *so deafening*. She couldn't escape it. Like the world around her was normal, and everything bad was inside her. And she couldn't escape out of her own insides, her own body.

A grating sob forced itself reluctantly past her lips and she watched her tears fall with soft *plinks* into her mug of tea. She held her head in her hands and dug her fingers into her scalp, until it hurt too much physically to focus on the hurt below the surface.

More tears fell and she moved so her tea wouldn't get too salty. She stumbled across the common area into the opposite wall, pressing her forehead against the cool, rough brick. She'd been so insistent on living in an apartment with large windows and exposed brick walls.

Stella'd joined in on her wish list and they'd bought yards of more string lights to add to their existing collection, and wrap them around their entire apartment. They'd even gotten quirky, mismatched dinnerware, hadn't they? Even though their boastful collection of mugs was now decimated to broken pieces and two plain ones from the dollar store that they'd gotten out of necessity.

Kash pressed her entire face against the wall, relishing in the way a sharp edge of brick dug into the bridge of her nose.

It's too far, too late, too cold.

She wanted to hurt more; less of the hurt that was clawing up her insides, and more of the hurt that she could bear on her skin.

Abruptly, the stupid old telephone rang loudly and she jumped at the shrill sound, slightly scraping her face on the brick.

The pistachio green chrome of the landline shined palely in the meager lighting from outside as Kash walked over to it apprehensively. They'd found it at an antique store and Stella had insisted on installing it, because what would complete the picture of exposed brick and sunlight and cityscapes better than having a vintage rotary dial telephone?

Kash snorted at the thought and reached for the handheld just as it stopped ringing. She paused, hand hovering over it for a few moments until a radical idea entered her mind.

Her breath hitched and she went over the combination of numbers she knew by heart even to this day. Although, they were probably useless now, weren't they? Had he kept the same number since high school, even overseas?

Kash sniffled and rolled her eyes.

No, he wouldn't have, he's not an idiot like you.

She hadn't seen him in years, and the last time he had visited, she'd been overtly stubborn to appear unbothered by him or their past, *stupidly.*

Another sob racked through her, and she slumped into the sofa with a heavy thump. She curled her knees up until she could wrap her arms under her legs and burrow into herself. Whimpers escaped her mouth as she tried to *stop.* Stop crying, stop feeling, stop the stupid incessant ache that hadn't let up since before she could remember.

Is this how you felt? Is this why you ran away across the ocean? Did you find an escape?

Kash screamed silently through another full-bodied sob.

Why didn't you take me with you?

She groaned out in effort, clenching her jaw to stop heaving and whimpering desperately. She uncurled her fists to dig her nails into her skin until her breathing came out shakily and her lashes were wet enough to blur her vision.

Are you a stranger now, too?

Her heart skipped a beat when she remembered what Raza had written in her notebook at Christmas and she got up with a sudden fervor. She made her way, clumsily, down the narrow hall to her bedroom.

Her notebook was on her desk, its whereabouts like a constant sixth sense in her mind. She grabbed it gently and flipped through the pages until she found Raza's telltale chicken scratch handwriting.

She stared at it, blinking only when her eyes started to burn unbearably. Nostalgic betrayal overtook the emptiness and she found herself falling into the feeling willingly. She let the old anger flow into all the places that had ached so painfully for so long. It was lightening, distracting in the worst way, and she sighed out into the stillness of her bedroom.

"I wonder if you'll pick up?" she asked out loud, absent-mindedly, as she ran her fingers across the page. She slumped onto her bed with the notebook and fished her phone out from under the sheets with effort.

She sighed out shakily, aftershock tremors of sobs still running through her, as she dialed the number carefully. It took her a long taxing moment before she pressed the call button and then immediately hung up.

Her heart raced as she sluggishly walked back into the common area and reached for the stupid dial phone. She spun in the numbers as slowly as she possibly could and pressed the handheld telephone to her ear.

It rang once. Twice.

"Hello?"

Kash choked and slapped a hand to her mouth before she could betray her presence.

You picked up.

"Hello?" Levi repeated through the speaker. His voice was staticky and wide like an old radio.

"Um, hey," her voice trailed off meekly. She squeezed her eyes shut and pressed the palm of her hand against her sternum.

"Sorry, who's this?" Levi asked, a hint of impatience in his voice.

Kash couldn't help gaping. His voice had even more of a foreign lilt than it did more than two years ago.

"I, um, I'm sorry. Are you busy? Am I interrupting?" Kash asked quickly.

"No," Levi said skeptically. "But I dunno who you are?"

Kash cleared her throat. He was going to make her say it. Of course, he wouldn't recognize her.

"It's, uh, it's—" Kash steeled herself, and spoke through gritted teeth. "You're Levi, right?"

"Right."

"Right. This is, I mean, I'm Kash."

She heard Levi's sharp intake of breath and unconsciously copied the gesture herself.

"Kash. Like middle name's Mercury, Kash?"

She laughed despite the gnawing anxiety in her stomach. "Yes, Kash as in Kashvi Mercury."

"Oh. Fuck, um," he sounded breathless and stunned. "How—why—"

"I'm sorry, Raz gave me your number this past Christmas," Kash blurted.

"Raz? Wait, why're you apologizing?" Levi asked and Kash could just picture the furrow of his brow.

"I don't know," Kash sighed out, lying down on the couch and taking care to stretch the coiled cord carefully so she wouldn't swing the phone off the coffee table.

"Don't apologize for calling. I've been—I just was looking forward to it, so… I'd prefer if you didn't apologize for it."

"Sorry."

"I could never regret you calling, Kash."

"How are you?" she asked before she could fall into the rushing familiarity of Levi's voice.

"I'm, uh, I'm okay. I'm good. Just walking back to the flat right now. It's a bit—*freezing*—and I forgot my gloves, so my fingers have become popsicles but other than that I'm good."

Kash smiled to herself at the sight of Levi getting swept up in the cold January winds, his hair flying and fingers and cheeks red, skin glistening with frost.

"Sounds tough."

"Winters in London are definitely leagues better than winters in Massachusetts," Levi said with a huffing laugh.

"I'm not in Massachusetts," Kash said softly, playing absently with the phone cord.

"Oh. Where are you then?" Levi asked, voice increasingly breathless as if he were running a marathon while speaking.

"New York."

"New York," Levi repeated, a hint of awe in his voice that Kash immediately felt the need to douse.

"I'm a writing assistant, nothing fancy. Doesn't even pay the bills. I've got freelance work and Stella to thank for that, so far."

"Who's Stella?"

Kash froze.

"Um," she floundered. "She was my roommate in college. Since freshman year."

"Ah, so you're flatmates."

Kash wrinkled her nose. "Yeah, I mean. That's how we met."

"She's willingly dealt with you for six years?" Levi teased. "She sounds nice."

Kash scoffed. "Right, she hasn't run off and left me."

She regretted the words as soon as they left her mouth, but the old betrayal she'd kept at bay with feigned indifference started to fester again.

Levi paused, breathing heavily over the speaker, and Kash listened carefully as something jangled and clicked.

"Are you," he started before another louder click interrupted him. A thud sounded distantly before his heavy breathing returned and he said, "I mean, are you more than flatmates, is that why you're getting so defensive?"

"What?" Kash said loudly, surprised. "No!"

Except you are—friends? Best friends? College friends? Or just college roommates?

Levi chuckled, the sound especially warm and crackling, like a nostalgic campfire. "Oh, I see," he said.

Kash wished she could travel through the phone line and slap the knowing smirk she knew he was wearing off his face.

"I definitely like her much better than you," Kash bit out instead.

"Oh," Levi sighed. "Is that why you called?"

"What do you mean is that why I called?" Kash bristled.

"You've called to finally get angry at me," Levi said.

I've been angry at you since the day you left.

She heard him sigh out amidst some soft rustling and she imagined him taking off his coat and setting it down somewhere.

"What does your *flat* look like?" she asked, mocking the word.

"It does the job. I imagine yours is messy and cluttered, like you've always been."

"Fuck off."

"Is it?" Levi asked, like he already knew the answer.

Kash gritted her teeth. "Unlike you, Stella is clean without shoving it down my throat."

"I've never shoved anything down your throat," Levi said caustically.

"No, of course not, you just fucked off across the world without giving me the honor of a warning," she venomously blurted out into the stillness of her apartment.

A silence stretched between them, and each moment left Kash more enraged than the last. She fisted her hands, nails digging into the flesh of her palms.

"What?" she bit out, goading him.

"I didn't leave to hurt you," Levi said, anger coloring his tone, too.

"No, you just didn't tell me or pick up my calls because you were so fucking *kind*," Kash snarled.

"Fuck off, I'm so very sorry I was such a fucking coward back then."

"You're a coward even now."

"You don't know me now."

Kash couldn't help the sharp gasp that escaped her lips before she pressed them together hard enough for her teeth to dig into the flesh. She felt hot, heavy tears overflow her lower lids, leaving cool tracks down her cheeks and collecting under her chin. A sob racked through her again and she clamped a hand against her mouth to stop the fresh wave of hysterics from before.

"And I don't know you," Levi said softly, sadly, after a few minutes of quiet.

Kash squeezed her eyes shut and held back another bout of tears. She wanted to fire back, to tell him that he couldn't say things like that, he couldn't sound like he was drooping with sadness, because he was the one who left.

"You're not the only one," she admitted instead, voice wet and higher than usual.

"What does that mean?" Sincerity overwhelmed the lingering anger in Levi's voice.

"Why would you," Kash deflected, "I mean, you talk to Raza and not me?"

Levi sighed out shakily. "It's—" he paused like what he was about to say had the potential to be fatal "—easier to talk to him."

Kash tried, unsuccessfully, not to let that hurt her as much as it did. "When did it—why did it become *hard* with me?" she asked in a small, anguished voice.

"I'm sorry."

No explanation. Again.

"I am too, I guess," Kash said spitefully, voice breaking. "Sorry it's so hard to talk to me. Shall I hang up? To make it easier for you? Never talk to you again, if it's such a *hardship*."

"No!" Levi's voice turned grainy with volume.

"You acted like things were normal just fine when you came and visited in junior year. I was stubborn to stay angry with you and play along," Kash sniffled pathetically.

"I know," Levi said softly. "Fuck, you're going to make me cry."

"Good," Kash demanded. "Fucking—you made me cry first. Do you know the amount of, of heartbreak? Like I couldn't fucking breathe."

The space between them filled with frayed tears.

"I…" Levi trailed off, sniffling before his voice returned closer to the speaker, "I felt like I was doing this terrible thing. I didn't know how to tell you because it felt like the only way to tell you was to say goodbye, to just spring it on you, and that's kind of a shitty thing to do."

"You know what's a shitty thing to do?" Kash asked with offense.

"I know, I know," Levi said, a hint of fondness in his voice that tugged at Kash's heart painfully. "I ended up doing exactly that, didn't I."

"You know I would've never forgiven you either way," she admitted, continuing with slight petulance. "You ran away without me. We'd made plans and you left."

"We were never going to run away together, Kash," Levi said. "You know that. That's just—childish. You were going off to college because it was the expected thing to do, not because you'd made plans to. I just. I have the bad habit of not being able to do things for the sake of others."

You're still as pretentious as ever.

"I mean, you left Levi. You told me what was going to happen and then you turned everything on its head without saying anything. Fine, forget running away together." Kash rubbed her cheeks roughly as she spoke, to get rid of the tear tracks tickling her skin. "You stopped being my *friend.*"

"How could I be your friend when I didn't know what the fuck I was doing? When I knew you'd have questions and I didn't have answers," Levi said harshly. "You know who doesn't fucking ask questions or fucking—interrogate me? You know who I don't feel the need to fucking answer to?"

Kash bit her lip to stop from screaming at him.

She had met Levi first, when they were barely three, before Raza had even entered the picture. Sure, they were all childhood friends, but her and Levi's friendship preceded theirs by a year, and she was very insistent on this fact anytime Raza and Levi claimed to be closer than her.

"You didn't talk to him at first, either," Kash said. "Not him, not me, not Lani."

"Look, I wanted to become someone new, all right? Wash myself of everything I hated about who I was and where I was. It was like cleansing myself of things I left behind for good."

"So, you needed to cleanse yourself of me."

"No! For fuck's sake, you take everything as a—I'm not talking about you. I've told you before. You are one of the very few things I never want to move on from and that remains true and will always remain—"

"You did move on from me. Why else—"

"Why did you call me, now, Kash?" Levi asked firmly.

"Why did you pick up now?" Kash fired back. "When you didn't every other time before?"

"Honestly?" Levi said, cruel honesty turning his voice rancid and spiteful. "Because I didn't know it would be you on the other end."

I didn't want it to be you.

Kash couldn't help the angry sob that escaped her then. "And do you like who you've become now?" she asked, forsaking any efforts to not sound like a complete mess. It wasn't worth it. Not to someone she knew was just as messy.

"I don't know, Kash," Levi said exasperatedly. "Is that what you want to hear?"

Kash wanted to scream hurtful things at him, but she couldn't find the words, couldn't decide on something impactful and damaging enough.

"You idiot," she settled on pathetically, "I've wanted to hear your voice, properly, for so many years. Now you've got an accent and you talk like you know everything, still as arrogant as ever. It's only endearing until it becomes tiring, Levi. When your grandparents—*grandparents*, Levi—told me where you went, I fought the instinct to get on a plane and find you just to strangle you. You insult me by giving me the excuse that it's 'too hard' to talk to me? You fucking prick? What about caring for someone is easy, Levi? Since when was being honest ever fucking easy? It's not. It's difficult. That's the whole fucking point. Everything is so fucking difficult—" She caught herself, clamping a hand to her mouth as she descended into silent hysteria.

"Kash," Levi said her name softly and gently, like a kiss good night.

"The first time I could take a breath without the weight of you closing me up," she said slowly, deliberately, "was when I woke up that first morning after moving into my dorm room."

"You know it took me a long time to breathe without you, too," Levi said. "You know that. I was an asshole, and I don't regret it because where I'm at now isn't great but it's better than before. But you're too important to me for you to think that it wasn't the same for me."

"Fuck off, Levi. You're the one that never—"

"I know, fuck's sake, I know. I'm the one that fucked up, I'm the one that closed off at the most difficult thing I'd ever been faced with, I know." He paused before laughing in a self-deprecating way that made Kash's heart squeeze. "You're the most difficult thing I've ever been faced with—and that's a fucking compliment."

"I don't talk to anyone anymore," she admitted before she lingered too much on that last sentence. "That's why I called you."

"Why? Don't you talk to anyone, I mean."

Kash inhaled deeply, shakily. "I don't know how to. I know why you didn't—I'm just so angry at you, I've been bottling it for six years. Because it was a shitty thing to do, but I know. I think I do."

"You know why I left?"

"Yeah," Kash said, voice going high with the beginning of another sob, "I know why you ran away, I think. Or at least I know why you felt the need to."

"What's changed?"

"Because I've wanted to stop everything for… a really long time. I hate everything in a way that, I just want to get rid of it. And I feel like such a terrible person because I got almost everything I said I wanted. But I can't get up in the morning without feeling this pressure, in my chest, in my head, to play the part of someone I am so, so tired of. I'm so tired."

"You're not a terrible person," Levi assured her. It was redundant but she closed her eyes to believe in it just for a second.

"I don't talk to anyone, because I don't know how to play the part with them."

"You don't have to play a part with anyone, Kash."

She squeezed her eyes shut. He wasn't getting it. Nobody was getting it.

"I don't think I can handle you being a stranger anymore, Levi," she said softly. "I have so many strangers in my life. I've estranged myself."

"Then don't be," he said urgently. "I'm sorry, I know. *I* won't be."

"Okay."

"I need you, too, Kash," he said, like a soft confession. "I'm sorry for acting like I don't."

They both had similarly large egos, ever since she could remember. They would clash more than they would meet in the middle and she smiled wetly, fondly, at the notion.

She was still so angry, like a molten pit in her chest. Angry at him, angry at herself, angry that nobody seemed to know the messy turmoil inside.

But, then, he knew, didn't he? He'd always been one step ahead of her, she could admit that begrudgingly to herself, and sometimes that made him an insufferable, arrogant asshole, but. So was she.

"Are you free in, like, three hours?" Levi asked tentatively, carefully, like he was carrying a glass filled to the brim.

"Why?"

"Can I call you back then?"

Kash caught her breath. She was so stupid.

You're so stupid, selfish.

He had a life, he was busy, had a job, had friends, and an apartment. She had just barged in on that, hadn't she, like it didn't matter more than she did to him.

"Sorry," she said quickly. "Yeah."

"Okay," he said in the same careful, warm voice, "I'll call you."

"Actually, not on the landline—"

"I have your number, Kash," Levi said, and she could perfectly picture the confused frown on his face. "I didn't delete it."

"I kind of assumed that you did."

Levi sighed. "Right."

"That's your fault," Kash told him pointedly. "I thought you blocked me, deleted me from your phone, your life. I called you a million times at least, and you didn't pick up. I might be more hurt to think that you actually rejected every call."

"Jesus, I know."

She waited for him to say something more, but the line remained silent.

"I don't know how to end this call with you," he said after a while. "I want to talk to you, hear you yell at me, yell back at you, for hours. But I've got to go."

"Then go," Kash said simply.

Levi paused on the other line before saying, "I don't think I would've picked up if I saw your name on the caller ID."

"I didn't want you to know it was me."

"I know I said earlier that I," he sighed heavily, like it was hard for him to articulate what he wanted to say, "I just—that doesn't mean that I didn't want it to be you. That I didn't want to—I know you won't like it. But it took everything from me not to come running back because where you are, where you and Raz and Mam and Pops are, is comfort. I would just, stare at my phone as it rang and I'd stare at your name, and I'd—I'd just have to keep telling myself to stay where I was, where I am. I was an asshole, I know that. I'm almost entirely sure that's still true. But. I know that I was the one who went. That I was the one who wanted to. And maybe you understand that, maybe that doesn't always guarantee we'll like it in the end, you know, doing what we want. And maybe you understand that there is no one in this world that is more difficult nor more essential to me than you."

Kash squeezed her eyes shut, bit her lip as hard as she could, and sank farther into the couch, curling and uncurling her fingers and toes.

"Kash?"

"Yeah?"

"Okay," he said, "I wasn't sure if you were still there."

Kash twirled the phone cord between her fingers and resisted the urge to disappear from existence.

Levi cut the line after another pause and a soft, "Three hours," and left her completely dumbfounded.

Doesn't mean I didn't want it to be you.

She frowned at that and tried to ignore the fluttering familiarity in her chest.

I wanted it to be you. No one in this world that is more difficult nor more essential to me.

You're essential to me.

Kash set the droning handheld back in its place and adjusted the phone on the coffee table, so it wasn't sitting precariously on the edge anymore.

She pressed the heels of her palms against her eyes and muttered, "Fuck, fuck fuck."

He'd picked up and she'd cried and raged at him, and he had cried and raged back.

"Fuck," she said one more time before getting up and walking over to her tea. The ache throughout her had shallowed and she wasn't sure if it was because she'd yelled it all out or if it was because of him. She wasn't sure which one was worse.

i want to call you secret names in front of future guests.

"Tell me how things will turn out, in a year or two," Kash said. She closed her eyes as a breeze blew gently past.

They were both perched on the monkey bars. The students weren't supposed to go off school grounds during free periods but the empty playground down the street was one of Kash's favorite places to escape to.

"I don't know. What do you want?" Levi asked, picking apart a purple wildflower.

Kash looked at him and watched as he flicked away the delicate petals.

"We should start a band," she said.

Levi laughed. "We're not musicians. Not good ones."

Kash shrugged. "I can ask my brother. I'll write songs and you can play the guitar and he'll lead. We can go on tours, live in a bus for half our life and stadiums for the other half. Screw college."

Levi raised an eyebrow. "And what?"

Kash smiled. "And you'll be the John Hughes boy with your hair in your face while you play guitar, and everyone will fall in love with you."

"Really?"

"Really. And I'll be the quiet stranger that writes words for no one. And Raf will turn them into songs and sing them like the stupidly talented goblin he is."

Levi shook his head and laughed. "You're crazy."

Kash frowned and lay down on her back against the cool metal bars, feet catching against the railing, so she stayed in place. "I'm being real."

"We're not going to start a band, Blue," Levi said. He leaned forward on his elbows, legs dangling below him, and stared at Kash.

"We could," Kash mumbled stubbornly.

They sat in silence for a bit. It was quiet enough to hear the breeze and Kash closed her eyes to relish it. It wouldn't be this calm, this private, for long. The PE classes would come out soon, to the game of capture the flag that was set up in the parking lot across the street.

"Would you live in a castle with me?" she blurted out.

Levi snorted.

Kash looked up at him questioningly.

"Yeah, sure." He nodded. "In *the* castle, why not."

"You would?"

"Yeah," he said, "we'd fill a room with books stacked floor to ceiling—"

"And plants."

Levi wrinkled his nose. "No."

Kash looked at him imploringly.

Levi rolled his eyes and conceded, "We'll have one of those huge greenhouses."

"On the grounds," Kash said.

Levi laughed.

"On the grounds," he said, looking at her warmly.

Kash smiled. She sighed and tilted her head up to look at the sky. It was clear, no clouds interrupting the vast blue. It was plain and beautiful.

"Thank you for indulging me," she said to Levi softly.

"I'd live anywhere with you, Blue."

She looked up at him.

"You're my best friend," he continued, "I'd go anywhere you go."

Kash's heart skipped a beat.

"We should have nicknames for each other for when we come home," she said casually.

Levi laughed. "We already do." He waved dramatically and yelled, "—Blue, I'm home!"

Kash joined in on his laughter, shaking her head.

"What about Lani and Raz?" she asked.

Levi paused, grin fading.

"Uh," he frowned, "I don't—know."

"We'll think of something for 'em," Kash said after a moment, waving her hand dismissively.

"Yeah," Levi muttered under his breath, nodding.

"I wish I could fast forward," Kash mused. "Wish we could just skip to the good parts."

"Assuming there are good parts to fast forward to," Levi said and Kash looked at him, watched the furrow between his brows deepen and then shallow out. "I guess, we just assume there are, then."

"Maybe." Kash nodded distantly. "Maybe that's what we do."

indulge my whims.

"What are you doing right now?"

Kash tucked her nose under the upturned collar of her jacket and shivered. "Battling the winds."

"Ah." She could hear the grin in Levi's voice. "Sounds intense."

Kash laughed softly, her breath fogging ever so slightly in the early blue winter sunset. In contrast, the passing storefronts and occasional trees all glowed warm with lights and decorations.

"It's all lit up here," she murmured. "Christmas lights everywhere. You should see it." Her eyes widened and she looked down at her thick black boots in embarrassment.

There was rustling from Levi's end followed by a soft thump that sounded a lot like falling into bed.

"Are you sleeping?" Kash asked.

"No, I'm still here."

She made an uncertain noise. "You can sleep. It must be late for you."

"I usually stay up until the ungodly hours anyway. Might as well spend my time talking to you, I'm doing it now already.

"Okay."

"It's *fine*, Kash."

"*Okay*." She switched hands to her left, tucking her frozen fingers into her pocket to warm up.

"It's like that here too, you know, with the Christmas lights and decorations everywhere. Can't walk five seconds without seeing Santa Claus or his reindeer, or his *elves*. But it has its moments. I was—," he started, breathing in and out like he was debating how best to tell a story, "—uh, like a year ago, walking back to the flat—"

Kash scrunched her nose fondly.

"—and I stopped at this sweet shop. I don't know why. I just didn't want to leave the holiday atmosphere just yet. And. There were so many kids inside, little feet running all over the place. You know those shoes your mom used to make you wear for our school holiday concerts?"

"Yeah," Kash said. "I hated those."

"I know. And there was this little girl, she had this hideous, adorable red dress with puffy sleeves, and she was wearing those shoes. With little green socks. I thought of you, of us. You, me, and Raz in our itchy holiday outfits, singing in front of a crowd of parents."

"A daunting sea of camcorders."

"Yeah," Levi laughed. "Yeah. Mamo might still have some tapes somewhere."

"God forbid those ever see the light of day," Kash said with a grin and hopped over another puddle, extending her front leg out in a leap.

"I don't know. I kind of miss being a child, Blue."

Air escaped her. "Oh."

"What? D'you step in slush or something?"

"No. What." She stumbled before racking up all the courage and eloquence she could apply. "No, just. Blue." She cringed and fisted her hand in her pocket, squeezing her eyes shut and tilting her head to the sky.

"Oh," Levi said softly, a warm fuzzy realization coloring his voice. "Oh, yeah. Is—that okay? It just. I'm just."

Kash dug her nails into her palm and bit her lip as hard as she could. She tasted blood not long after and dragged her teeth across the flesh of her bottom lip.

"I have you saved as Lovie," she blurted. "On my phone."

"Oh."

"It was a whim."

"This was too."

"Calling me Blue?"

"And picturing you in your seven-year-old glory. And likely a lot of things I do in regard to you."

I do a lot of things in regard to you.

"Likely a lot of things you do, in general," she countered.

Levi laughed and Kash realized she hadn't heard him laugh this much, this naturally, in a lifetime.

"You called me first, on a whim," he challenged.

"I called you first because I was being atomically pulled apart, and you seemed like my only option," she said before she could think. She paused on the sidewalk, eyes wide and heat blooming under the skin of her cheeks and ears and neck.

"If you hadn't been in danger of said atomic dismantling, would you have ever called me?" Levi asked, voice careful but almost earnest.

Kash held her breath until she reached her apartment building, all of thirty seconds or less. "I don't know," she said. "Maybe. Yeah. Eventually, somehow. Something would've still brought me reeling to you."

"Why?"

Kash shrugged. "You live on whim."

"So, we've decided."

"And I live on contemplation. And—," she took a deep breath, "—there's no way I would've been able to even play at sanity, when all of my contemplation leads to you, in some way, shape, or form." Her voice hung in the air, saccharine and heavy like some kind of whipped sugar. "And I'm not good at being insane. I'm quite insane now and I'm on my knees."

"That," Levi said, "almost sounded romantic."

Kash blanched at that, recoiling. "Insanity's romantic to you?"

Levi scoffed. "Okay. Don't be dramatic."

Kash barely tamped down the need to provoke him more and spiral into another argument. "Wait a minute," she muttered from between clenched teeth, before slipping her phone into the pocket of her jacket and wrestling her keys out. Her apartment was too warm, and she looked around to see Stella's jacket still missing from their standing coat rack. She hung hers up, keeping Levi on hold in her pocket for a few more moments while she leaned forward on the kitchen counter and tried to expel her anger through long, heavy sighs.

Her knees fell onto the waxed wood floor with a loud, painful thud and Kash heaved, chest rising and falling too fast, before pressing the back of her hand against her mouth and squeezing her eyes shut.

A distant ambulance siren brought her back into her body and she reached up clumsily into her coat pocket, fumbling a bit before her fingers closed around the cool surface of her phone.

"Kash?" Levi's voice was distant and shallow in the quiet air of the apartment.

She almost pressed the red end call button.

"Yeah, I'm here," she croaked.

Another siren went by, the sound reverberating from one end of the apartment to the other.

"I think someone's in trouble," Kash mumbled.

"Kash."

"*Yes.*"

"You—go on a whim."

Kash frowned. "What?"

Levi sighed, the sound cutting out in the grainy audio of Kash's phone. "Stop contemplating and go on a whim with me. Come here."

Go on a whim with me.

"Come… to you? To London?"

Levi laughed nervously and the sound surprisingly made a corner of Kash's mouth twitch up. "Yeah, yeah. Like, if you want. Not if you want, I mean, yes but. Please."

Please.

"You want," Kash said slowly.

"I want, Blue."

I want you.

Kash nodded. "Now?"

"Would you—would you get on a plane now, if I said yes?"

Kash laughed tiredly. "I think yeah, I would, maybe."

Levi made an aborted noise that pulled at Kash's heart so sharply she had to hunch over and hold her chest.

"Okay," he said, like he was about to make an indicting confession. "Yes. Please."

Kash inhaled sharply and nodded, chest expanded and agonizingly full, overflowing, with want and retrospect. "Send me your address."

"I'll send you a ticket."

Kash frowned, a smile creeping onto her lips a moment later. "Think I can't afford it?"

"No. You just. You focus on packing and getting to the airport on time."

"And what should I pack for?"

"This is a whim," he said with a short, breathless laugh. "Don't think too much."

Kash squeezed her eyes shut, fisted her hands, and made a face. She scrunched up her nose, grinned wide, almost a baring of teeth, and hunched her shoulders, hair falling over her face.

"So, I'm finally following in your footsteps, huh?" she murmured. "Following you across the world in a split second."

"It's hardly the world."

Kash hummed in acknowledgment, looking down at a chipped nail on her right hand. "Does feel like it, though."

She imagined he had a crumpled look on his face now, and guiltily savored the feeling of making him hurt a little while longer.

"Sorry," she said after a moment, wincing.

"No, you're right. It does."

It's okay to hurt me. I deserve as much.

let's run away, like, together.

Kash let out a relieved sigh as she ran over to the wooden bench by the tetherball pole.

Levi followed close behind, his footsteps crunching mutedly on the dried grass. He slung his backpack onto the table before sitting down with a heavy groan.

Kash sat on the same side as him, briefly leaning her face down against the rough wood of the table and savoring the small pricks from the worn, splintery surface.

"God, I haven't even started *Catcher* yet." Levi shook his head. "I have to read two chapters by tomorrow. And I have English Lit. first thing."

Kash rolled her eyes. "I sort of hate that book."

Levi leaned away, surprised. "You've *finished* it?"

Kash shrugged and simply said, "Yeah. Read it a long time ago."

Levi groaned again and slumped against the table, head between his arms and voice muffled against the sleeves of his puffer jacket.

"You have an *incredible* ability to pull things out of your ass, you'll be fine tomorrow." Kash laughed. "I'm the one that struggles, even if I know what I'm talking about."

Levi lifted his head, peeking out from behind his arms. His eyebrows were raised high, and Kash knew he was smirking.

"It's better to be actually smart than fake-smart."

Kash snorted.

"You're not *fake*-smart, Lovie," she said with a sarcastic grin.

"Just give me the low-down of what happens in the first three chapters." Levi gestured conversationally.

"It's not that hard to read, it's fine, it goes by quick. And the main character's angsty and sarcastic, and annoying, so that should be familiar."

"Hm, back at you," Levi grinned toothily. His cheeks were flushed from the late fall weather, and the light pink color made his freckles appear darker than usual.

Kash rolled her eyes and nuzzled farther into her jacket against the cool outside air.

"Sometimes I don't feel smart," Levi mumbled.

Kash frowned. "You have better grades than me. And I have good grades."

Levi shook his head with a smile. He sat up with a sigh and slid down the bench smoothly until he was pressed up against her.

"What are you doing?"

"I mean sometimes I feel inadequate," Levi continued.

"Why do you feel inadequate?" Kash asked, mouth curling into a confused frown.

"Like I'm acting you know? I don't like school, but everyone thinks I do because I try to do well most of the time. And sometimes I feel so unmotivated to do anything. Like I've used up all my, my, motivation energy on school and now I've got nothing left to do what I actually want. Like all I am is who I am at school, but that's fake. I'm pretending to like something that I really don't. And I don't want to be known for something that I don't like."

Kash stared at him, trying to process and understand what he was saying. Slowly, bits and pieces came together only for her to lose them again.

"What?" she asked dumbly after a moment.

Levi chuckled and shrugged. "I'll tell you again when I understand it better."

Kash nodded skeptically.

"You're not one-dimensional," she said. "If that's how you feel."

"To you, yeah." Levi gestured to her. "But not to, like, everyone else."

"Does that really matter?" Kash smiled knowingly and nudged him.

"I don't know, maybe it doesn't," Levi said, shaking his head.

"What do you want to be to everyone else?"

Levi looked down at his fingers, walking them back and forth across the table.

"I've been talking to Pops. I think I want to be a lawyer," he said.

Kash leaned away, scanning him for any sign of joking. The image of Levi as a lawyer was hard to conjure. Lawyers were hard and professional. Suits and perfect hair and sharp voices. She took in Levi's unruly red curls and overly chapped lips and old sacramento green jacket that occasionally shed soft white feathers.

She smiled. He was anything but.

"So, you're going to grow up and wear suits and every-thing?" Kash blurted out, trying to hide her grin.

"I can be a lawyer without wearing a suit." Levi wrinkled his nose.

Kash hummed thoughtfully, trying to downplay the cheeky grin on her face. "I don't think so. Dress shirts and slacks at the least."

Levi rolled his eyes and waved his hand dismissively. He made a sound of disinterest and assured, "I'll break the rules. Be a revolutionary lawyer. It'll work out, trust me."

Kash snorted. "*Revolutionary* lawyer?"

"Yeah. What do you want to be to everyone?" Levi asked quickly.

Kash blinked, taken aback by the question.

"I never said I wasn't already who I wanted to be," she said defensively.

Levi gave her an unimpressed look. "Come on," he drawled, "you're fourteen. There's no way you've already figured it out."

"So are you, Mr. Revolutionary Lawyer," Kash countered.

"Blue," Levi coaxed.

Kash rolled her eyes. "I don't know. I was always pretty open about writing, I guess, I love it and *Nanna*'s kind of always made sure I kept that."

"It takes a really cool parent, I think, to be like your dad," Levi said wistfully.

Kash shrugged her right shoulder nonchalantly. "I mean," she started, furrowing her brows as she looked up at the gray sky coming in through the surrounding mess of foliage-free branches, "it's a bit much right? *Nanna* gets so… I mean I tell him I like writing and now I think he expects me to do everything I can to be great at it. Like it's not just something I love, it's what I have to pursue *because* I love it."

Levi nodded intently, eyes fixed on her as she spoke. She looked away awkwardly and sighed out with a trill of her lips.

"I want to just love something, you know? That's it. No pressure to *do* anything—like I'm a freshman, I have no idea what I want to do and, I have to decide *now*, then what happens when I want to change, because that'll definitely happen."

"You're sure you're gonna want to change?" Levi asked.

Kash picked at a splinter of wood covered in a meager layer of moss. She pressed her fingertip against the point just hard enough to feel a blunt prick.

"Won't I?" she asked.

Levi curled his mouth down in a sign of "maybe."

"Rafi used to hide his songs when we were younger," Kash said softly. "He told me why but I mostly chalked it up to him being my weirdo ingenious older brother. I get it now, though."

Levi laughed at that. The sound echoed and Kash instinctually looked behind her and the school building to make sure nobody was coming out to check what was going on.

After a moment to confirm they were good, she shushed him sharply and got slightly distracted by the laughing flush on his cheeks. He was paler in the winter, so the dark pink color stood out more along with his freckles.

"You have less freckles in the winter," she murmured without thinking. An embarrassed warmth washed over her immediately and she sunk into her coat with a wince, zipping the collar up around her chin.

"Less sun, less freckles," Levi said. "Thanks for noticing after all these years, though."

Kash scoffed and shoved him away playfully.

He let out a sound of disbelief and fell back dramatically, back bending over the bench far enough for his head to touch the ground and his Adam's apple to protrude uncomfortably.

He swallowed and laughed dryly, the sound gurgling from his position. Kash made a face of disgust.

"The world looks better upside down, I think," he mused. His voice was tight and tinny, and the blood was starting to rush to his head. Veins bulged in a simple pattern along his temple and forehead. Kash grabbed the front of his jacket with a fond eyeroll and yanked him up harshly.

He cursed from the suddenness and cradled his head in his hands for a moment before confronting Kash with a mean stare.

She hadn't let go of the front of his jacket. She gripped it tightly, crumpling the soft synthetic material in her hand. The zipper line dug into her palm, but she ignored it in favor of focusing on the proximity of Levi's face to hers.

It was cold out, so the warmth of his breath was all the more apparent as it rushed against her chin. She frowned as her eyes darted between each of his. The bright gray daylight made him seem almost silvery, despite the golden strawberry color of his eyelashes and brows. His eyes were shiny, slightly watery against the cold and because he hadn't blinked since they'd frozen like this.

"Blue," he murmured. His breath was slightly metallic, and she looked down and noticed his bottom lip had split slightly along the right.

"Your lip's bleeding."

"Yeah, they're really chapped," Levi laughed softly and then winced as the split in his lip widened. "Probably opened up when I—" He made a gesture to mimic going upside down.

Kash nodded like it made sense.

"We should get away from it all," Levi said.

Kash tilted her head. "That's why we're skipping class."

Levi shook his head. His nose barely missed hers as he leaned forward a bit.

Her heartbeat quickened as she stayed rigid instead of moving away like her mind was screaming at her to do.

"No, I mean, like run away."

Kash widened her eyes and stared at the boy in front of her incredulously.

"Like, proper run away?" she asked in an unintentionally high-pitched voice.

"Yeah, yeah. I don't know. Maybe. Someday. Soon." Levi's voice grew smaller and smaller as he spoke until he was barely above a whisper.

Kash bit back a smile.

"Like, together? The two of us? Or the three of us?" she asked.

"Who, Raza?"

"Yes!" she laughed out loud.

Levi flinched gently against the puff of air from her laughter. The curly baby hairs along his crown fluttered slightly and Kash became enamored with them for a short second.

"I was thinking the two of us, but. I think I might love Raza a little more than I love you anyway, so I'd actually rather run away with him," Levi said cheekily.

Kash let go of his jacket to push him away and watched in fond amusement as he fell back against the bench with a cushioned thud.

"All right, let's run away together, then," Kash said matter-of-factly. "Let's do it, Lovie. I'll pack the bags, you steal your grandparents' money, Raza'll come with his mom's food, and we'll run away with a few suitcases and an icebox."

Levi narrowed his eyes at her. "Don't patronize me. I'm serious, I'm pretty sure I hate this place. I've been here too long. I want to move on. Preferably with you because you're one of the few things I don't want to ever move on from."

Kash froze in shy awe. She smirked at him and bit the inside of her cheek. Her hands clenched the fabric of her baggy denim pants and she let out an embarrassed, disbelieving laugh.

Levi nodded pointedly, features schooled into a serious, sincere expression.

"You and Raz," he said, "sometimes Mamo and Pops because they're everything and raised me when no one else would and I'd be terrible if they weren't on the list."

Kash nodded back in agreement. "Yeah. Who else?"

"Nobody."

"Nobody?"

Levi shook his head and looked at her earnestly, but she couldn't decipher if it was genuine or not.

"Oh, and—" he cut himself off.

Kash frowned. "What?"

"And your dad," he added with an unmistakable air of false sobriety. "He's my favorite member of the Narahari-Blue family."

Kash spluttered before slapping him upside the head and descending into incredulous laughter.

I'd run away with you in two seconds.

I'd hesitate for one and grab your hand within the other.

"When we grow up, it'll be away from here," Levi sighed out after they both calmed down.

Kash looked out across the field between the school building and their bench. The grass was practically grayscale, dead and dry and covered in a thin crunchy layer of frost.

"We're fourteen, what do we know," Kash murmured. "Except for breaking the rules and wanting to run away."

"Nothing I guess. At least we're not complete delinquents," Levi said.

Kash laughed softly. "No, we're not. We've got a good… facade going, right?"

"Right."

Kash nodded decidedly, eyes still wandering across the faraway details of the school building they'd been going to for the past three and a half years. Another three and a half to go.

tell me how, then.

She walked out of Levi's bathroom, right hand holding her hair up in a ponytail. The plane ride over was still weighing on her eyelids and she tried to blink away the heaviness. Her feet padded dully against the wood floor. Fancy, she thought, for such a simple space. The walls were plain white. She figured Levi would have at least one wall of exposed brick but so far she was disappointed.

"Is it not what you expected?"

She looked up as she walked into the kitchen and noticed Levi leaning against the counter with his arms crossed. She shrugged.

"No."

His eyebrows rose, mouth opening slightly in surprise. He'd been joking, then.

A part of her felt immediately guilty for being so blunt.

"I mean," she mended, "I just got here. I'm just taking it in."

"Oh," Levi murmured, nodding to himself. He looked down into his mug of tea, as if he were about to dive into it. She wondered if he'd ever actually tried. To disappear into the dark liquid, into the aromatic nothingness, and never come back up for air.

"Do you have an extra elastic, by any chance?" Kash asked awkwardly, indicating her meaning by lifting her hair. Levi looked up suddenly, with such abruptness and force that it made Kash take a startled step back.

"Oh, yeah. Of course." He began nodding vigorously, head bobbing like one of those dancing dolls her mom kept on the fireplace mantel. It was comical to watch, and she felt a fond smile briefly turn the corners of her mouth.

"All right, don't break yourself," she murmured under her breath, feeling obligated to nod with him.

"What?"

"Hm?"

"You said something?"

She stared at him, contemplating for a long minute.

"I said don't break yourself," she repeated loudly. There was a pause then. Both of them stared at each other with wide, calculating eyes. Just as she began to admonish every time she had ever opened her mouth to form words—

Levi laughed. A bright, red-cheeked laugh that ignited something familiar in the space between them.

"Right, yeah," he breathed out, still laughing, "sorry. Just can't believe you're here is all."

Kash smiled back and they both stood there like happy, absentminded children.

After a few moments, the ache in Kash's arm throbbed too much to ignore and she lifted it in emphasis.

Levi's eyes darted to her hair and his brows arched up toward his hairline.

"Right," he blurted and then gestured for her to follow him into the bathroom.

She watched as he opened the top right drawer underneath the sink and revealed an array of hair ties and clips.

"I think you have more accessories than me," she commented with a raised eyebrow. Levi scoffed and grabbed a blue scrunchie, offering it to her with slight petulance.

She couldn't help but grin. She dropped her arm and let her hair fall down her back. She turned to face the mirror and gestured to Levi.

"You tie a mean bun," she said, nodding to the way his hair was tied together haphazardly.

He rolled his eyes and stepped forward, coming close enough for his toes to bump against her heels. He gathered her hair gently in his hands, raking his fingers from the crown of her head up into the ponytail.

"'S grown," he said quietly. "I mean, it was long before obviously, but I thought you would've cut it more in the meantime."

Kash shrugged.

Levi carefully wrapped the scrunchie around her hair, curling it around and slipping it through the loop of the scrunchie.

Kash glanced at him through the mirror before settling on her own reflection. She didn't like how conscious she was of how she looked right now, tired from the plane ride over and nervous about being inches away from Levi after so long. It had been years, and a part of her knew that she was not the same person he had memorialized in his mind. Nor was he the same boy she had memorialized in hers.

"There you go," he murmured, his hands settling on her shoulders for a moment before he swallowed and stepped back with a slight jolt. "You can fix it if you want," he said before walking out of the bathroom.

Kash sighed out, slumping slightly. She took one last look at her reflection, tightened her bun, and flicked the light off as she left. She walked back into the common area and found Levi looking out the window. She looked around, taking in the kitchen area and the TV in one corner just barely concealing a mess of cables behind it. She settled her gaze on Levi, taking in the large flat planes of his shoulders and back. She remembered being able to curl her fingers easily around his bicep, with just one hand. Now, Kash thought, she would have to use both. She traced her eyes along his silhouette and then darted her gaze to the window. The dark night sky allowed a clear, warm reflection of the interior. She could see herself in the window and saw the exact moment Levi noticed her. He turned around.

"Are you hungry?"

"You asked me that in the car."

Levi shrugged. "Just making sure your answer hasn't changed since then."

"It hasn't."

She couldn't stop herself from staring at the queen bed situated opposite to the TV. She still couldn't look at him, even as she sensed him tilt his head to get her attention. It was decorated with messy blankets and assorted pillows, and she focused on the dark folds and creases of his gray bed sheets.

"Do you want some tea?" he asked.

She shook her head. She heard him sigh out slowly and imagined him rolling his eyes.

The last time she saw him roll his eyes was almost three years ago.

"Are you not going to look at me at all?"

She tried to. Burning tears began to distort her vision. Bed sheet folds turned into blurry lines, blending gray into darker gray.

"Hey, is something the matter?"

She shook her head. "No, no, I'm fine."

Her voice wasn't shaky, there wasn't an ounce of upset in her tone. Maybe that's what allowed him to stand there and not walk over to her and brush a thumb against her cheek.

A loud, needy part of her wished he would.

"What time is it?" she asked. Tears overflowed, surface tension breaking, and she brushed them away as soon as they spilled down her cheeks. Her vision cleared and she willed herself to look at him one more time, gaze successfully landing on him. She blinked, expelling any future tears.

"It's eleven?" he said, like a question.

"I'm a bit sleepy," she said carefully. His eyebrows furrowed, eyes lighting up with understanding. His mouth formed a full-lipped "o" and he walked over to her with measured steps.

"I've only one bed," he said slowly and gently, perhaps to test the waters.

"You told me that in the car."

"I know, but I feel like I have to say it again. You know, just to make sure."

"Make sure of what?" she asked, inching closer to him by scrunching her toes on the floor and pulling her heels forward.

"That you're okay with it. If not I can totally sleep on the floor—it's just cold is all." He ran a hand through his hair and looked down shyly. It was uncharacteristic of him to feel bashful about anything.

"We've slept together before," she offered and immediately wanted to take it back. A deep, burning embarrassment washed over her as Levi's gaze darted up. Wide hazel eyes stared at her and she winced.

"Not like that, I mean—"

"I know what you mean," Levi murmured, eyes still wide and unnervingly unreadable. His golden lashes blinked slowly.

"When we were kids," she explained, still caught in his trance-like gaze.

He blinked and grinned suddenly before saying, "Well, we're not kids anymore."

Kash shook her head.

Levi grabbed hold of her wrist and led her over to the bed.

His bed. Not a sleeping bag on the floor or a pile of blankets in a makeshift fort. His own bed that he slept in.

"Your flatmate won't mind—what's his name again?"

Levi looked at her over his shoulder, eyebrows slightly furrowed.

"Oh. We… had a falling out. This is just my place."

Kash paused and stared at him. Her hand fell out of his grip. He had not told her this.

"I thought you were—"

"Nope," he said, popping the "p."

Kash threw her hands up, looking around as if she could find an answer for his idiocy somewhere in the flat.

"Why did you not, like, I don't know, *tell me*? What happened? I know *nothing*."

Levi shrugged nonchalantly and she bristled.

"I just did. Now don't be dramatic and get in bed. I'll turn off the lights."

Kash spluttered, "I'm not being dramatic."

Levi raised an eyebrow and pinned her with a pointed look.

"Then why'd you bring it up?" he asked.

Kash shrugged, feeling called out and thoroughly embarrassed.

"You know, just to make sure," she parroted.

Levi let out a breathy laugh and shook his head like he knew what was going on, like he'd already read her mind and found whatever he'd learned highly amusing.

"Make sure of what?" he answered back with twinkling eyes.

She felt an overwhelming urge to slap him upside the head and tackle him onto the ground. He was tall now, almost a head above her which she didn't expect. They'd always been close in height, but she reminded herself that it had been more than three long years since the last time she'd seen him.

"That I'm not intruding on anything," she admitted softly, unable to look at him. She scrutinized the pilling along his sleeve and watched as his arms moved slightly as he sighed out.

"What could you possibly be intruding on? I told you to come. So obviously I'd make sure you weren't."

She looked up at him then, a sense of betrayal hanging low in her chest.

Levi's eyes widened in recognition, and he immediately began shaking his head. He grabbed hold of her upper arms and tugged her closer.

"No, no, no, no, no," he said quickly. He was shaking his head so violently that his hair began to fall loose from his bun, and soon his face was framed by messy red curls, falling just below his jaw. "Not because of you."

She felt hot where his hands squeezed her upper arms. Bony fingers in soft flesh.

"Let's go to sleep," she croaked, looking down at the bed in tired apprehension.

"Blue," Levi coaxed, a scared tinge in his voice. He didn't relinquish his grip, even as she took a step back.

"It's been a long day." She looked up at him, focusing on his eyes. They were almond-shaped and hazel and brilliant just like she remembered, probably the only thing about him that remained the same. Her gaze fluttered around his face, taking in the smooth baby hairs and curly locks. He'd grown it out to a properly royal length, like a prince.

She pressed her hands to where he gripped her arms and wiggled her fingers underneath his. With a bit of effort, she peeled his hands off her skin and held them, interlocking their fingers like a second thought.

Levi kneeled on the mattress first, backing up clumsily to the far side. Then Kash joined and only until the last second before they lay down did she let go of him.

She felt a need to apologize. The words wouldn't come out, though, so she stayed silent. She usually did more damage trying to fix things anyway.

"I have to turn off the lights," Levi muttered into the heavy quiet.

Kash looked over at him.

"I'll do it." She felt responsible, like a new guest. Which she was, she thought, she was a new guest in his new life in his new flat in his new bed.

She got up quickly, ignoring the painful head rush making her vision swim momentarily. She began walking, ending up in the hallway, before realizing she didn't know where she was going.

"Um," she breathed out, blinking, and looking around.

"By the sink, just to the right. It's underneath the cupboard," he offered with a fond smile, waving his hand in the direction of the kitchen area.

She huffed and walked purposefully over to the sink, feet thudding loudly as she scanned for a switch. She found a pair and reached out before pausing, fingers hovering over both.

"The right one," Levi called.

She pressed the right one. The lights went out and suddenly the only things visible were illuminated with faint gray moonlight. She looked over at the bed and held in a breath.

His silhouette was outlined in a soft glow, like old black-and-white film. His eyes twinkled and she faintly remembered how blinding they were in the sun, reflecting sunshine like two all-seeing prisms. She tilted her head and regarded him for a reverent moment. They weren't as blinding now, more like twin fires, reminding her of a long-lived connection.

She made her way quietly over to the bed, flicking her hair over her shoulder before leaning down onto the mattress. She climbed into the mess of blankets and lay down on her back, aware of Levi watching her. She heard him fuss a bit and looked over to see him turning on his back, intently staring up like he was tracing constellations in the white plaster. They stayed like that, trying to ignore the heaviness surrounding them.

After a few fragile moments of withholding, Kash couldn't stop herself. "I don't want to ruin or derail your life."

She pressed her lips together, using all of her willpower to not add more. One sentence was damaging enough. She felt Levi tense beside her, bedsheets moving minutely with small rustling sounds.

After a painfully long minute, he confessed softly, "You could never."

She held her breath. There was no way. He must know that all she'd ever done was barge into his life and take what she wanted and then leave everything in a mess.

"I know I have," she insisted quietly, letting her breath out in a long, shaky sigh.

Levi scoffed and shook his head. "Don't be like that."

"Like what?"

"Like," he paused, probably searching for the right words, "you're the cause of every problem."

Kash winced. "I don't intend to be self-pitying."

"You're not."

Kash nodded. "Okay, good."

"It's just," he started. He reached a hand up toward the ceiling, wiggling his thin fingers. After a few seconds, he continued, "I mean, it's a two-way street. You know, obviously you're important to me but that wouldn't matter if I wasn't important to you."

You're important to me.

"Why wouldn't it matter?"

She felt him shrug.

"Because you wouldn't be here if that wasn't the case. You wouldn't have—you didn't *have* to come. I've asked for a lot of things that you've refused, so you didn't have to come. I mean, if anyone is derailing anyone's life, it's me derailing yours."

Kash frowned. "No, you're not. What's there to derail?" She momentarily remembered that the only warning of her absence she'd left Stella with was a sticky note on the fridge. A part of her thought maybe she wasn't any better than the boy in front of her.

"And," Levi continued, "you wouldn't be worrying about possibly ruining my life."

"I always worry about that now." The words escaped her before she could stop them.

Levi stayed silent for a moment, eyes trained on the ceiling. She watched him, mesmerized by the quiver of his lower lid. He looked upset for a minute. She could tell by the clench of his jaw.

Then he turned over on his side to face her and blinked once, slowly.

"That's a terrible way to love someone."

His words hung in the air for a moment. A sense of accusation itched at her.

How do *you love someone, then?*

She almost opened her mouth to voice the question out loud. Boldly ask him the route he might advise on how to best love someone. How most *efficiently* to love someone, she thought viciously. The path of least resistance.

She asked him in her mind, demanding him to answer her somehow. She swallowed sand as he closed his eyes and turned on his back to face the ceiling once more. She watched his chest rise and fall, air flowing in and out of his nose at a steady pace. Occasionally, the pattern would break, staccato interrupting the smooth inhale, and for a second she would stupidly anticipate something.

An hour could've gone by. Two. Three. Four. No more than six, she confirmed blankly, since the sky outside remained black. She had moved back to staring at the ceiling sometime in that blurry period of time. Drying tracks traced down her temples and saltwater pooled uncomfortably in the conch of her ear.

She could unnervingly sense Levi sleeping. She felt each of his light breaths like spiders crawling on her skin. She shivered in disgust. Her face scrunched up, throat constricting painfully. The familiar broken glass lump formed in the back of her throat and the welcome painful burn ignited in the corners of her eyes. She drew in a shaky breath and pressed the back of her hand against her mouth. She squeezed her eyes shut, tears once again forming rivers down dried track beds, and spilling onto the pillow beneath her. She tried her best not to make a sound, aware of the delicate sleep the boy next to her was in.

She wondered how he could sleep so simply, disregarding whatever he'd meant by his last words. She had an urge to shake him awake and pull the answers out of him, but she stopped herself by digging her nails into the side of her thigh and pressing her fist harder against her mouth until her teeth pushed painfully against her lips. Her muscles were clenched, every part of her body painfully tensed, and half of her wished Levi would wake up right now and hold her face and explain to her *how*. The other half of her screamed and yearned to quietly sink into the mattress without Levi ever knowing she existed. A thought pulled at her, like jewelry caught on a sweater. Tiny pin pricks all along her spine, across her cheeks, and down her stomach.

I don't know how to love someone.

i can['t] put it in words for you.

It was a casual affair. After dinner, Kash had said she needed air. Levi had agreed to come along. Now they were facing a dotted white, slippery expanse of pavement and slow vehicles and Kash was using the quiet sereneness of a mild snowstorm to confess her thoughts.

She glanced at Levi. He was all bundled up in a dark blue wool coat. His chin was hiding under a soft red scarf that matched the stray curls escaping his unruly bun. He was looking at her with wide, puzzled eyes.

"So, you—I'm sorry, I'm still lost," Levi sighed heavily, scratching his head in endearing confusion.

Kash shook her head. "It's fine. I just mean—" She took a deep breath. "—At least, it's not black and white. It's kind of blurry. A gray area."

Levi nodded attentively.

"So, you didn't like being with Evan?" he asked. "Or anyone else?"

Kash sighed, "I don't *know*. I've wanted too many people in my life to think that I wouldn't ever go through with it. It's just, as soon as I start to go beyond wanting, as soon as I start to… as things get real—"

"You want out," Levi finished.

Kash nodded.

"So, you don't like being more than friends. Or more than the space in between friendship and a relationship?"

Kash winced. "Uh. It's… like for example, I like being your friend."

She paused and glanced at him nervously, gauging her next words. "And I like being more. Or the idea of it, or whatever," she added quietly.

Levi frowned and nodded again.

"But," Kash continued, "it's not—it's neither romantic, nor platonic. It's in between. But also, neither? Honestly, it's just… tiring to be anything more. But that doesn't mean I don't want to be with someone. At all."

No response.

"Does that make any sense to you? Or am I just—"

"No," Levi said, "no, it makes sense. I think."

"Okay," Kash said, watching him carefully. "It doesn't make any sense to me."

He pursed his lips and shook his head slowly as he said, "I don't, um, I don't really like being your friend, by the way."

It was a private admission that was dampened by the swirling snow, but it registered to her ears nonetheless.

She breathed in slowly, taking in the sharp cold air. "Well, that's alarming considering we've been running this our whole lives," she said lightly.

Levi scoffed and pushed her away with two gloved hands. They both laughed softly, basking in a fleeting warm familiarity.

"I know I've said it's beautiful here before, but I'm not sure if I like the snow," Kash mused. "It makes it look too much like home."

"I think it's nice."

Kash nodded, agreeing, "Yeah, it is." She looked at him and added, "Don't have to like it if it's nice, though. You can think something is nice without wanting it."

Levi shrugged and nodded thoughtfully, and they both spent the next few moments watching occasional headlights illuminate beams of falling snow in growing and fading movements.

"I do think about you sometimes," she confessed quietly.

"What?"

They'd been standing on the side of the street for over an hour. It was likely dangerous.

"What about me do you think about?" Levi asked.

"I don't know," she said, reaching one arm out and turning her palm upward to face the sky, collecting snowflakes on the black fabric of her mitten. "Should we go?"

"Do you think about me as someone you want?"

Kash didn't dare move, didn't dare answer.

He waited a moment before letting out a resolute sigh. He looked at her through the corner of his eye and said, "Yeah. Let's go."

They began walking, feet crunching through the slushy snow. They were quiet for the short walk back to Levi's, carefully crossing streets and passing other people.

Kash tried to ignore the similarities between here and New York City but focusing on the differences was almost just as bad, if not worse. London felt homey, though, where New York felt foreign.

Warmth bled in through the layers of clothing between their skin as she kept her arm looped through his until they were standing in front of the old brick building. She wondered, anxiously, if passing people took them for a couple. With the snow, and their perfectly in sync cadence as they walked, she almost made the same mistake multiple times until they were standing in front of the old brick building Levi lived in.

"You know, you've not changed at all," he said, looking down at her. She frowned and dropped her hands from his arm.

"'S a good thing," he reassured her, grabbing her hands and placing them back where they were. "Mostly."

Kash raised an eyebrow and he answered with a doltish grin.

They entered the building, dusted their boots off on the mat, and clumsily made their way up the stairs side by side, laughing softly.

"I don't like being your friend," he repeated gently as he turned the key in the lock of his door.

"I heard you the first time."

Levi sighed and shrugged. "But we've been crossing that line for a while now, haven't we? And I'm fine with it," he added quickly, like a disclaimer, before continuing, "I just—I think maybe this is an opportunity? After, running this our whole lives, as you said?"

They both walked into the flat, taking off their jackets and winter accessories.

"You don't…" Kash started, a panic rising and squeezing her lungs. "What, so you want to finally get together like normal people? Is that it?"

Levi wrinkled his nose like his answer was the most obvious thing. "I mean, yeah?"

Kash blanched.

She hadn't expected him to actually say *yes*.

"Did you even comprehend what I told you?" she practically yelled.

Levi nodded dutifully.

Kash threw her arms up helplessly, "*Levi*. I like sleeping in the same bed as you. You're always so fucking warm. I'm always freezing. It works. And it's nice because we're close, we're best friends and all that."

Levi opened his mouth. She held her hand up.

"But," she continued, searching for words to make him understand, "I don't—I can't just, I mean—I have no idea what to do when we're kissing."

He looked baffled. "Wha—we're not kissing *now*?"

She groaned. "That's not what I—I know. But we would, right? That's what normal people do? And I don't, I don't know how. I don't know what to do."

The right corner of his mouth curled up teasingly. "Are you telling me you don't know how to kiss?" he asked. "After all these years?"

Kash stared at him, at his boyish demeanor, at the way his brows rose suggestively and the way his impish grin lit up his face.

"That's not—" Kash let out a frustrated sound, a small fond smile sneaking its way onto her face, "Oh my *god*. You haven't changed one bit, either. Still as fucking annoying as ever."

Levi lifted a shoulder indicatively and grinned. "It's been too long for things not to've changed, Blue," he murmured.

Kash hummed in agreement and threw her coat and gloves onto a nearby chair.

Levi did the same and looked at her.

"I won't ask for anything, okay? I just—I miss you. You're like home to me," he said sincerely. "And three years is a long time to be away from… you."

You're like home to me.

Kash felt the air in her lungs dissipate into nothing. She clenched her fists involuntarily and dug her teeth into her bottom lip. A familiar force coaxed her forward, and she stumbled closer to Levi.

"Lovie," she sighed out, using the nickname as stable ground to stand upon. She reached out and wrapped her arms around his torso and pressed into him, squeezing firmly. She felt Levi hesitate before he reciprocated. They both settled into the familiar hug, like falling into place.

It had been six years since she'd hugged him like this. It felt like rushing back into childhood and growing up all at once.

"'M sorry, you know," Levi admitted softly. "I realize it's my fault."

Kash huffed against his chest. She looked up at him, digging her chin lightly into his sternum. "Still can't believe you're taller than me now," she muttered.

Levi rolled his eyes.

"I was running away when I first called you," she confessed quietly, tucking her head back underneath Levi's chin. "Missed my best friend, yeah. I hated who I was, who I am."

"Why?"

Kash shrugged slightly.

"I get it," Levi said softly, voice slightly lower than before, like he was reluctantly revealing a secret, "I'm not a fan of myself, either, to be honest."

"For the past six years," Kash said, "I pictured you with this perfect life. I believed that picture. That you're absolutely content and far better than everyone you left behind."

"I'm not, obviously."

Kash nodded. "Yeah, well, picturing you happy somewhere far away was good fuel to hate you."

Levi stiffened.

"Because I was so, so sad," Kash continued, swallowing the lump in her throat with difficulty, "and it's so much easier to be angry."

Levi squeezed her tightly, and she melted into him.

She'd forgotten how good he was at hugging. They hadn't even touched in years. She wanted to keep touching him until all the tightness in her chest and shoulders and feet eased into nothing. He was capable of that.

"Can we hug for a little longer?" she asked in a whisper. "You're warm."

"Yeah," Levi pressed his cheek against hers, "yeah, of course."

She whispered a thanks.

"And," Levi said softly, voice hesitant but sincere, "you know I'll always want you."

Kash squeezed her eyes shut.

I want you.

"I don't how to do anything more than want," Kash said. "Anything more and suddenly I need to run away, I don't know why."

"Is that what happened with Evan?"

Kash nodded. "It's what happens with everyone."

And yet, here I am.

"Lucky I'm the type that runs away, too, then," Levi said.

Kash laughed and slapped his back playfully.

Of course, you are. We're the same, aren't we?

"I know you are," she said, smile fading into a serious gaze. She looked at him leisurely. It was the first time in years she'd looked at anyone that way, taking her time to travel across every inch she could see.

"Would you ever?" Levi asked.

"Ever what?" Kash frowned in confusion.

"Be okay with, you know, me and you."

Kash hummed, looking into familiar hazel eyes that were now wide with sincerity. She leaned out of the embrace and grabbed both of his hands. "Come with me for a second," she explained softly.

Levi followed as she led him gingerly to the bed. He gave her a confused look and she nodded with assurance.

They both lay down side by side, sinking into the unmade bed.

Kash was acutely aware of the inches of distance between their hands and bodies. She braced herself and sighed out shakily.

"In another universe," she started, voice soft and timid and earnest, "I have you. In every way. We're lying on the floor with all the windows and doors open and it's raining outside so we let it in."

She could hear her breathing turn heavy and loud and tried not to pay too much attention to it. She squeezed her hands into fists before uttering her next words.

"I love you," she all but whispered.

Levi inhaled slowly and Kash listened to the uneven sound as he exhaled.

"And you love me," she continued. "And it's *even*. There's no higher ground, no giving or taking. We just—we exist in love with each other. It's just a constant state of being—like breathing—so there's no way you could love me more than I love you because that would mean you'd have to *exist* more than me and that's just—," Kash laughed nervously, "—that's just nonsense."

Levi was silent as Kash mustered up the courage to continue.

Her heartbeat blended together into a continuous pressure in her chest. She almost thought she'd forsaken the need to breathe, because it didn't feel like she was. Every minute detail of the way she was alive itched at her consciousness.

"Okay," Levi murmured after what felt like a lifetime. "Go on."

Kash steeled herself and continued, "We'd be on the floor and our fingers would touch—," she entangled her fingers with his before she could second-guess it, "—and we'd stare up at the ceiling and it would be covered in creeper vines like an old stone house."

"You still want to live in an old house?" Levi cut in.

Kash faltered and shrugged. "I mean, I guess—I want to live in a place with history? And… I want to live anywhere you are."

She could hear Levi's smile in his voice as he spoke.

"So," he said, "we're lying on the floor in our house of history with creeper vines and rain. What else?"

"I turn over and look at you—"

She turned over and looked at him just as he did the same.

"And suddenly the roof cracks and the rain seeps through and lands on your face and I," she hesitated, "I kiss you."

The surprised look on Levi's face made her smile.

"Normally," she said. "It's ordinary and meaningful like it happens every day. Like it's nothing and everything at once, yeah?"

"Yeah," Levi whispered.

"And that's it. We're young and in love in the rain."

"Are we happy?" he asked.

Kash paused before answering, "Yes. Of course. Existentially."

"Imagine that," Levi said, a certain reverence in his tone. He reached a hand out to curl around Kash's cheek.

She relished in the warmth and leaned up into it.

"But for now, in this world," Kash whispered, "wanting is enough. Or it isn't, but it's all I'm ready to do. Everything else is… unknown and not for me."

"I understand," Levi said.

Kash turned over on her side to face him.

"You remember in freshman year," he said, "we were sitting on the bench next to the tetherball, and we made a—"

"—plan to run away," Kash finished. She watched Levi bite down on his bottom lip nervously.

"Would you, I mean, obviously I know we've both got jobs and whatnot now, and it's a bit simpler when you're teenagers, but," Levi paused, taking a deep breath, and capturing Kash's eyes with his own. His fingers ran over her skin as he moved his hand down to frame her neck gently. Bony fingers in soft flesh.

Kash's heart raced. "Are you asking me to run away right now?" she asked, a combination of awe and amusement making her voice light and breathy.

Levi shrugged. "In a sense. If you want. For the night, for the week. For the month, even, if you're up for the damage control that'll require after."

Kash stared at him like he was crazy, like he was her other half, like he was all the right things in all the right places.

"Where to?" she murmured.

The smile Levi awarded her was beautiful and nostalgic and it brought out a delicious ache in her chest and suddenly they were children again and he was chasing her through the woods and she danced in and out of the sunlight sneaking in through the foliage, and she looked back at him and he grinned at her in the familiar way that filled her stomach with butterflies and she relished the feeling.

my destination is you.

They had been walking for a while, side by side. Both of them were dressed warmly against the cool morning air. It wasn't even fully light out, but Levi'd woken her up around four in the morning and insisted that they leave to a destination that was still unknown to her.

Kash was still cranky with lingering sleep and Levi was annoyingly awake and lively, and she had to stop herself from hitting him for it multiple times on their trek over to the parking space down the street.

Once they reached it, Levi ushered her toward the left side of the car.

"Get in, get in," Levi coaxed gently.

"Please tell me where we're going, it's so early," she whined. She frowned at the brightness in his eyes and the way his freckles stood out against his skin in the fresh morning light.

"When did you become a morning person?" she asked grumpily, settling into the cold car seat with a full-bodied shiver.

Levi laughed as he turned on the engine.

"Since I'm finally running away with you," he said with an impish grin.

Kash froze. All the sleepiness evaporated and suddenly she felt a chill run through her body. The kind of chill she felt before something equally exciting and terrifying was going to happen.

"We're actually doing it?" she asked incredulously.

Levi nodded seriously, eyebrows raised, like a child.

Kash poked her tongue against the inside of her cheek to quell the smile sneaking onto her face. "We haven't packed anything."

Levi shook his head. "Don't worry about that."

"How long're we heading out for?"

"That's not important right now."

"All right." Kash leaned forward and asked with a teasing grin, "Where are you taking us, Kissinger?"

"Just, don't fall asleep. The car ride's the best part, what makes it actually feel like we're running away."

Kash smiled and shook her head. She reached a hand out to tuck behind Levi's back, pressing against his shoulder blade, and looked out the window peacefully.

This felt like old times, but to her happy surprise, it didn't hurt. She breathed in the feeling deeply, inhaling and exhaling without any pressure in her chest or hunger for more.

They drove for an indistinct amount of time, but Kash figured it'd been a couple of hours when she unwittingly fell asleep and opened her eyes to the sun midway in the sky.

"You fell asleep on me," Levi said with playful accusation.

"Sorry," Kash muttered, wincing as she stretched as much as the confined space let her.

"You want some crisps? I picked up some sustenance while you were sleeping."

"Crisps?" Kash said skeptically, a teasing smile curling her lips.

Levi rolled his eyes and reached down behind his seat. He rummaged around before they heard the telltale crinkle of a foil chips bag. He threw it at her gracelessly and she shot him a look.

"You're gravely mistaken," Kash teased. "These are chips."

"We'll stop for lunch at the next travel plaza, if you want," Levi said, shaking his head at her in amusement. He had a bag of cookies in his lap, and he tossed one in his mouth with a smile, biting down with an audible crunch.

Kash looked out the window and noticed the land on either side of the highway was now snow-covered and vast. It was beautiful and infinite, going on almost entirely uninterrupted into the horizon line of distant hills and mountains.

"Wow," she sighed out.

"Yeah, I told you the drive was the best part. I could leave you here with a notebook if you want. You'd be a writer in the English countryside. It'd be fitting, if not cliché."

Kash pursed her lips and shook her head.

"I don't want to be a writer," she murmured. A part of her winced at the half lie. It was an oversimplification of the truth, of what was really going on, but the thought of having to explain everything was intensely exhausting.

"What?"

She looked at Levi and shrugged. "I mean, it's not like I don't want to write, I just…" She sighed, looking down at her fingers before looking up at him with a cheeky smile. "I'm not an author or anything. Isn't the cliché being an author in the English countryside?"

Levi shrugged, eyebrows furrowed seriously. "A writer in New York is just as cliché," he said, biting down on another cookie.

Oh.

Something heavy pulled at Kash's heart and she felt it sink into the moving road below them, becoming a painted streak on the cold pavement.

"I, um," Kash started. Everything in her stopped the words from coming out, but the sincere look in Levi's eyes reminded her just how many of her secrets he'd held onto in the past. She nodded weakly.

"I don't want to go back," she admitted. "To New York. Ever."

"Ever?" Levi asked with a frown.

Kash shook her head and let out a self-deprecating laugh. "It's stupid, because I'm the one that fought to go, but I don't know."

"Just because you wanted something, doesn't mean you're going to actually end up liking it. It's not—you're not stupid, Kash."

"Yeah, I know, but. Like, sometimes I feel like I'll never fully want something forever? That I'm just meant to be nomadic in every aspect of my life." She looked at Levi apprehensively, who was watching her with an infuriatingly unreadable expression.

"Are we supposed to have static desires?" he asked.

The question hung in the air, and she looked over at him.

He looked back at her in darts, eyes struggling to multi-task and focus on the road while meaningfully meeting her gaze.

Kash made a face, not tearing her eyes away from Levi's even if the constant motion was making her dizzy. "Well, I mean, yeah, right? Marriage. Jobs. Kids. They're pretty fucking permanent."

"So, you don't like writing anymore?"

"No," Kash immediately said, defensive. Her fingers twitched against her thighs, and she pressed her lips together while she strained to try and gather her thoughts. "No, it's not that I don't like it," she explained. "It's just—I'm tired of it. I'm starting to, I think, I just tire of things really easily even if I like them. Even if I love them."

"Are you going to grow tired of me one day?"

His question was a punch to her gut. She choked out and clutched at her stomach.

I don't want to ever grow tired of you.

She looked up at him in confusion, wondering if he truly believed the possibility. "I don't want to grow tired of anything, or anyone," she said in a small, solemn voice.

"But you just said you can't—"

"Do you know how exhausting it is to have to rediscover everything over and over again? To have to find what I want, again and again, because I just can't make up my mind no matter how many times I try?"

"No, I don't," Levi said, voice rough, eyes fixed on the road.

"And a part of me is so terrified that I'll get tired of wanting things altogether, and then—where does that leave me? Wanting's all I have. It's—it's what drives me. Fucking insane."

"Is that what brought you here?"

"Well, yeah."

"Wanting?"

Kash paused and looked at him. "Yeah," she whispered. "But not like. Not like that, you know? I just didn't want to feel like a creep anymore. Wanted to be familiar. And you're familiar. In a way I think I'm inclined to rely on for a bit."

Levi sighed and switched hands on the steering wheel. He used his newly freed left hand to rest against the edge of Kash's seat, like an invitation. "I'm not saying just wanting things is bad. I'd be a hypocrite. But being stuck wanting things and watching the world pass by as others get there first, doesn't sound like a—a content way to live," Levi said.

"I don't want to be content. I want to be *normal*."

"Why?" Levi asked. "Why do you think *normal* people are any better off than you? Why do you even want to be normal, that's so fucking bland."

Kash laughed wetly and blurted out, "Because I'm so tired of feeling so fucking estranged from everyone around me. I feel like I don't know how to act, how to be."

She held back a sob and instead opened the bag of chips in her lap and shoved one into her mouth.

"You know," she started, stuffing two more chips to muffle her words, "when we said we'd run away, I didn't intend to cry over a building lifelong identity crisis."

Levi laughed. "We're in our twenties, obviously we're gonna have dreadful identity crises. Then we'll have another set of 'em in our thirties, and so on. I don't think people ever properly work out who they are. It'd be counterintuitive."

"Well, that's something to look forward to," Kash said, tilting her head indicatively. She looked down at his hand with purpose and thought about how it would feel on her leg. She grabbed it, put it where she imagined.

Levi squeezed his hand around her thigh as soon as she placed it there, like it was an instinct to do so. She immediately pulled his hand away and settled it casually in her lap, curling her fingers in between his.

"Are you going to stay here?" Levi asked suddenly.

Are you going to stay with me?

"I want to," she said. "But it seems like it's better to be fleeting? Making home somewhere almost always takes away its allure."

Levi exhaled roughly and said nothing until he pulled over into a viewpoint shoulder overlooking a vast forested valley that glittered in the sun.

He stopped the engine, the heating cutting off as well, and looked at her with a kind of forthright intensity she imagined she'd only ever looked at others with.

"We grew up together, Kash. I spent practically my whole life with you and over half of that time longing—" his lips curled downward, face taking on a serious candor "—for *more*. That can't be fleeting."

Kash gazed at him, an unknown emotion fluttering in her stomach. She found herself nodding dazedly, eyes still not leaving his.

They were almost childishly bright now, shining exactly the way they always had since the day they met in a small school cottage surrounded by a large playground, two preschoolers competing at every chance they got.

She smiled at the memory.

"Of everything that hasn't changed," she murmured and pressed the back of her hand against his temple briefly, her fingers brushing against the shape of his eyes, skimming the wiry ends of his gold-spun lashes.

His eyes fluttered closed, and she couldn't help the widening of her smile as she moved her hand down his face to mold against the shape of his jaw, cupping the sharp bone with quiet reverence.

"Skive off work," he said, voice meek and firm at the same time. "Cancel all your plans. Pack everything into boxes and suitcases."

Kash nodded along, hand moving down to grip at his shoulder. It was muscled now, and she wondered if she could still keep up with him. She hadn't played soccer in a while, but she still spent hours at the gym. She wondered if Levi had too, why he had. Was it to find reprieve from the constant tension knotting his body up? Was it to escape the fact that he had gone too far down the wrong path for the sake of others?

We're the same.

"I'll do it, too," Levi continued, eyes still closed and slightly squinted in focus, like he was reciting an incantation. "Take all my things, the stuff that matters. We'll pile it in the boot along with yours, on the roof, tie everything down. I'll drive as steady as I can when you write in your notebooks, so you won't scribble all over the place, and they'll fill the backseat like our own mobile library."

Kash listened in rapture, picturing it in as vivid a daydream as she could conjure.

In it, Levi's hair was tied back with a silly scrunchie that matched his old sacramento green jacket from high school. It fit him properly now, almost tight around his shoulders whenever he lifted a box above his head to rest on the roof of the car.

Kash helped, too, loading their suitcases and fragile cardboard boxes into the trunk. Her hair stuck to her face with sweat and Levi teased her for getting tired quicker than him. But his hair was damp around his face too, curling delicately in soft darkened red strands.

Levi's voice brought her back to the present. "We'll stop when we want to. No pressure, no strings."

She opened her eyes and met his gaze with a hitched breath. The hand that gripped his shoulder slowly traced up to tangle into his unruly, unbrushed hair.

She knew the longing, melancholic look in his eyes and was sure the same was reflected in hers. She used her hand to bring his head gently forward until their foreheads touched tenderly.

Every part of her yearned to fulfill the picture Levi painted. It was an overwhelming ache in her chest that was both sharp and dull and pulsed with every beat of her heart.

This boy in front of her was the only thing that had come back as clear and keen as before. The only part of her that she slowly realized she could never move on from. Everyone else—they were there, far beneath the surface. But here, in front of her, breathing heavily enough for her to feel it on her skin, was someone who was also fighting to stay afloat. Someone she could wholly, trustingly hold onto without a second thought or later regret.

"You ran away once already. Across the ocean from me," she reminded him. There was no malice in her tone, not anymore.

Levi shook his head, eyes crossing slightly to look into hers. "Won't do it again," he murmured. "Not without you."

Kash inhaled shakily at that and nodded, her skin rubbing against Levi's. She slowly reached up to where her hair was tied up with one of Levi's elastics and pulled on it until her hair fell around her face like a black drape of tangled vines. She reached out to Levi's topknot and gently pulled the elastic out of his hair, so it fell in chunky curls around his face.

They were hidden behind a dual curtain of black and red, foreheads still pressing into each other like it was the most intimate gesture.

Kash closed her eyes again, savoring the feeling of his skin against hers and the rhythmic puffs of his warm breath that felt like small reassurances their plans would come true.

"I don't think—" she flashed a playful smile "—I mean, at some point in our lives, I'm going to drag you back home, back to the woods behind your house, and you'll give chase like before."

Levi laughed, the sound and feeling rushing at her face deliciously. "Yeah, Blue," he agreed fondly. "I'll be a child with you."

She grinned at that and couldn't help it as she angled herself entirely to the right and lunged over the console, wrapping her arms tightly around him.

Levi hummed softly with surprise before hugging her back fiercely.

"Please don't ever become a stranger to me," she whispered earnestly into his ear. "I don't think I could bear it. Everyone else is—you're my—just please don't become someone I remember as much as I regret."

"I won't," he said, his chin coming to rest on her shoulder, the words firm and short like he was struggling to express exactly how he was feeling. "Shall we go appreciate the view before we move on?"

Kash laughed after a moment. "Yeah, fine."

The view was spectacular, although she imagined it would be even more so in fall. The valley dipped deeper than it looked, the chasm seemingly endless in a glittering sea of iced trees with tangled branches. A thick mist caught the tips of the forest and it looked like a cloud had descended upon the area.

Kash curiously looked down over the ledge they stood near, leaning against the railing to bend over as far as she could without risking anything.

It was dizzying. There was a drop-off a few feet from where she stood and as she looked down, all she could see was a foggy darkness that looked both enticing and menacing.

"I could follow it all the way down," she murmured.

Levi stiffened beside her but said nothing.

She leaned forward more, imagining falling into the icy forest depth that looked both jagged and brilliant, like she would get all cut up on the way down, but the beauty would be more than worth it.

"If I jumped," she mused out loud, "would you, too?"

Levi looked at her in stark confusion. "Seriously?" he asked.

Kash shrugged, a smile playing on her lips.

He nodded after a moment of watching her. His head jerked up and down resolutely and he looked out at the view in a long, scaling glance before saying, "Yeah, obviously. I'd follow you anywhere you want me to, Blue."

A painful feeling tugged at her. She couldn't take her eyes off him, off the flush of his freckled cheeks and nose, the pink tips of his ears and his fingers that peeked through his gauntlet gloves. His dark auburn brows were furrowed flatly over his eyes as he looked out ahead.

She reached out her hand, in a trance of taking all of him in, and gripped his arm. She tugged on him gently until he looked at her.

His eyebrows lifted slightly, revealing more of his hazel eyes.

Kash smiled when she saw a distracting reflection of their surroundings in them. She pulled him closer, familiarly, until he was right in front of her.

He looked down at her with an unreadable expression, face still stoic and flushed with the cold.

She looked up at him and pressed her nose into his arm, minutely nuzzling the wool fabric of his coat. She closed her eyes, turning her head so her cheek pressed against its slight roughness.

Levi lowered his head with a sigh and leaned against hers. His jaw jutted against her temple, but it felt deliciously natural, familiar, like coming home after a lifetime away.

She curled both of her arms around his, leaning into him so her shoulder pressed into his chest, pushing him away and pulling him into her at the same time. She exhaled into the fabric of his coat, feeling the damp warmth of it fan across her face.

"You're so warm," she said with a smile.

Levi laughed above her, his breath warm against her neck. He bent down to fit the shape of his jaw against hers, his warm cheeks and cold nose coming into contact with her skin.

She felt a semblance of ephemeral satisfaction rippling out from her chest down into her fingertips and toes and up through the tips of her ears. It made her shiver with novelty and bite the growing smile on her lips.

They stood there in soft quiet, holding each other long enough, maybe, to try and make up for the past seven years they could've spent like this.

Maybe this, standing in silence so they could hear each other's steady breathing, close enough to *feel* each other breathe, was a paramount intimacy. Maybe this familiarity that expanded in her and caught on all her edges, maybe the forgivable simplicity of it was the satiating feeling she'd been so hungry for.

Before the confusion could set in again, she slipped her fingers underneath the sleeve of Levi's coat and caressed the bare skin there.

"Your fingers're cold," he mumbled right next to her ear.

"Yeah, no surprise there," she retorted.

He laughed and she pressed her ear into his chest, away from the tickling outburst of his breath. A smile curled her lips despite the growing seriousness inside of her. She traced her fingers along the warm skin of his wrist and then farther up, feeling the veins that rose from his skin like topography on a map. She imagined what the soft patterns would read, where they might take her.

Maybe being with someone just meant this, meant tracing the rivers and roads and mountains along their body out of nothing but tender curiosity; meant finding all the possible ways to burrow under their skin, slip through the spaces in their bones and live inside them.

Kash sighed out into the quiet air. She gripped Levi's forearm tightly, fervently, in the only familiar way between them—

bony fingers in soft flesh.

note for levi (the start of our mobile library).

*Can I crawl in through the spaces of your ribs and curl up
between your lungs—*
    I'll breathe for you when you run.
    I don't want to kiss you,
    I just want to sleep next to you.

*Can I slip in through your pores and take up residence
behind your cheeks—*
    I'll blush for you when you speak
    I don't want kiss you
    I'd rather run my fingers through you
    Can I run my fingers through you

*Can I lean into your side and melt into your skin and just
exist within you*
    *Can I wrap around your neck like a small gold chain and
glint so softly upon you*
    I don't want to kiss you
    but I'm just dying to love you.

I don't want to kiss you
but I'm just dying to be loved by you.

Acknowledgments

Thank you.

The words are short, and I might be overusing them in the coming acknowledgments, but I don't know another way of saying this that conveys the sheer amount of gratitude I feel for everyone who made this book possible. So, thank you, in every language and every intonation and every meaning these words could possibly be said.

Thank you to my parents, Amma and Nanna, for—everything. I wouldn't be who I am without you, and I wouldn't have the courage to pursue what I want without your constant support and encouragement. Thank you for loving me with everything you are and supporting me with everything you have.

Thank you to my editors, Stephanie McKibben, Kristy Carter, Angela Mitchell and Anne Kelley, for encouraging me and making me a better writer, and for going above and beyond to support me regardless of circumstance, and for making sure I did my best no matter what.

Thank you to Casey, for being one of the most meaningful mentors in my life, for reading my long emails, for being someone I always look forward to sharing my work with, and for always supporting me in my creative endeavors, without which I wouldn't have had the courage to write this book.

Thank you to my ninth-grade mentor, Mr. Baillie, for being one of the first people to believe in my writing, one of the first people who gave me the courage to *believe* I could be an author. This book is a far cry from the horror gore-influenced stories I wrote then, but it would not have been possible without your early encouragement and mentorship.

Thank you to my friend, and sunshine incarnate, Santoshi, for listening to me ramble and vent about my book, and my life, for encouraging me in all caps with happy emojis even when I'm sure you're stressing out with your own stuff, and for being such a brilliant role model and friend.

Thank you to my adopted sisters, Sruthi for putting up with me texting emotional poems and chapter excerpts after midnight, being a beta reader, and supporting me unconditionally literally since my birth, and Sravya, for pushing me to be my best and to do things as an artist I otherwise would've never attempted.

Thank you to Sruj, another adopted sister of mine, for putting up with my anxious rants and last-minute self-doubts and for telling me to shut up and just *do* it, and Ramya, for being the older sibling I never had, and for being someone I look up to always.

Thank you to my friend Jared, for humming my song back in high school (I will never get over that), but mainly for always encouraging me and supporting me in what I do (you have no idea how much it means to me, really).

Thank you to my friend Abby, for being a constant inspiration, for reading my work and sharing yours, and being so incredibly supportive that I have no idea where I'd be without you.

Thank you to my author friends Alisha and Nina, for being an incredibly important source of motivation for me, for sharing dreams, and being a support group I could never have done this without (I can't wait for Europe and beyond).

Thank you to Declan, for being a vital mentor in my early days, supporting me even years after I was in your class, and giving me the confidence to pursue writing and more.

Thank you to Shiamin Aunty, for championing me, and my book, these past few months, and for being such an important mentor in my life, and an important role in how I learned and connected with my culture since I was a child. I would not be who I am without you and your support, and the community of ISW.

I'm incredibly fortunate to have so many people supporting me that I couldn't possibly name everyone single person in these few pages. Thank you to all of my friends and family who supported me all my life, and supported this book, spread the word, preordered a copy, donated to my campaign, asked me how I was doing in the process, and kept encouraging me with comments of how excited and proud you are. You are the reason this book is here, now, through the ups and downs of these past few years.

Thank you everyone below, who preordered my book and/ or donated, and in doing so, made this lifelong dream possible. This book, and my being a published author, is a product of your support. I couldn't thank you enough:

Naya Amin, Shana Hopkins, Lara Hill, Anandita Punnamaraju, Christine Regan Davi, Cynthia Noonan, Aizay Rashid Tariq, Snigdha Kalathur, Olivia Hewitt, Jared Penna, Shivanka Ruhela, McKenna C Poe, Kun Hong, Grace Delaney, Rhea Krishnan, Spandana Shankara, Vaishnavi Yalala, JP Slurzberg, Keerthan Ekbote, Arusha Anupindi, Clare

Hackwith, Jessica Cannon, Aimee Noonan, Nashwa Zaman, Declan Drapeau, Desira Pesta, Emily Podgorni, Nina Raman, Rupali Sharma, Emily Chu, Cassidy Samovar, Srujani Kolli, Praveen Kanuri, Kembo Matungulu, Kalyan Vemuri, Srinivas Vemuri, Sharoon Shetty, Sruthi Tanikella, Peter Gomez, Chakradhar Bonam, Shovan Mondal

Madhavi Chukkapalli, Sandhya Makkapati, Sahiti Bonam, Hasneet Kaur Chowdhary

Sandhya Nallajerla, Harvin Vallabhaneni, Sridhar Vallabhaneni, Becky Harte, Michael Byrum, Prardhana Chaliki, Ramya Tammisetti, Srujana Tammisetti, Santoshi Nadimpalli, Alisha Sehgal, Gautam Chopra, Akshaya Ravishankar, Krishangee Gauree, Callie Dennis, Divya Koduri, Sinduja Manchi, Eric Koester, Ragini Seth, Shiamin Melville, Nirmala Rajasekar, Levi Streb, Casey Haymes, Abigail Willson, Sergey Kochergan, Della Jennings, Caroline Noonan, Mahima Cielappa

And a final thank you to everyone at NDP—especially to Eric Koester, for creating this program, to Brian Bies, for working with me on the ever-changing game plan that is writing a book, and to Gjorgji Pejkovski and Max Yenin for giving my story a beautiful cover—for giving me the opportunity to meet and work with so many wonderful people, and enabling me to publish my first book. You are forever written into my journey as a writer, and I couldn't be more grateful.

Glossary

Telugu—A language spoken in India, mainly in the states of Andhra Pradesh and Telengana, where Kash and Raza's parents are from. Telugu is also the language that Kash and Raza's families speak at home.

Nanna—Father.

Amma—Mother.

Anna—Older brother.

Akka—Older sister.

Ammamma—Grandmother, maternal.

Nannamma—Grandmother, paternal.

Thattha—Grandfather.

Sambar—A soup-like curry dish made from lentils and vegetables, that is mostly popular in South India, and eaten with rice, idly, or dosa.

Pachadi—a.k.a. pickle, usually made with fruits or vegetables, and chilies.

Biryani—A popular dish that consists of meat (i.e., chicken biryani is made with chicken), curry, and rice, and is made with various spices and sometimes eggs.

Elaichi—Cardomom.

Raitha—A yogurt side dish made with vegetables, often eaten with fried rice or biryani.

Mirapakaya/mirchi bajji—Usually stuffed green chilies fried in batter and served with fresh cut onions, coriander, and squeezed lemon.

InshAllah—A Muslim phrase, meaning "god willing." also spelled Insha'Allah or Inshallah.

Deepavali—A major festival, celebrating the victory of light over darkness/good over evil, commonly associated with the goddess Lakshmi. Oil lamps, also known as *deepams* or *diyas* are lit and placed all along the interiors and exteriors of the house to illuminate the path for good and to keep any dark forces away.

Chichubuddi—A type of firework that comes in the shape of a cone. It's usually very loud and explodes in a huge firework spectacle.

Langa voni—A traditional piece of clothing consisting of a skirt, a long draping fabric piece, and a blouse, that can be worn as daily wear as well as for special occasions.

Kurta—A loose top worn by men and women across South Asia both casually and formally.

Cheera—a.k.a. sari/saree, a traditional South Asian piece of clothing usually consisting of a long draping fabric piece, a blouse, and a petticoat, that can either be worn as daily wear as well as for special occasions.

Jhumka—A type of earring that has a dangling piece in the shape of a cone, semi-sphere, or bell of some sort.

Devudu—God.